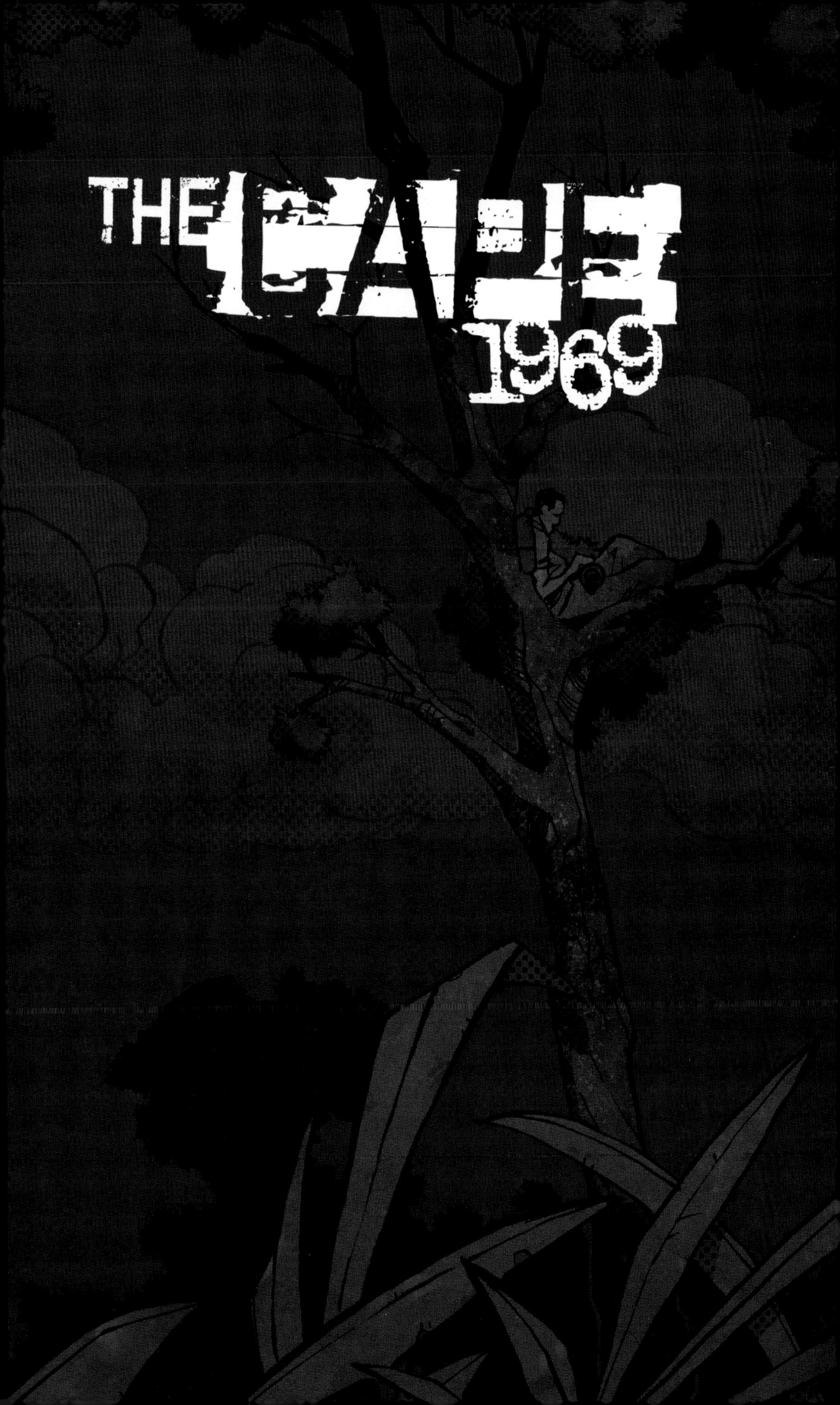
THE CAPE
1969

"For Ellen. With all my heart. Always."
—Jason Ciaramella

"For Lucca, Agustina, Vicente, Bruno and Pilar"
—Nelson Daniel

Special thanks to Ellen Croteau and Mickey Choate for their invaluable assistance.

IDW®

ISBN: 978-1-61377-545-5   16 15 14 13   1 2 3 4

www.IDWPUBLISHING.com

Ted Adams, CEO & Publisher
Greg Goldstein, President & COO
Robbie Robbins, EVP/Sr. Graphic Artist
Chris Ryall, Chief Creative Officer/Editor-in-Chief
Matthew Ruzicka, CPA, Chief Financial Officer
Alan Payne, VP of Sales
Dirk Wood, VP of Marketing
Lorelei Bunjes, VP of Digital Services

WRITTEN BY **Jason Ciaramella**

BASED ON THE SHORT STORY "THE CAPE" BY **Joe Hill**

ART BY **Nelson Daniel**

PAGE 5, PANEL 1 ART BY **Zach Howard**

LETTERS BY **Shawn Lee**

SERIES EDITS BY **Chris Ryall**

SERIES EDITORIAL ASSISTANTS **Christopher Schraff**

AND **Toni Kerde**

CREATIVE CONSULTANT **Joe Hill**

COVER BY **Zach Howard**

COVER COLOR BY **Nelson Daniel**

COLLECTION EDITS BY **Justin Eisinger**

AND **Alonzo Simon**

COLLECTION DESIGN BY **Tom B. Long**

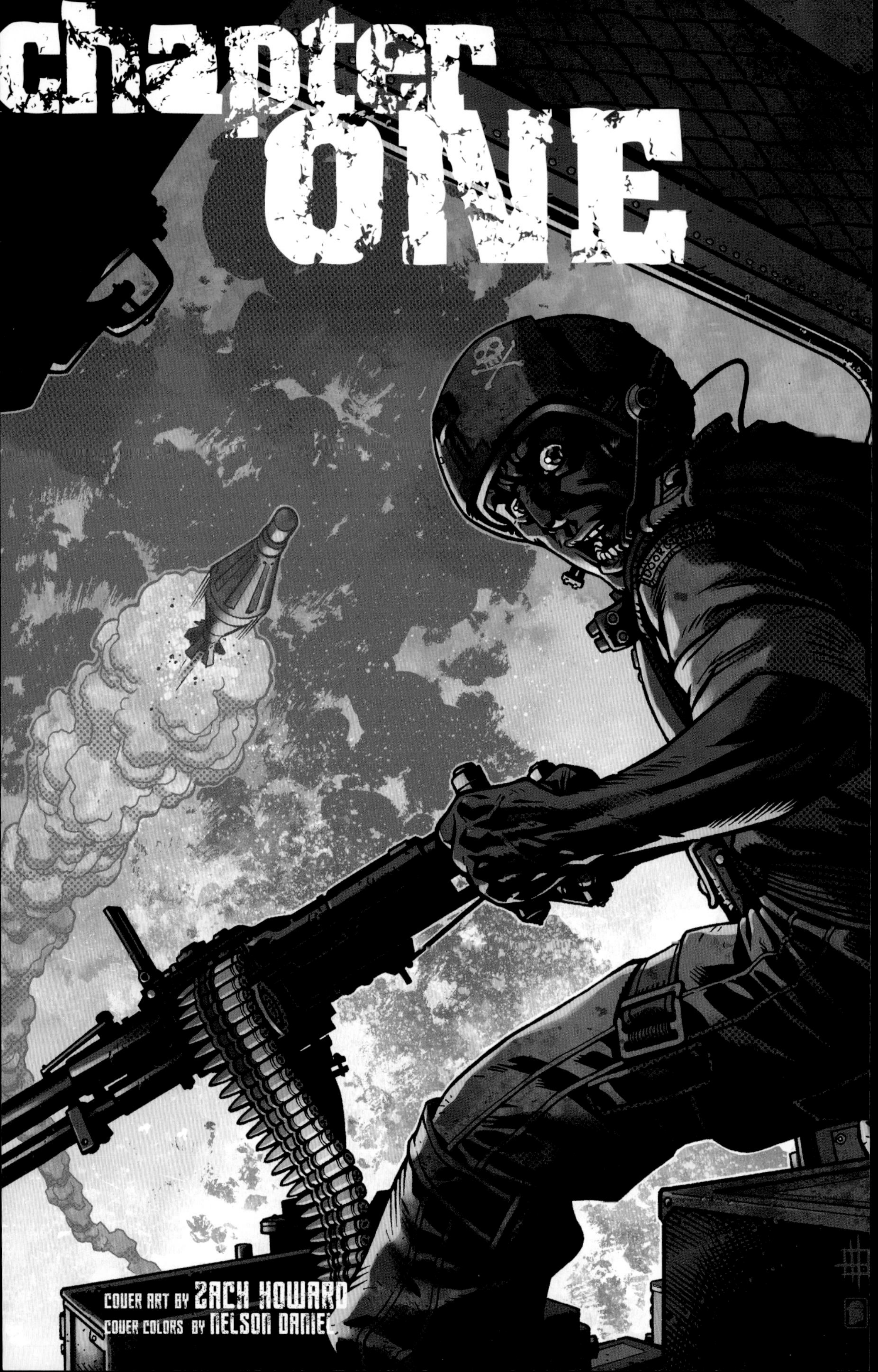
chapter ONE
COVER ART BY ZACH HOWARD
COVER COLORS BY NELSON DANIEL

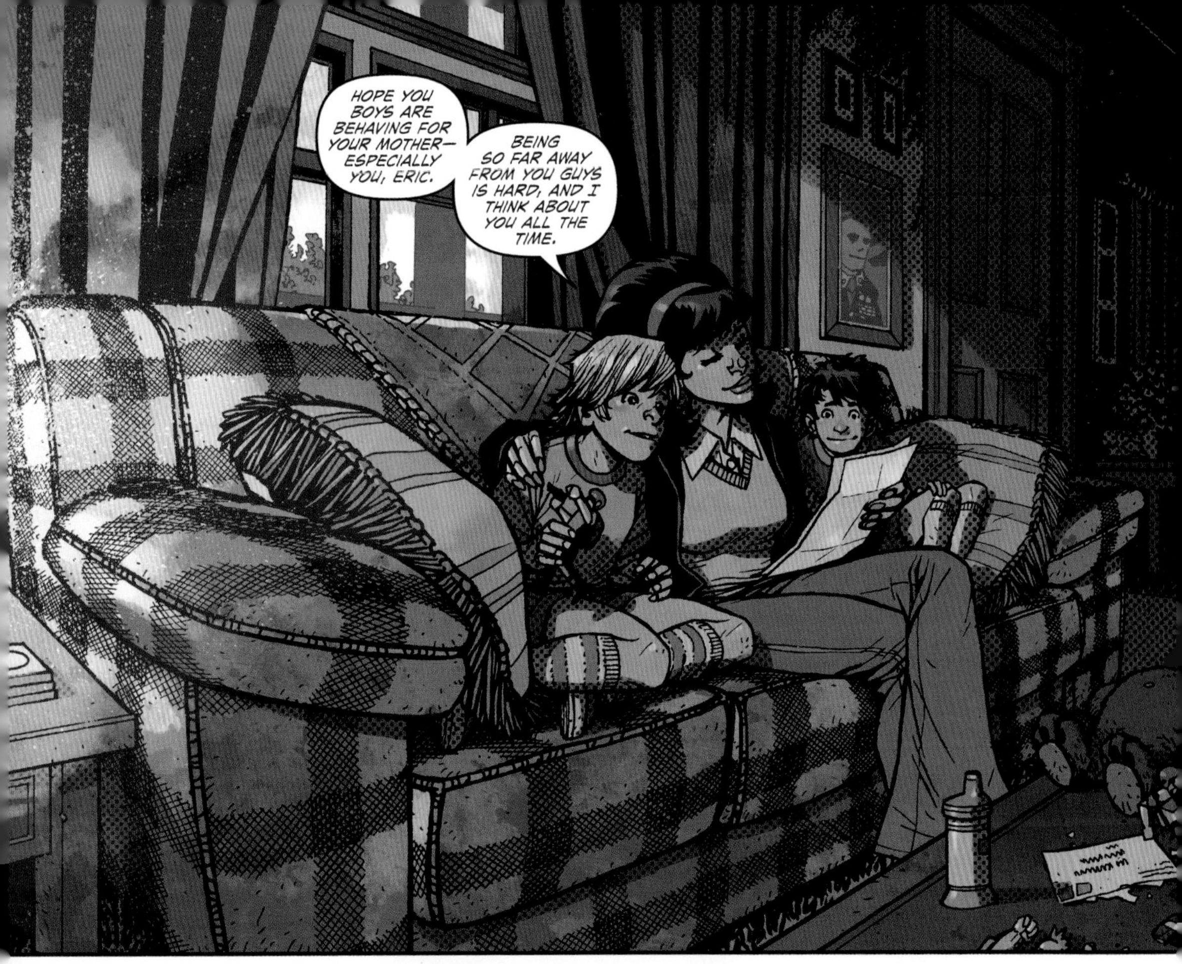
HOPE YOU BOYS ARE BEHAVING FOR YOUR MOTHER—ESPECIALLY YOU, ERIC.
BEING SO FAR AWAY FROM YOU GUYS IS HARD, AND I THINK ABOUT YOU ALL THE TIME.

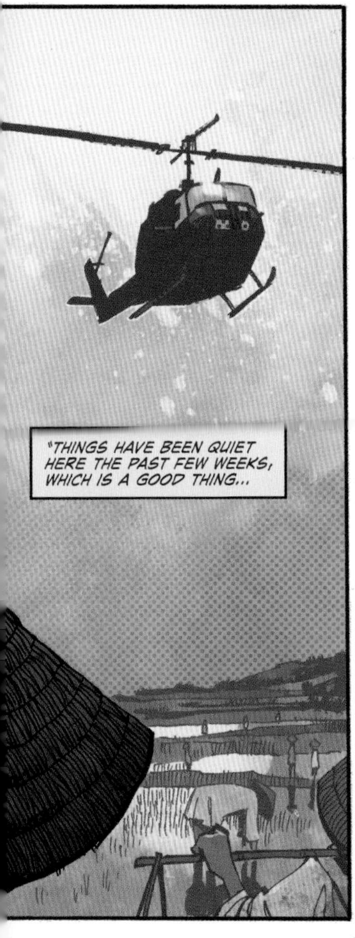
"THINGS HAVE BEEN QUIET HERE THE PAST FEW WEEKS, WHICH IS A GOOD THING...

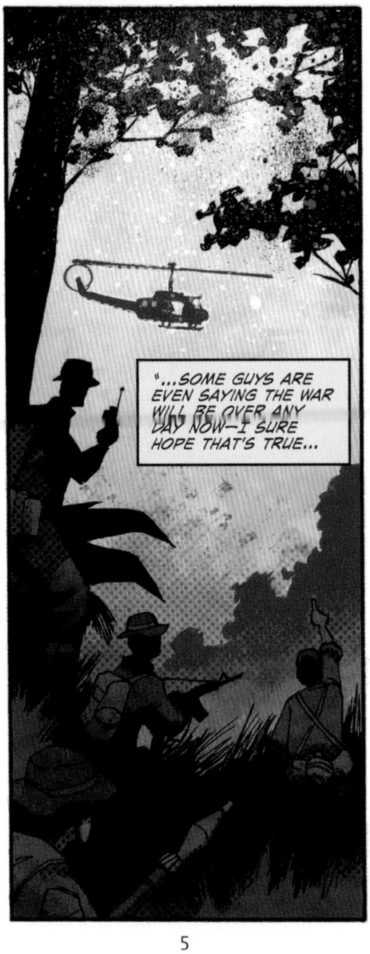
"...SOME GUYS ARE EVEN SAYING THE WAR WILL BE OVER ANY DAY NOW—I SURE HOPE THAT'S TRUE...

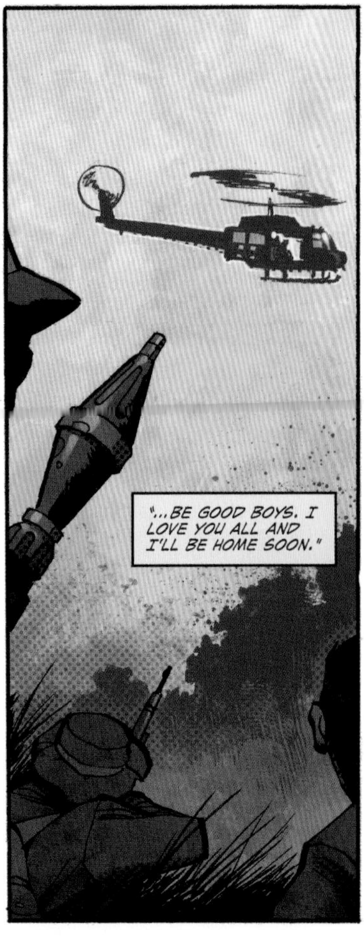
"...BE GOOD BOYS. I LOVE YOU ALL AND I'LL BE HOME SOON."

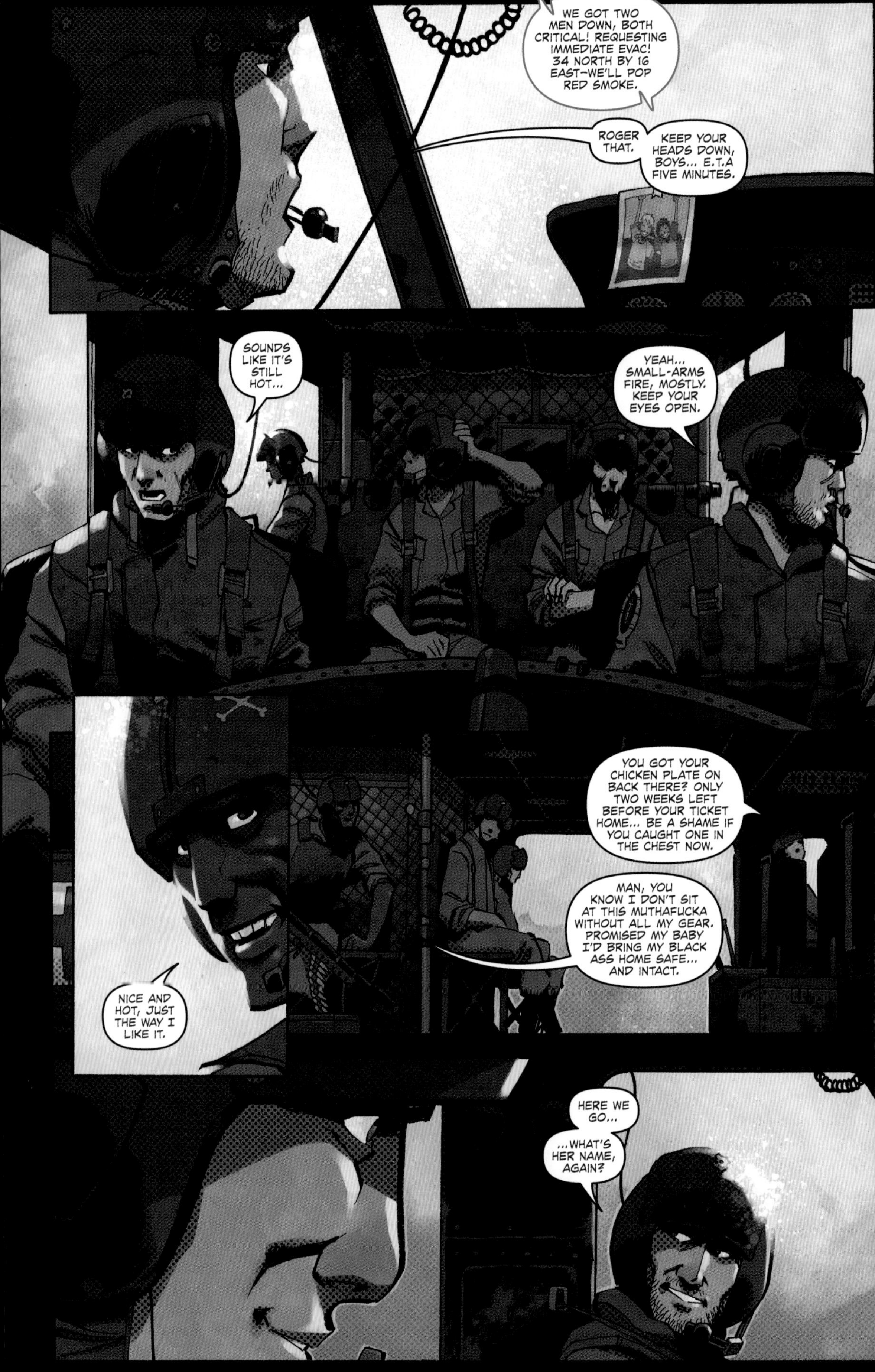

WE GOT TWO MEN DOWN, BOTH CRITICAL! REQUESTING IMMEDIATE EVAC! 34 NORTH BY 16 EAST—WE'LL POP RED SMOKE.
ROGER THAT.
KEEP YOUR HEADS DOWN, BOYS... E.T.A FIVE MINUTES.
SOUNDS LIKE IT'S STILL HOT...
YEAH... SMALL-ARMS FIRE, MOSTLY. KEEP YOUR EYES OPEN.
NICE AND HOT, JUST THE WAY I LIKE IT.
YOU GOT YOUR CHICKEN PLATE ON BACK THERE? ONLY TWO WEEKS LEFT BEFORE YOUR TICKET HOME... BE A SHAME IF YOU CAUGHT ONE IN THE CHEST NOW.
MAN, YOU KNOW I DON'T SIT AT THIS MUTHAFUCKA WITHOUT ALL MY GEAR. PROMISED MY BABY I'D BRING MY BLACK ASS HOME SAFE... AND INTACT.
HERE WE GO...
...WHAT'S HER NAME, AGAIN?

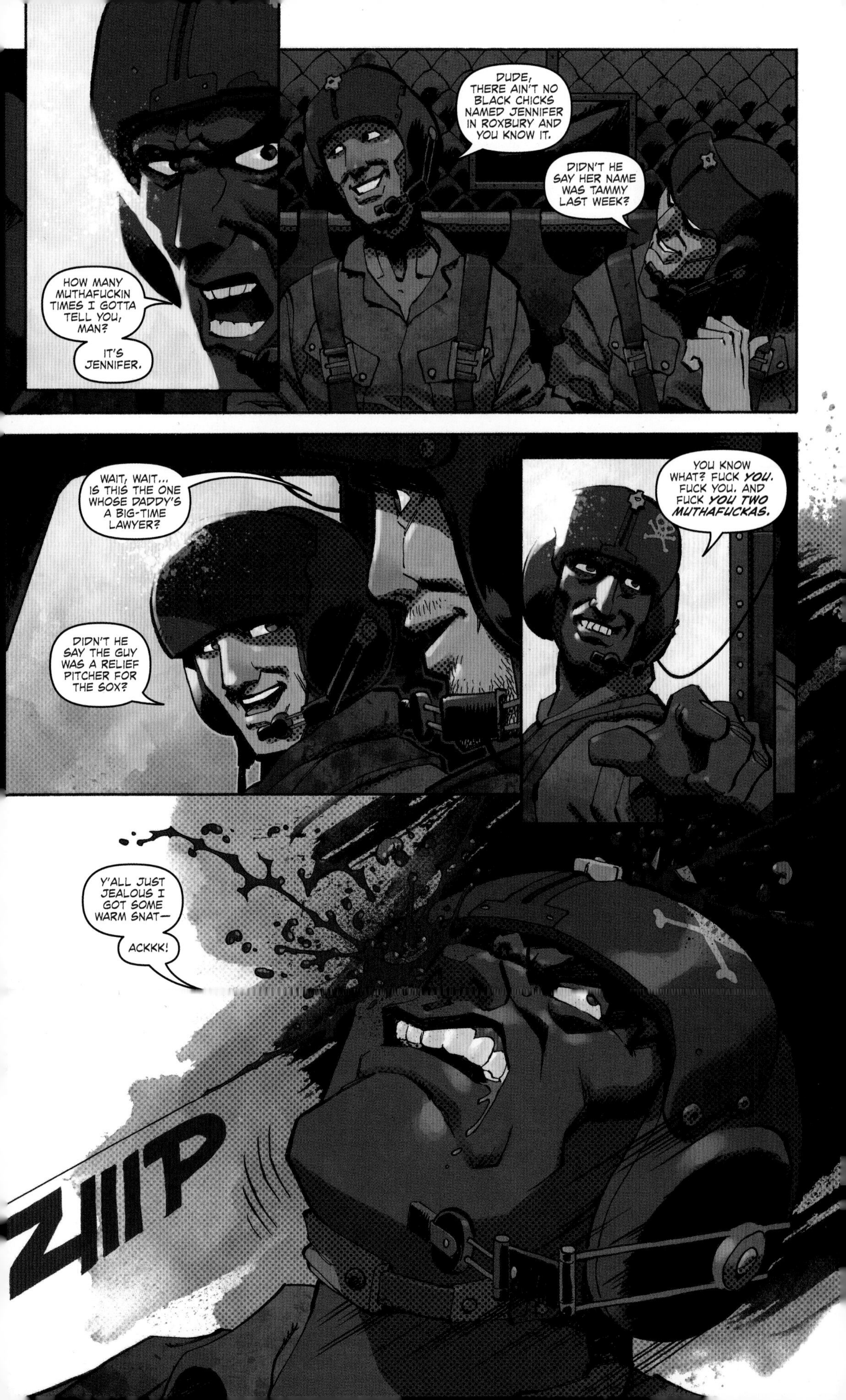

DUDE, THERE AIN'T NO BLACK CHICKS NAMED JENNIFER IN ROXBURY AND YOU KNOW IT.
DIDN'T HE SAY HER NAME WAS TAMMY LAST WEEK?
HOW MANY MUTHAFUCKIN TIMES I GOTTA TELL YOU, MAN?
IT'S JENNIFER.
WAIT, WAIT... IS THIS THE ONE WHOSE DADDY'S A BIG-TIME LAWYER?
DIDN'T HE SAY THE GUY WAS A RELIEF PITCHER FOR THE SOX?
YOU KNOW WHAT? FUCK YOU. FUCK YOU. AND FUCK YOU TWO MUTHAFUCKAS.
Y'ALL JUST JEALOUS I GOT SOME WARM SNAT—
ACKKK!
ZIIIP

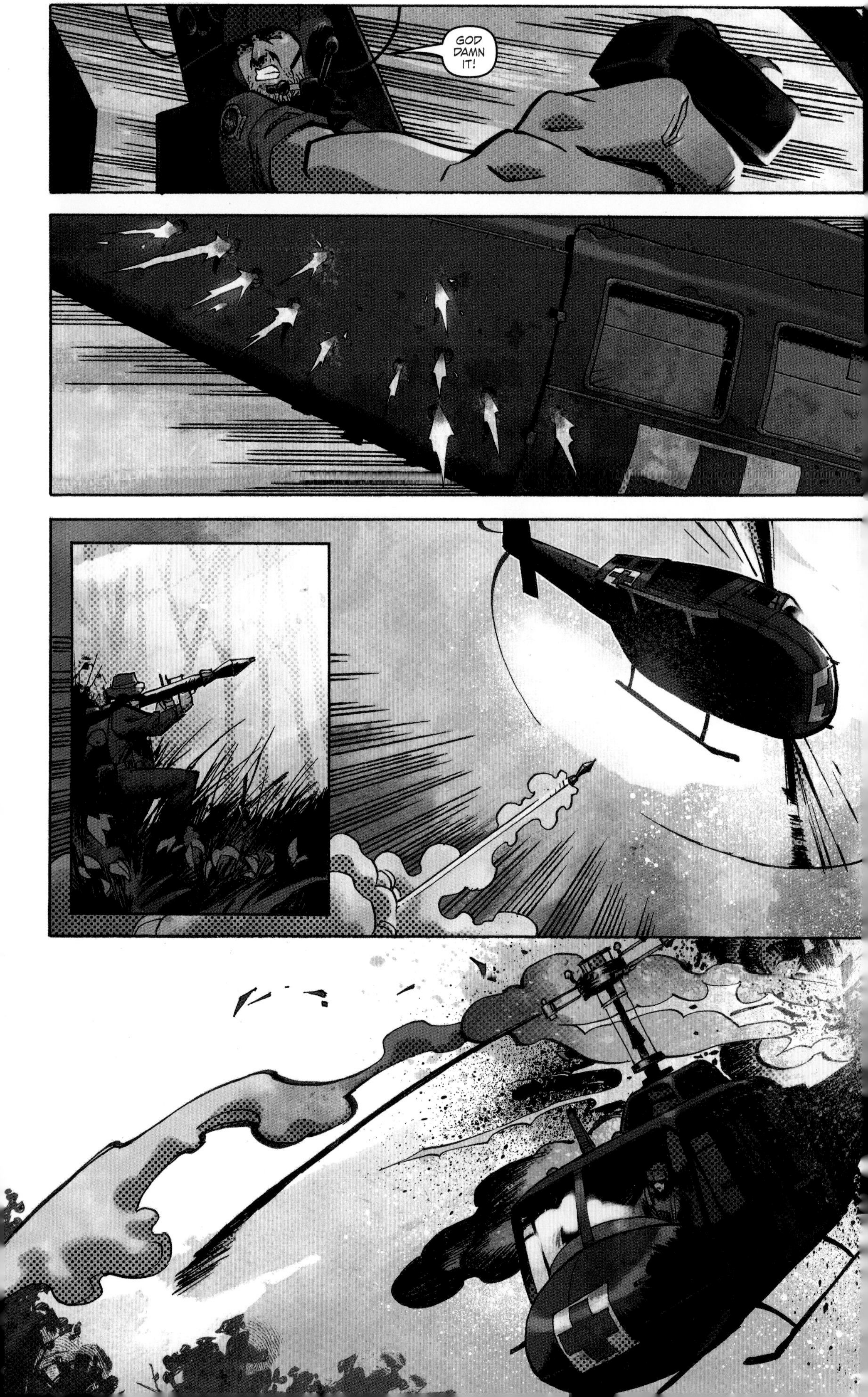
GOD DAMN IT!

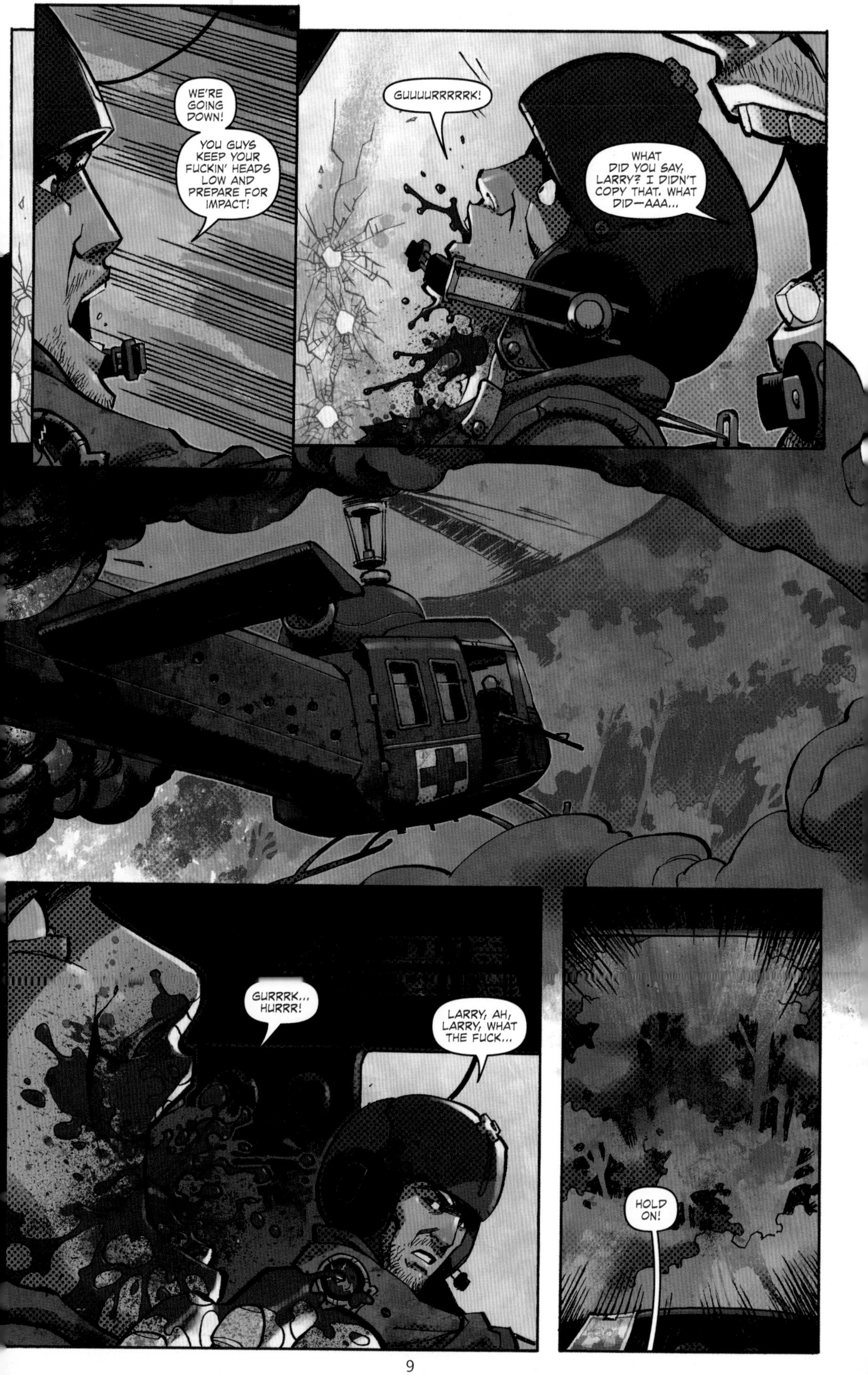
WE'RE GOING DOWN!
YOU GUYS KEEP YOUR FUCKIN' HEADS LOW AND PREPARE FOR IMPACT!
GUUUURRRRRK!
WHAT DID YOU SAY, LARRY? I DIDN'T COPY THAT. WHAT DID—AAA...
GURRRK... HURRR!
LARRY, AH, LARRY, WHAT THE FUCK...
HOLD ON!

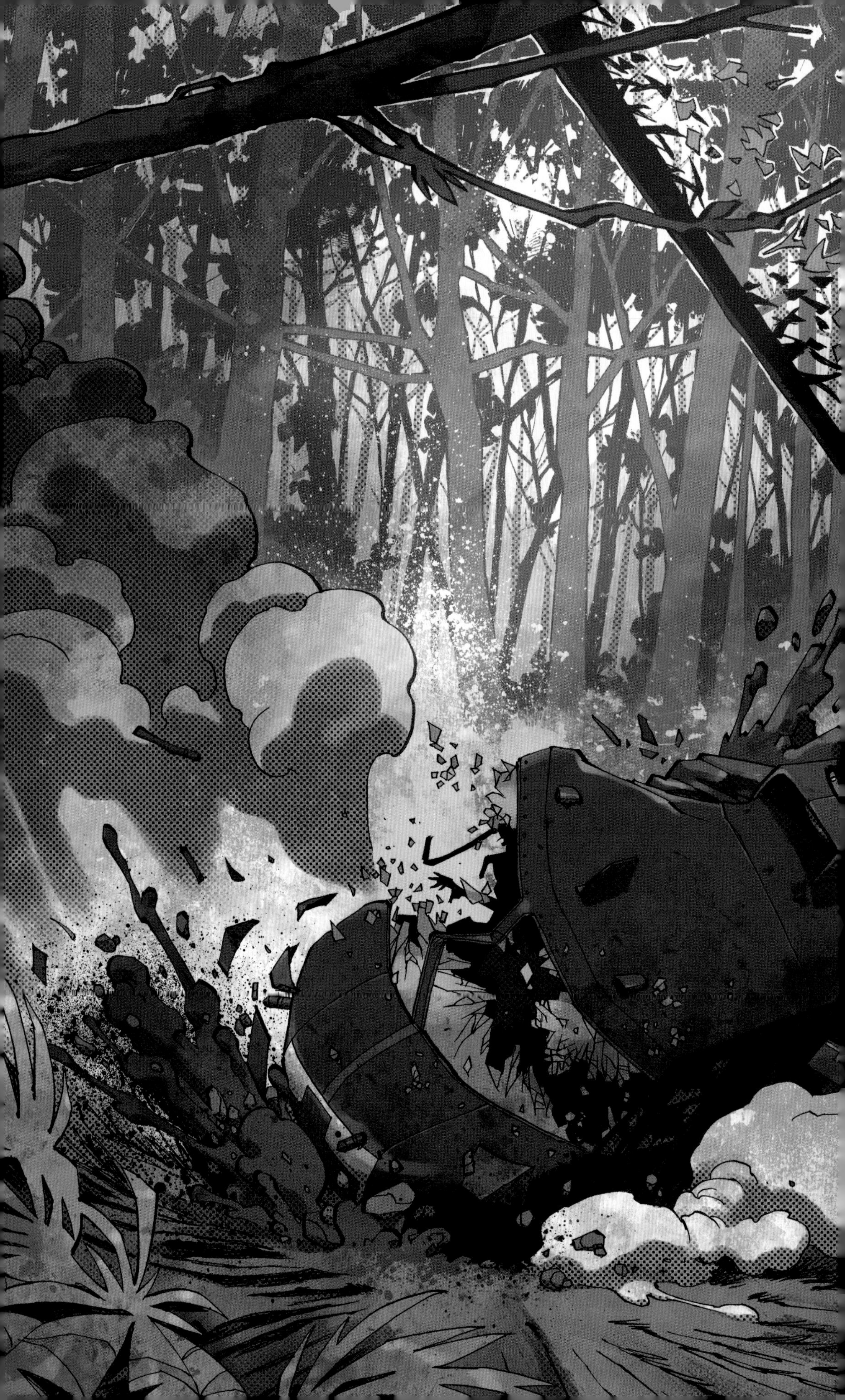

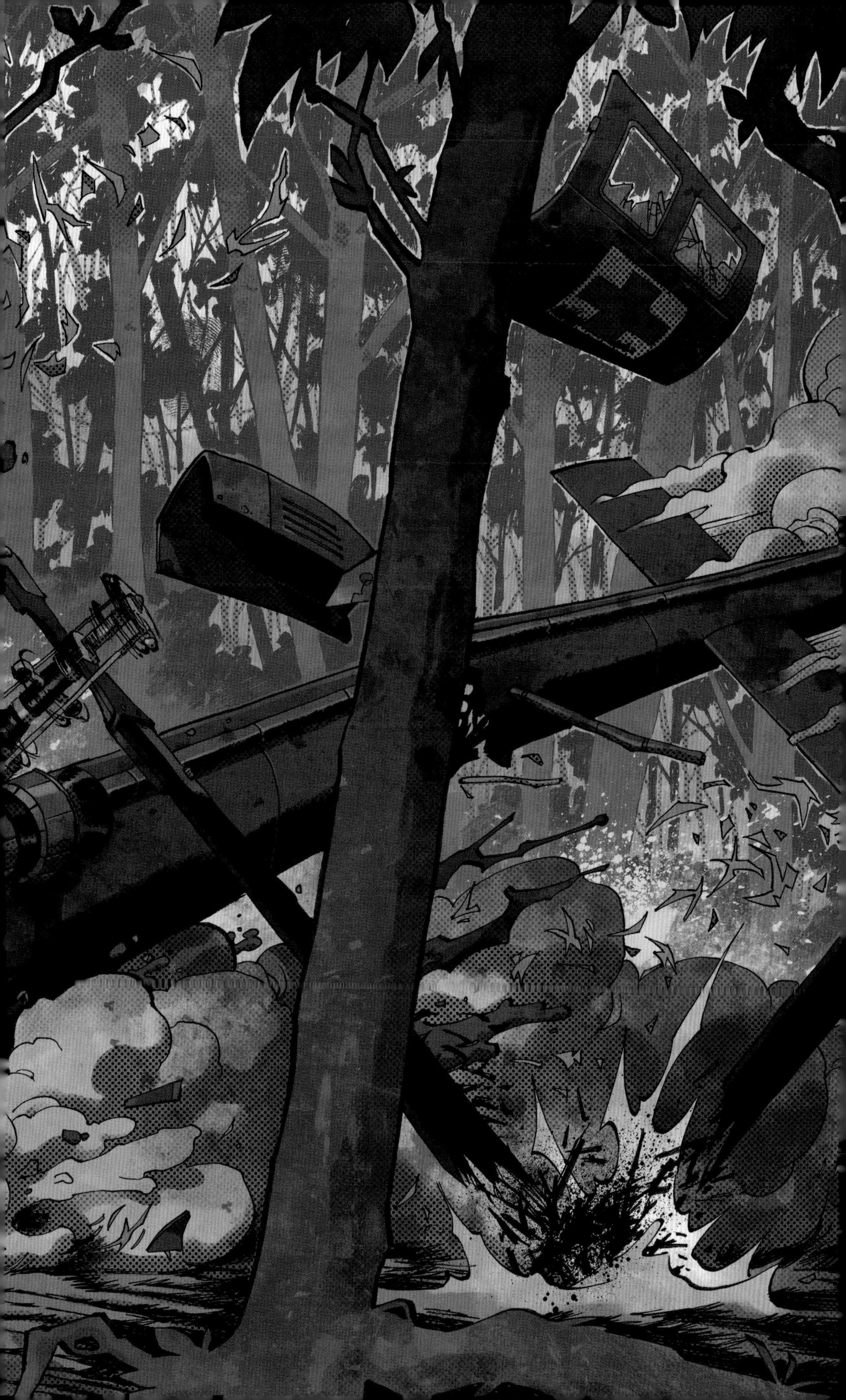

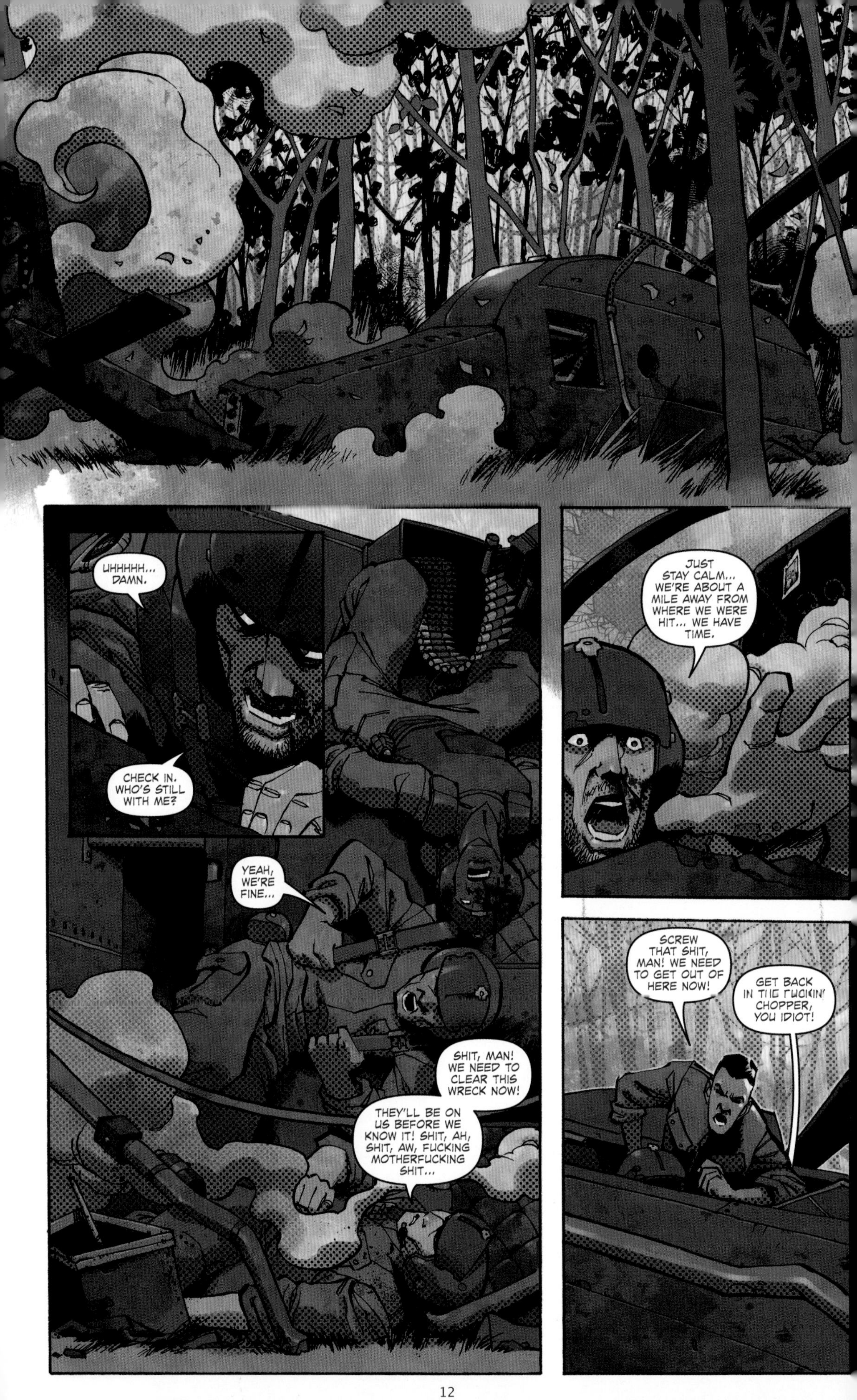
UHHHHH... DAMN.
CHECK IN. WHO'S STILL WITH ME?
YEAH, WE'RE FINE...
SHIT, MAN! WE NEED TO CLEAR THIS WRECK NOW!
THEY'LL BE ON US BEFORE WE KNOW IT! SHIT, AH, SHIT, AW, FUCKING MOTHERFUCKING SHIT...
JUST STAY CALM... WE'RE ABOUT A MILE AWAY FROM WHERE WE WERE HIT... WE HAVE TIME.
SCREW THAT SHIT, MAN! WE NEED TO GET OUT OF HERE NOW!
GET BACK IN THE FUCKIN' CHOPPER, YOU IDIOT!

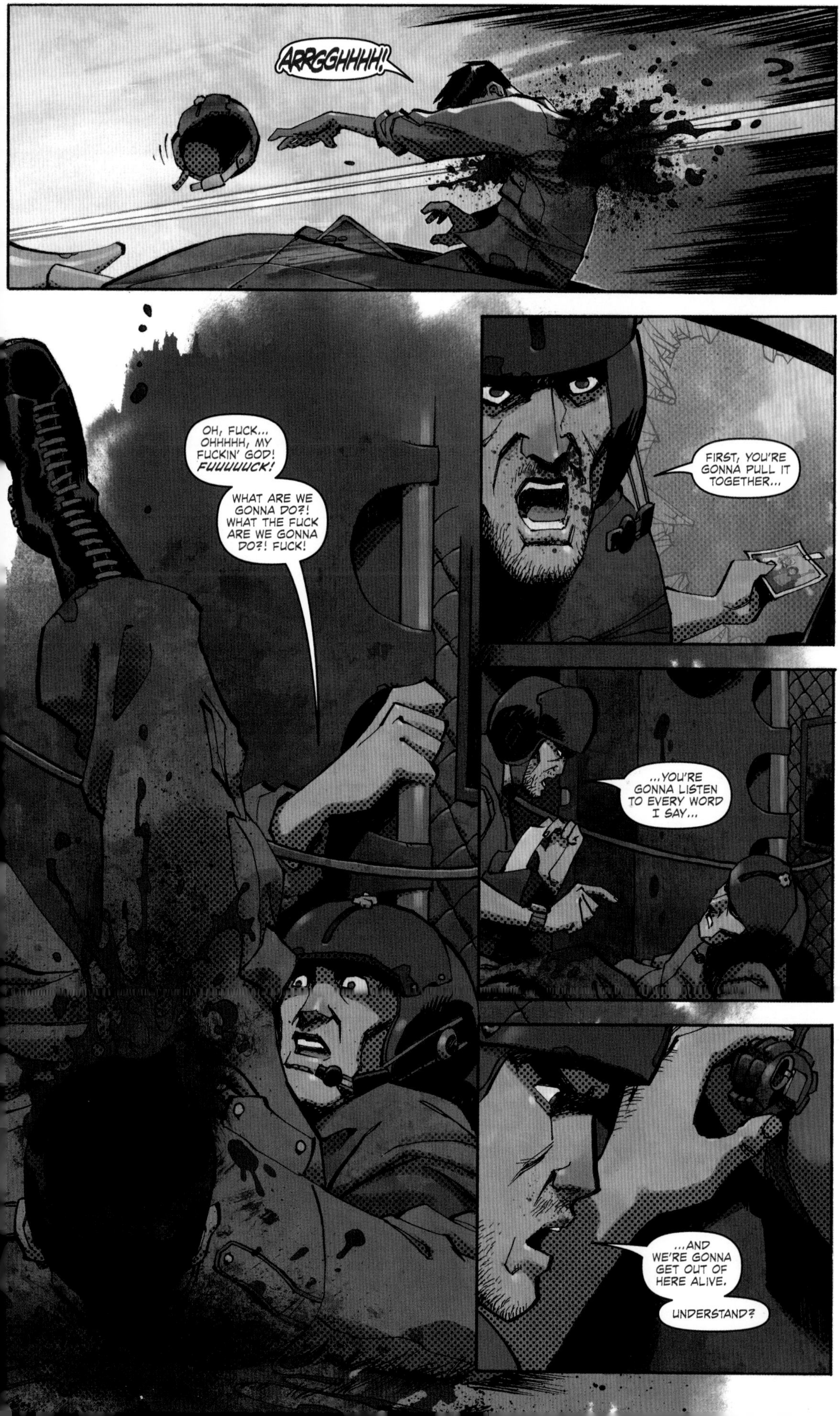
ARRGGHHHH!
OH, FUCK... OHHHHH, MY FUCKIN' GOD! FUUUUUCK!
WHAT ARE WE GONNA DO?! WHAT THE FUCK ARE WE GONNA DO?! FUCK!
FIRST, YOU'RE GONNA PULL IT TOGETHER...
...YOU'RE GONNA LISTEN TO EVERY WORD I SAY...
...AND WE'RE GONNA GET OUT OF HERE ALIVE.
UNDERSTAND?

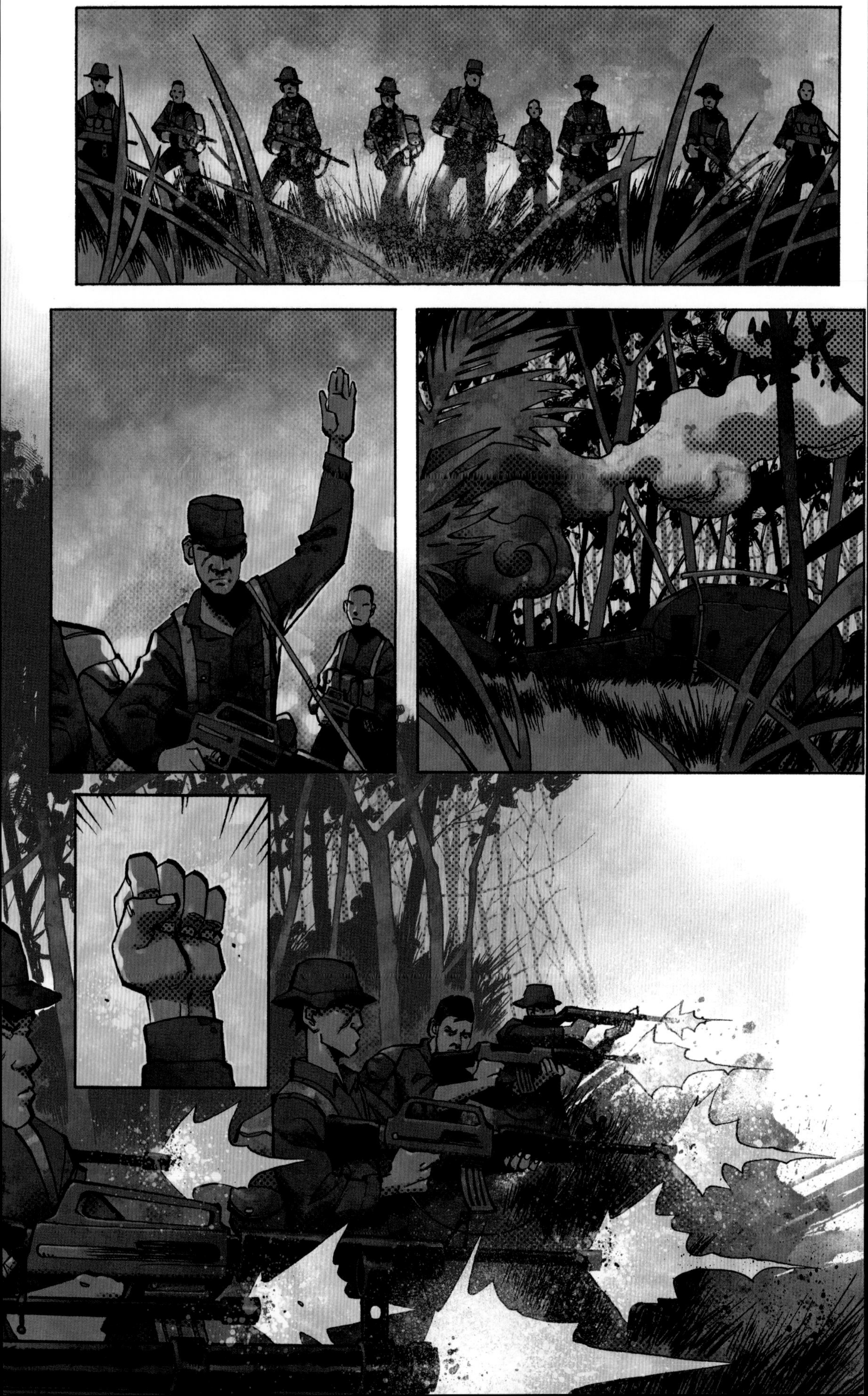

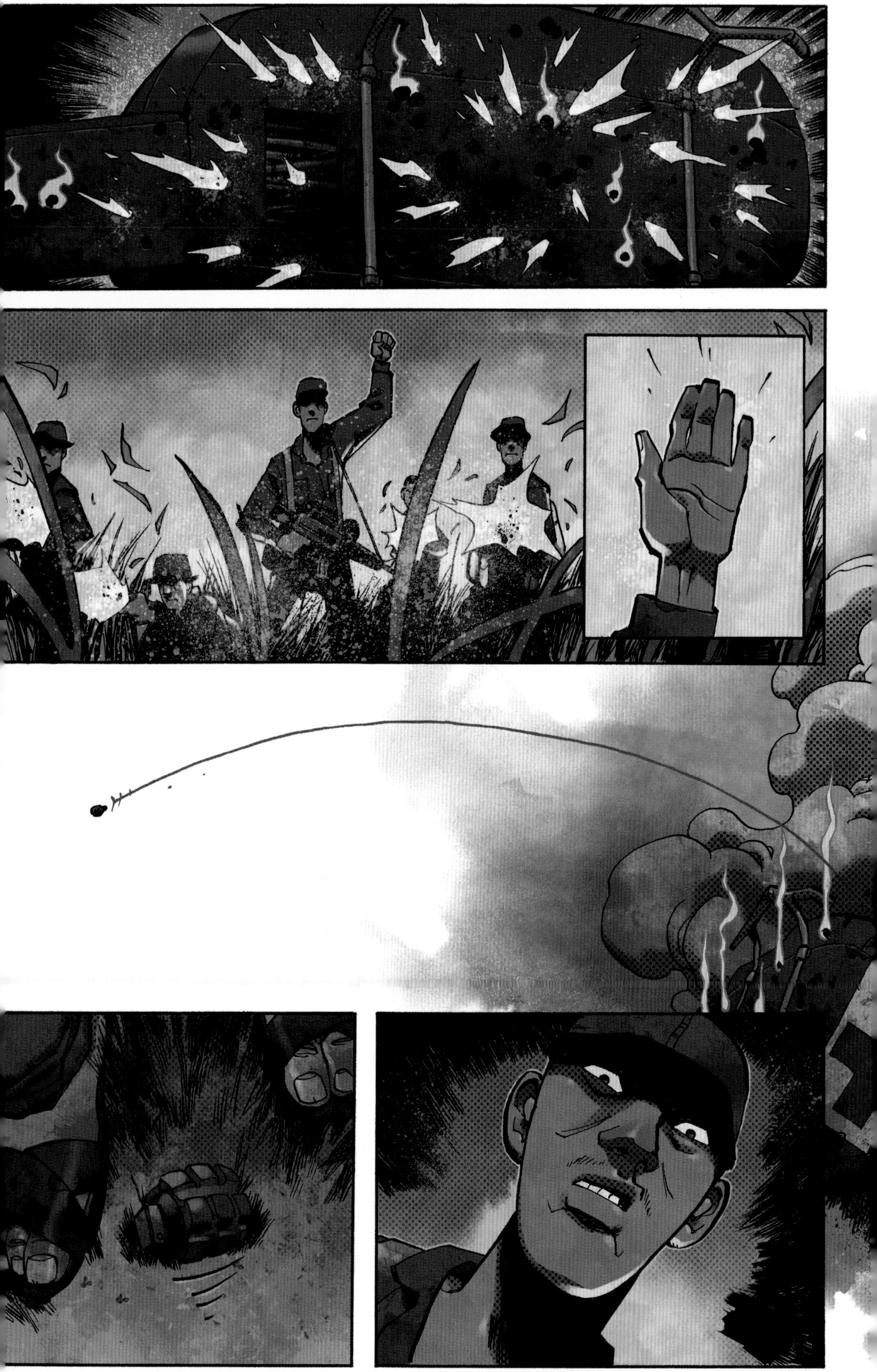

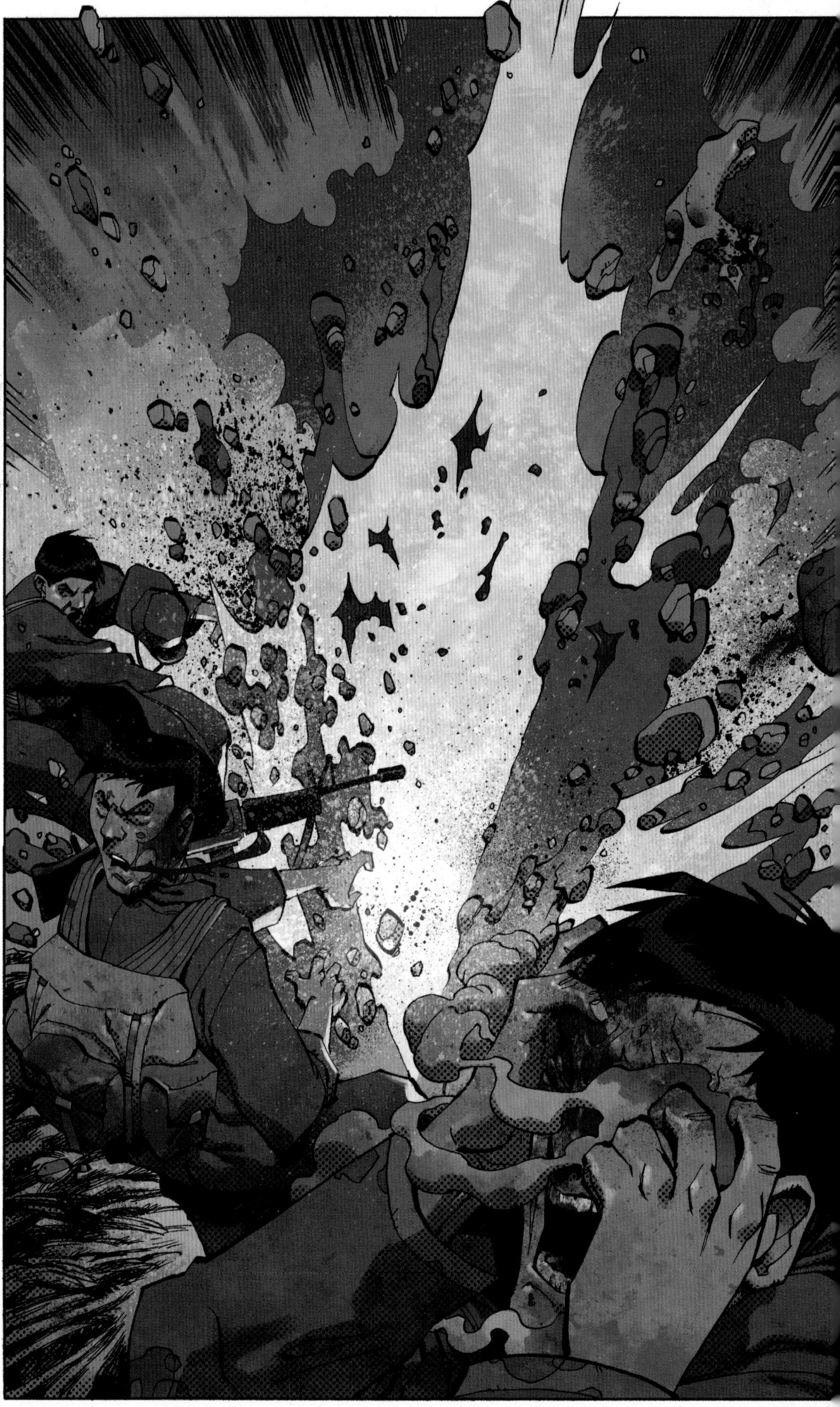

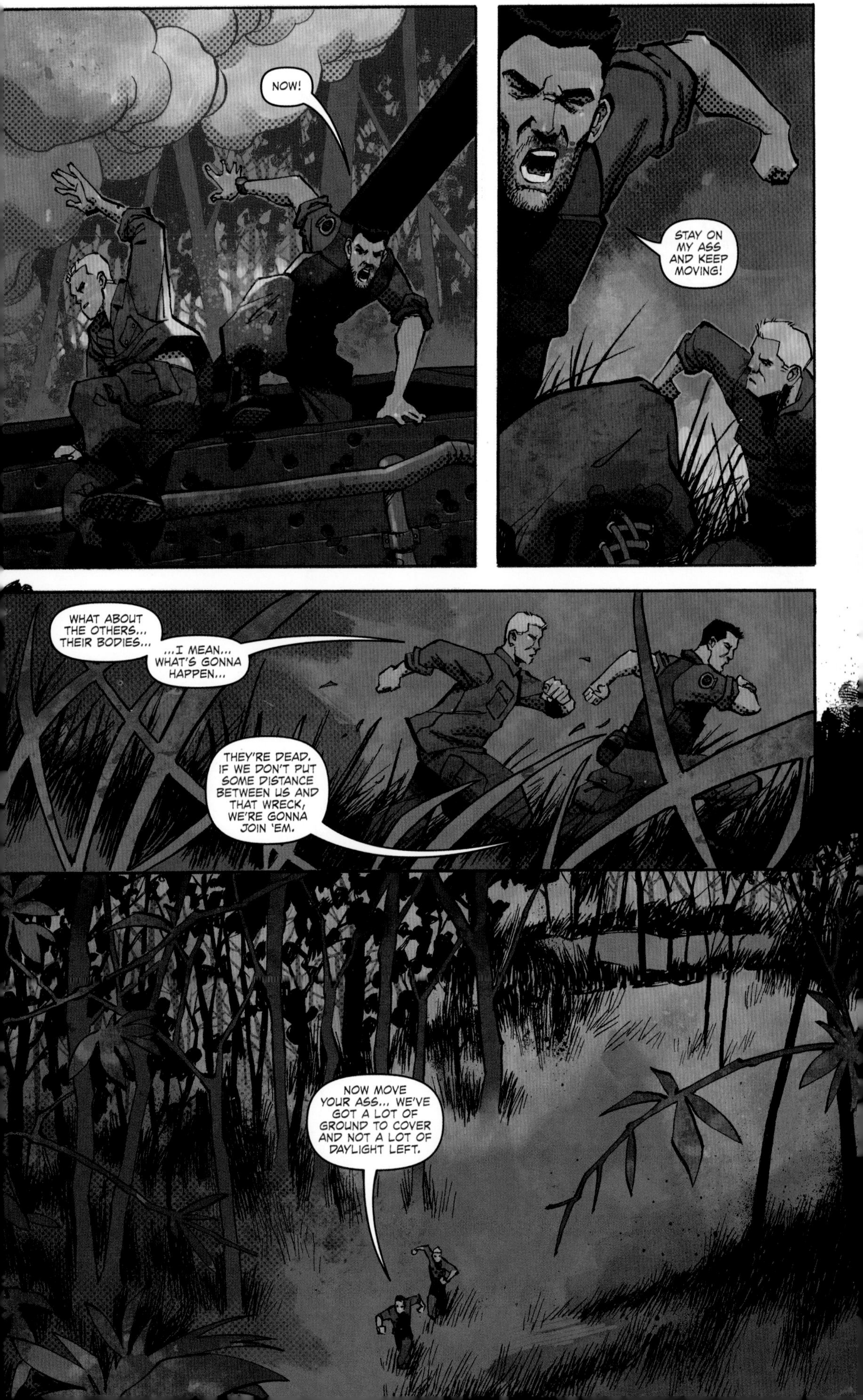
NOW!
STAY ON MY ASS AND KEEP MOVING!
WHAT ABOUT THE OTHERS... THEIR BODIES...
...I MEAN... WHAT'S GONNA HAPPEN...
THEY'RE DEAD. IF WE DON'T PUT SOME DISTANCE BETWEEN US AND THAT WRECK, WE'RE GONNA JOIN 'EM.
NOW MOVE YOUR ASS... WE'VE GOT A LOT OF GROUND TO COVER AND NOT A LOT OF DAYLIGHT LEFT.

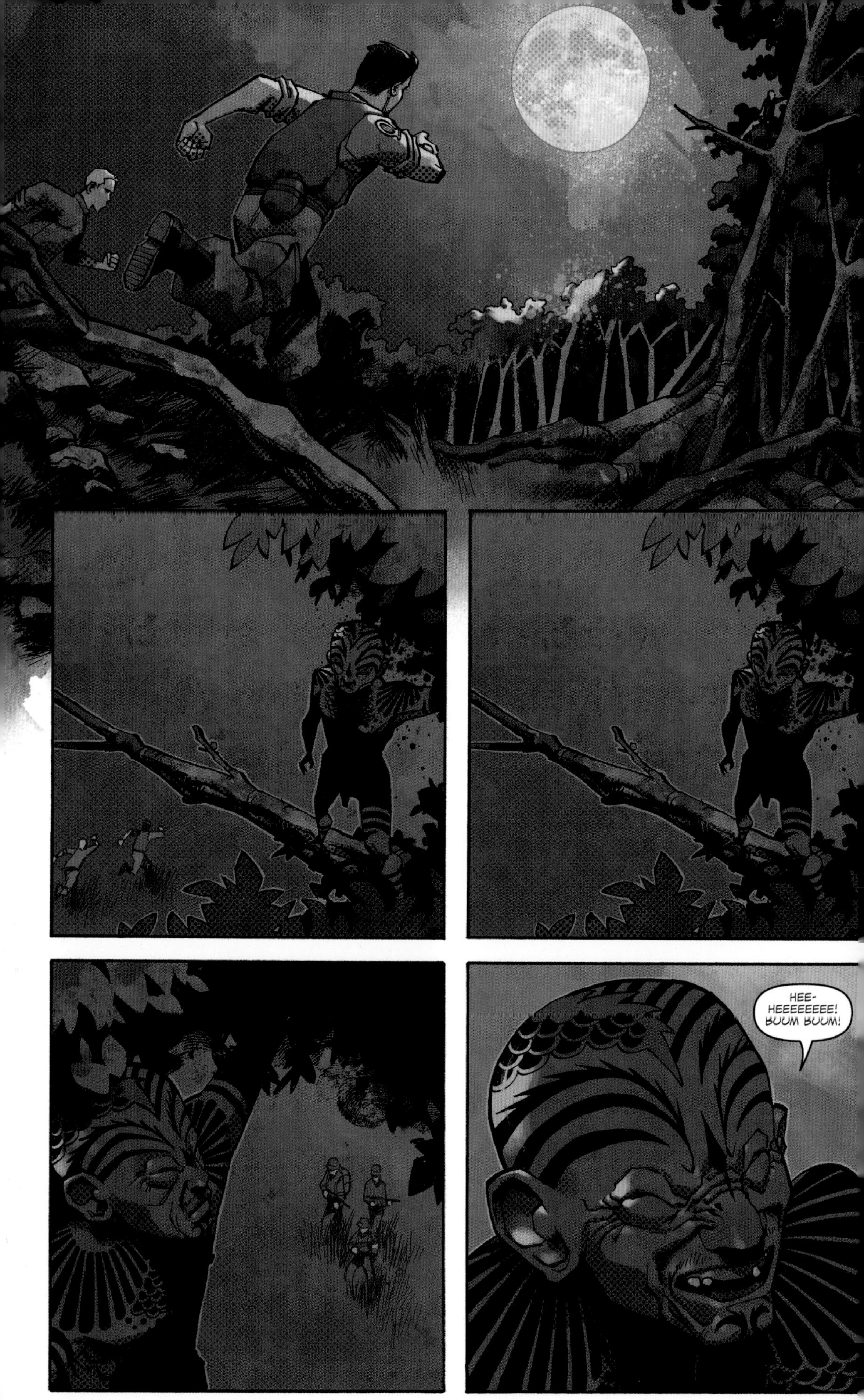
HEE-
HEEEEEEEE!
BOOM BOOM!

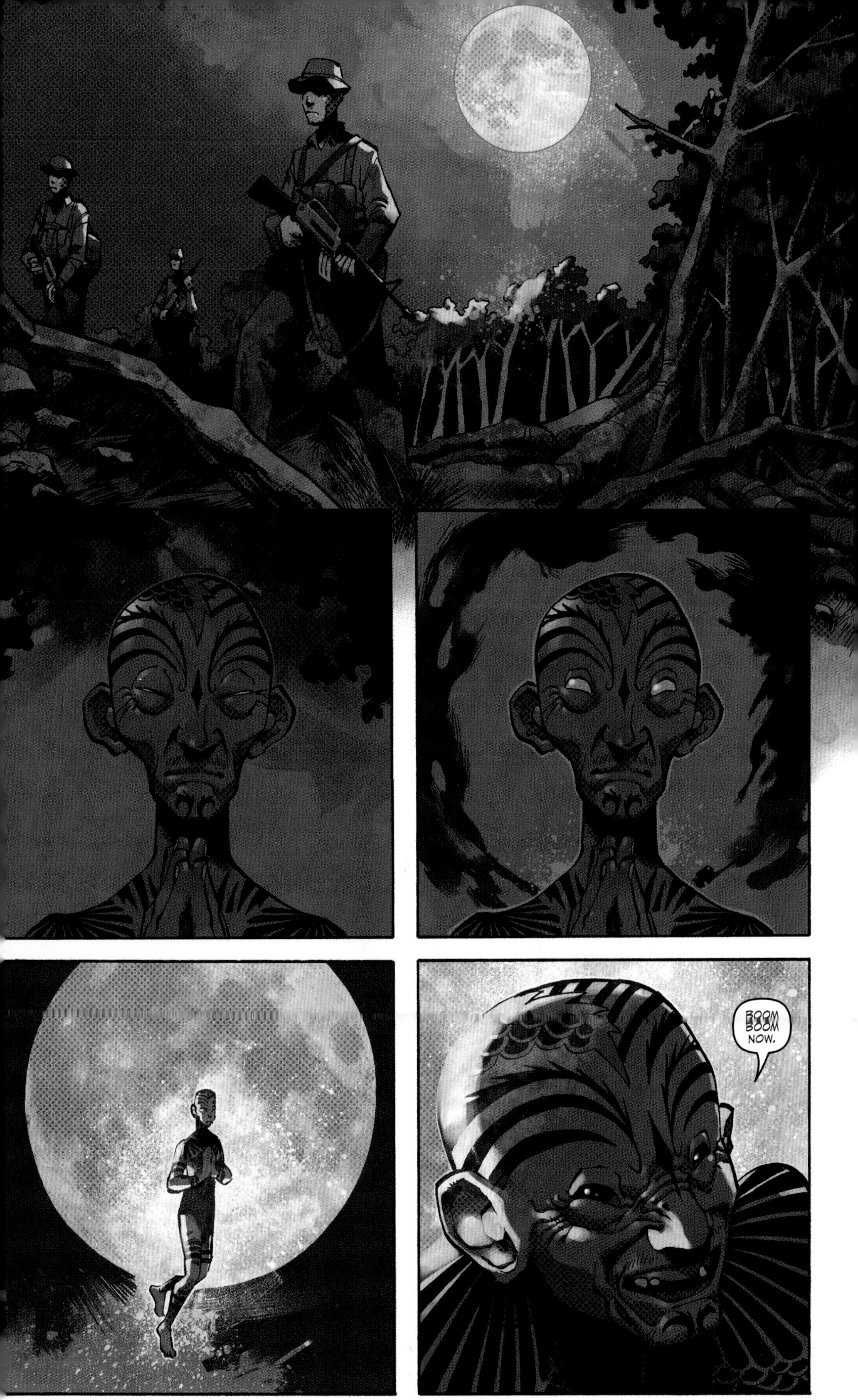
BOOM
BOOM
NOW.

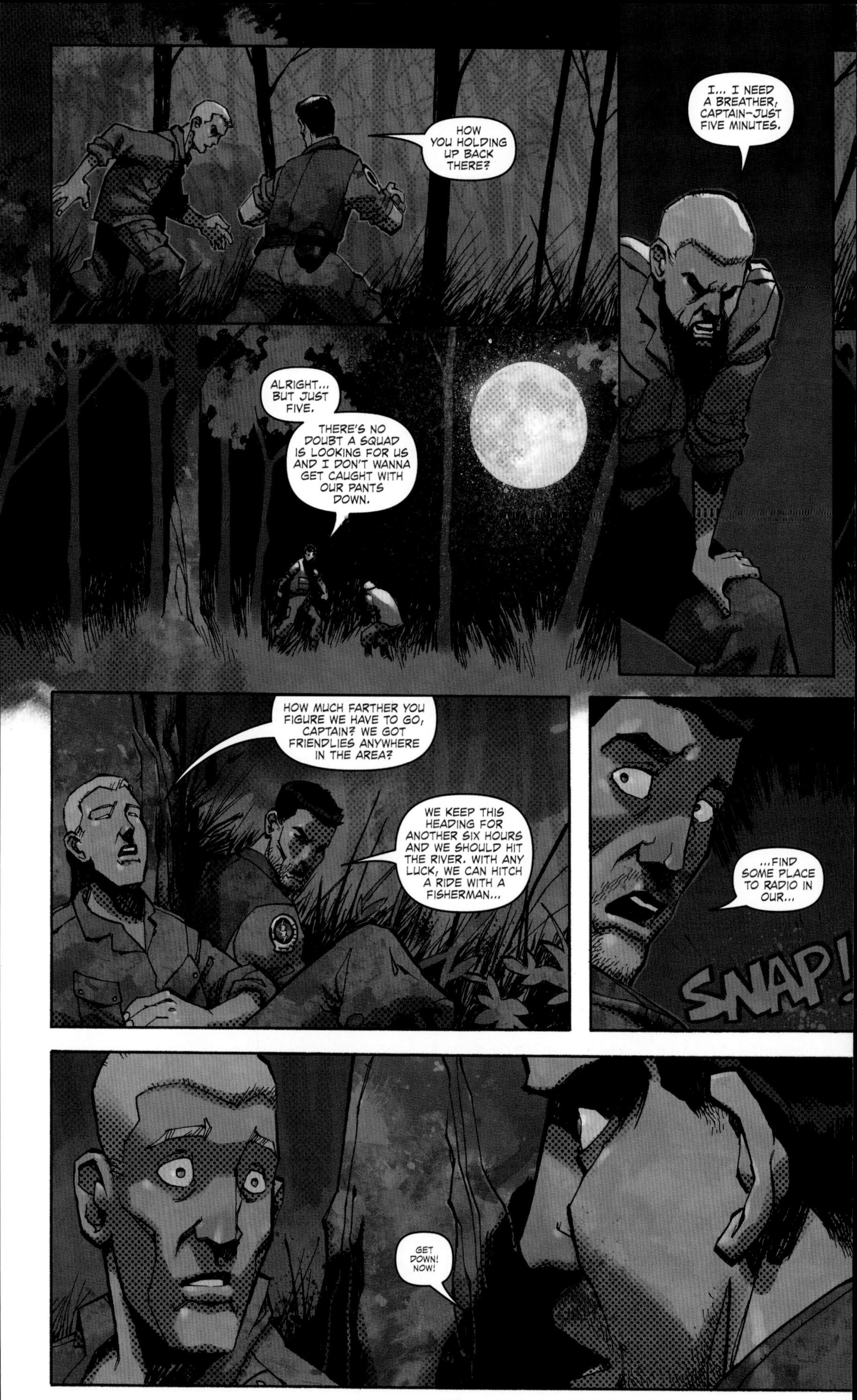
HOW YOU HOLDING UP BACK THERE?
I... I NEED A BREATHER, CAPTAIN–JUST FIVE MINUTES.
ALRIGHT... BUT JUST FIVE.
THERE'S NO DOUBT A SQUAD IS LOOKING FOR US AND I DON'T WANNA GET CAUGHT WITH OUR PANTS DOWN.
HOW MUCH FARTHER YOU FIGURE WE HAVE TO GO, CAPTAIN? WE GOT FRIENDLIES ANYWHERE IN THE AREA?
WE KEEP THIS HEADING FOR ANOTHER SIX HOURS AND WE SHOULD HIT THE RIVER. WITH ANY LUCK, WE CAN HITCH A RIDE WITH A FISHERMAN...
...FIND SOME PLACE TO RADIO IN OUR...
SNAP!
GET DOWN! NOW!

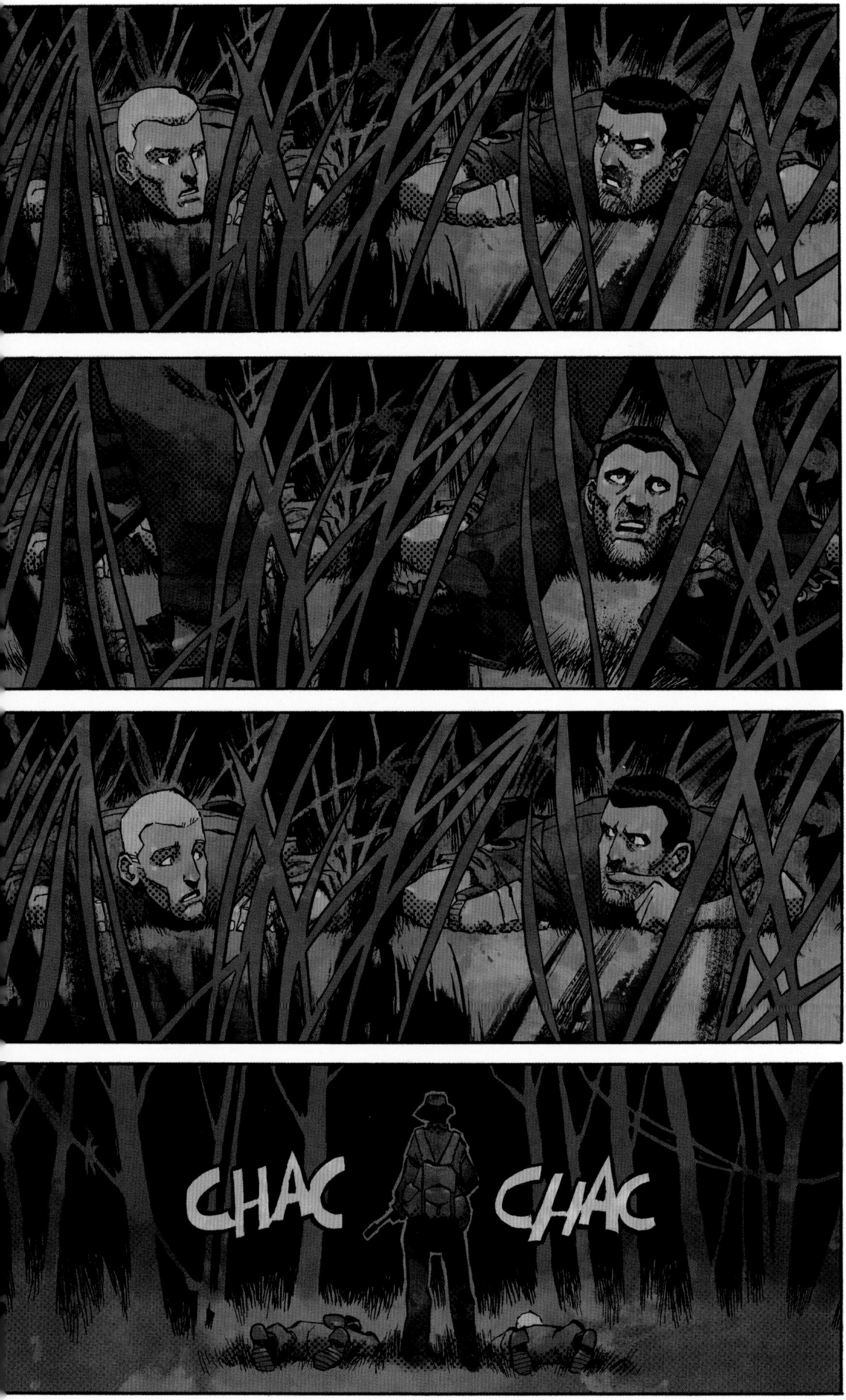
CHAC
CHAC

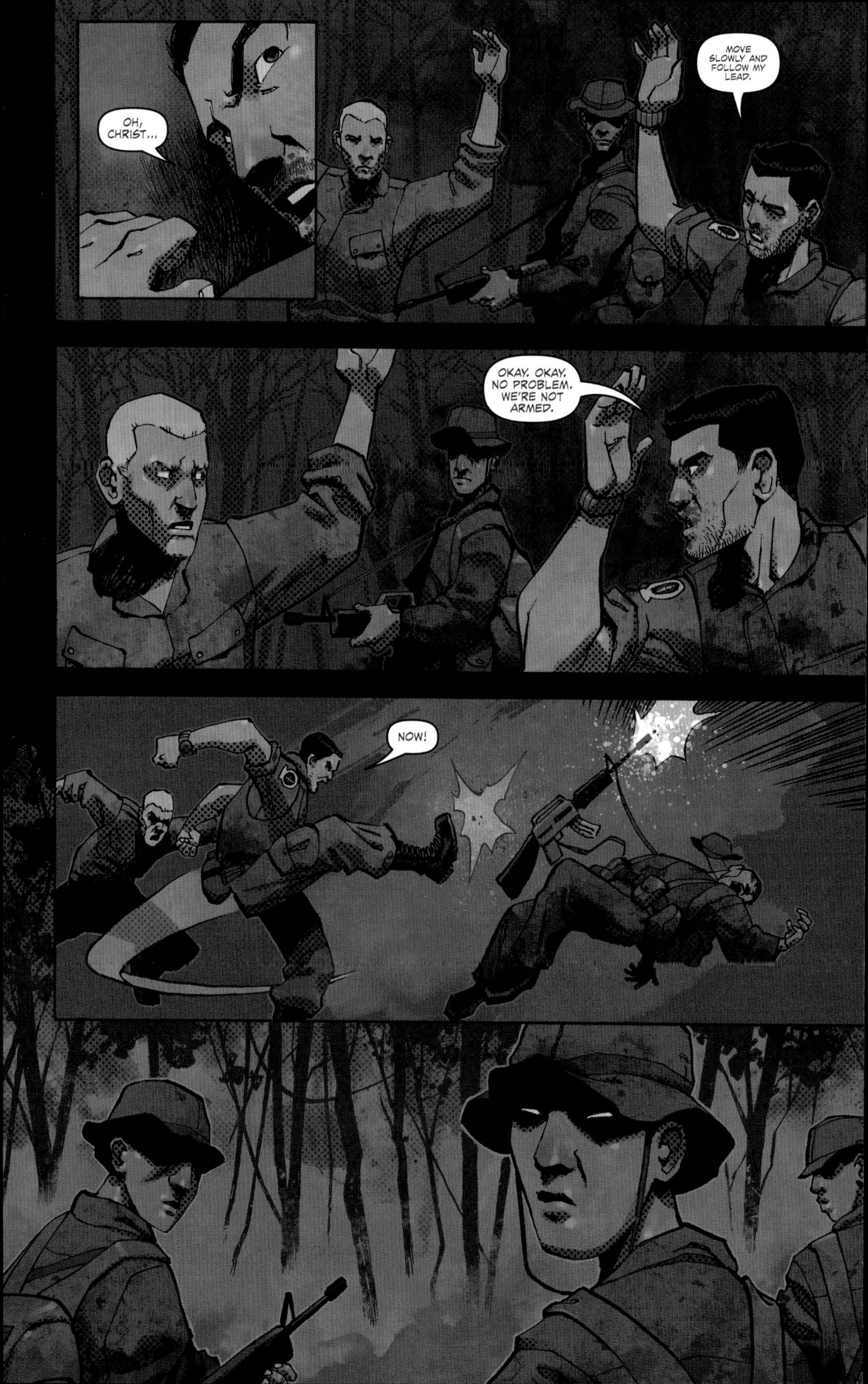
OH, CHRIST...
MOVE SLOWLY AND FOLLOW MY LEAD.
OKAY. OKAY. NO PROBLEM. WE'RE NOT ARMED.
NOW!

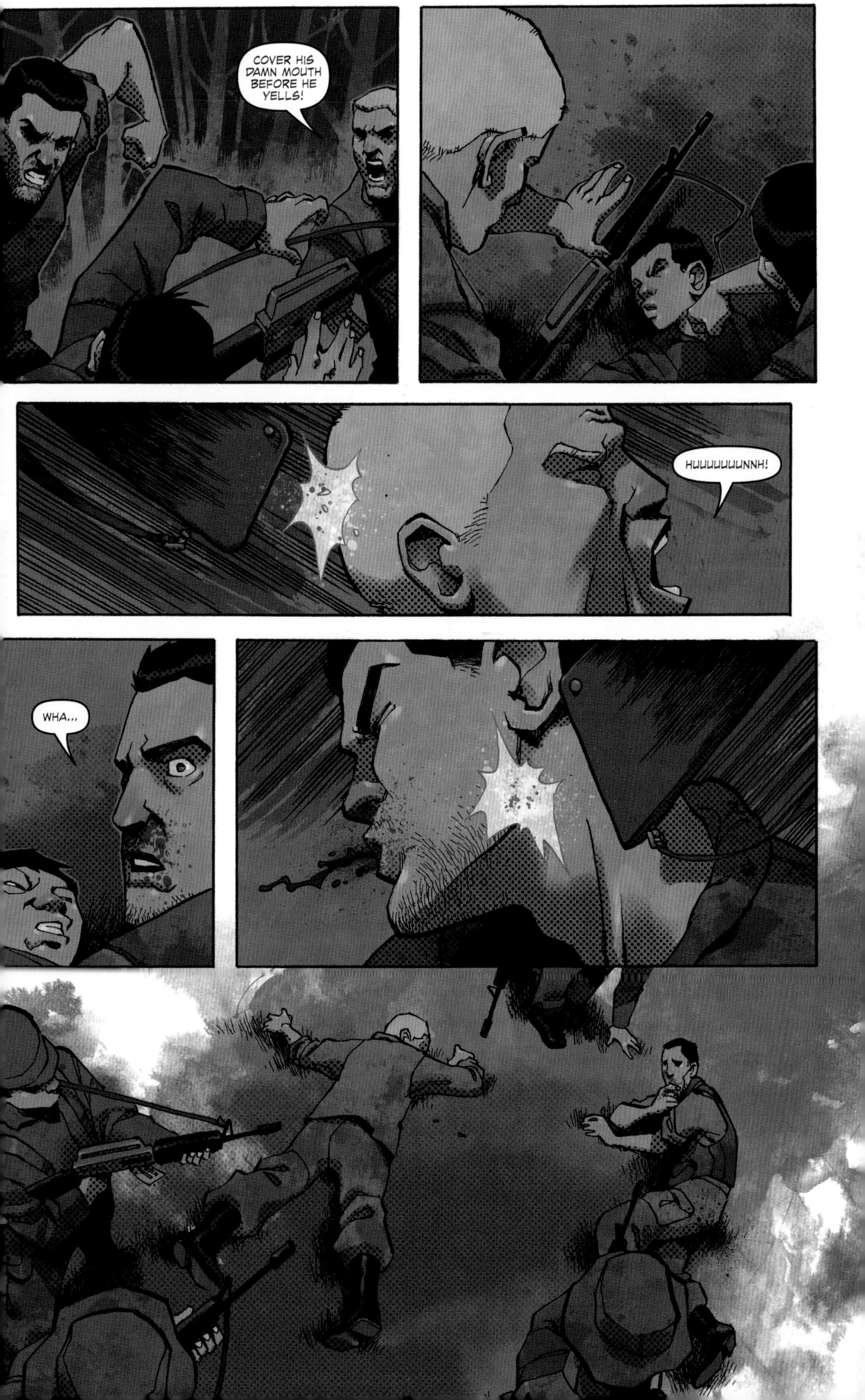

COVER HIS DAMN MOUTH BEFORE HE YELLS!
HUUUUUUUNNH!
WHA...

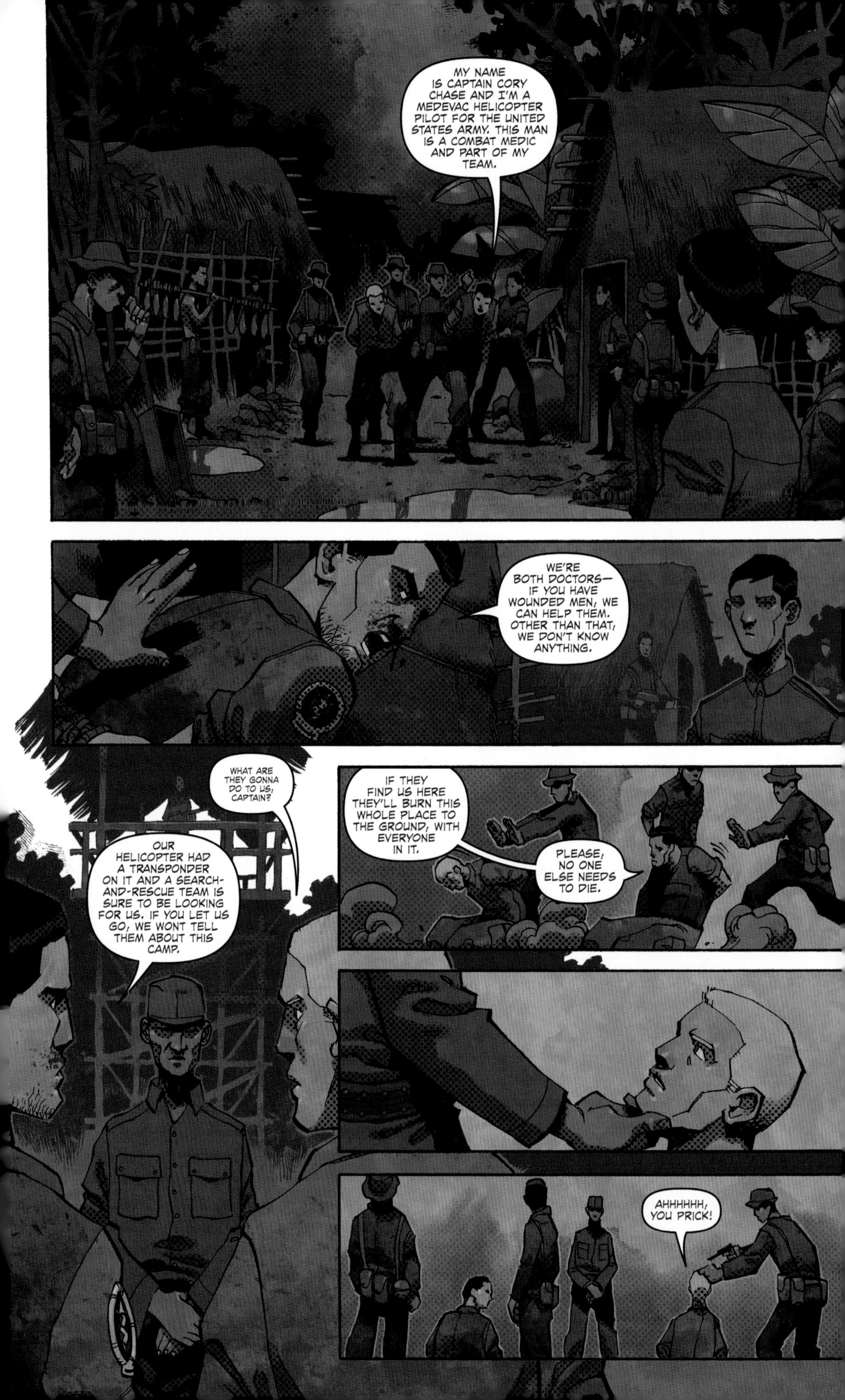
MY NAME IS CAPTAIN CORY CHASE AND I'M A MEDEVAC HELICOPTER PILOT FOR THE UNITED STATES ARMY. THIS MAN IS A COMBAT MEDIC AND PART OF MY TEAM.
WE'RE BOTH DOCTORS— IF YOU HAVE WOUNDED MEN, WE CAN HELP THEM. OTHER THAN THAT, WE DON'T KNOW ANYTHING.
WHAT ARE THEY GONNA DO TO US, CAPTAIN?
OUR HELICOPTER HAD A TRANSPONDER ON IT AND A SEARCH-AND-RESCUE TEAM IS SURE TO BE LOOKING FOR US. IF YOU LET US GO, WE WONT TELL THEM ABOUT THIS CAMP.
IF THEY FIND US HERE THEY'LL BURN THIS WHOLE PLACE TO THE GROUND, WITH EVERYONE IN IT.
PLEASE, NO ONE ELSE NEEDS TO DIE.
AHHHHHH, YOU PRICK!

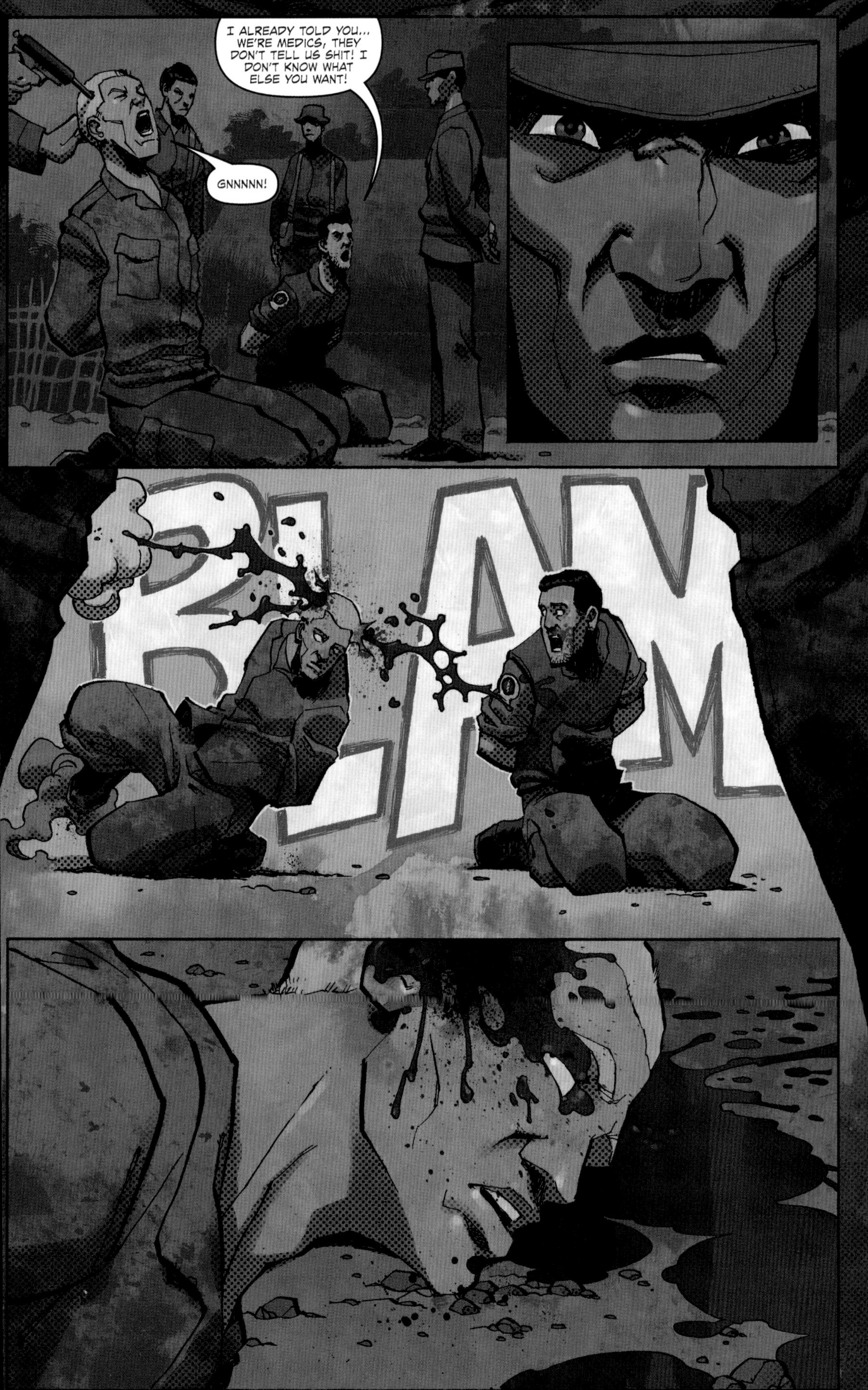
I ALREADY TOLD YOU... WE'RE MEDICS, THEY DON'T TELL US SHIT! I DON'T KNOW WHAT ELSE YOU WANT!
GNNNNN!
BLAM

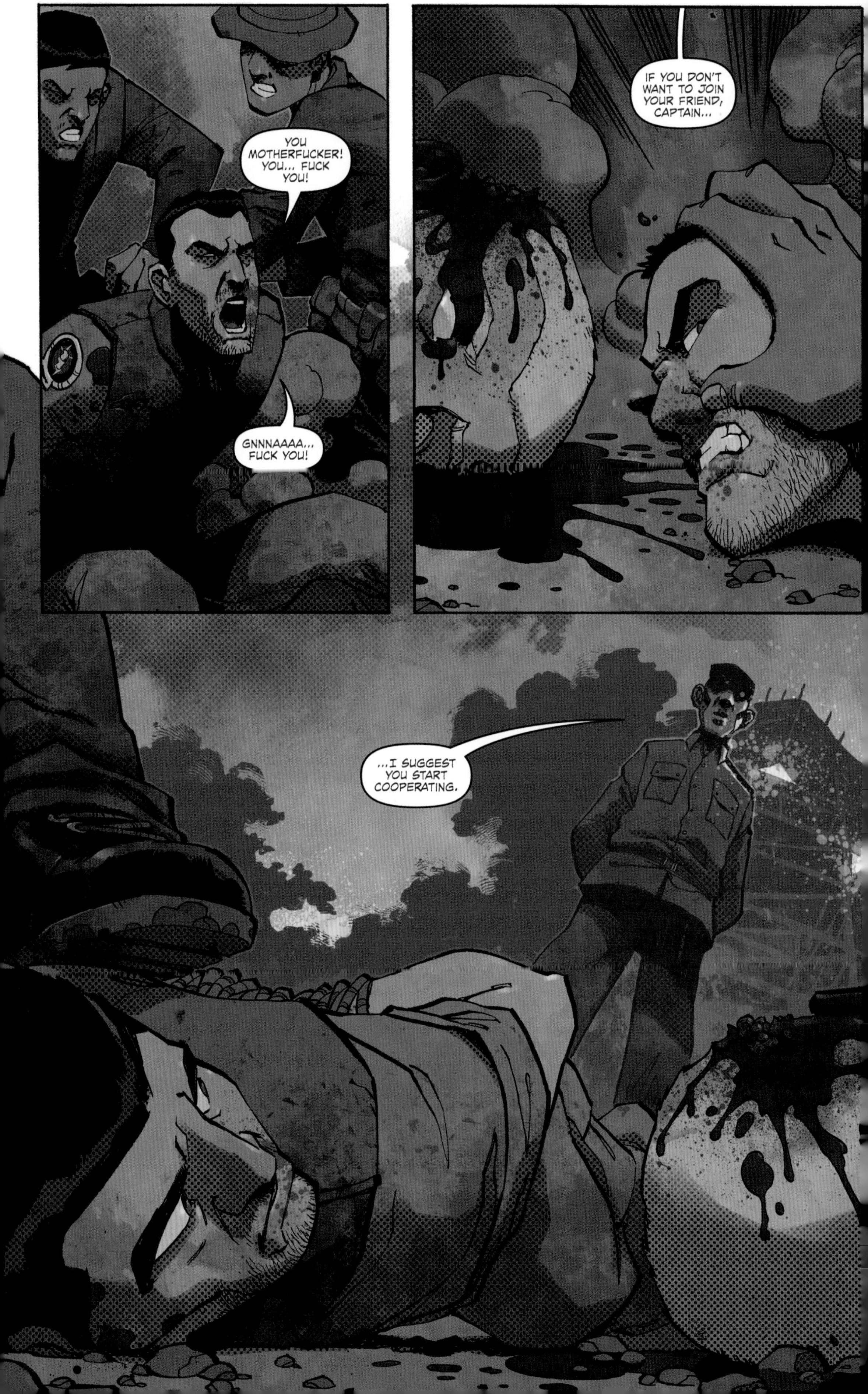
YOU MOTHERFUCKER! YOU... FUCK YOU!
GNNNAAAA... FUCK YOU!
IF YOU DON'T WANT TO JOIN YOUR FRIEND, CAPTAIN...
...I SUGGEST YOU START COOPERATING.

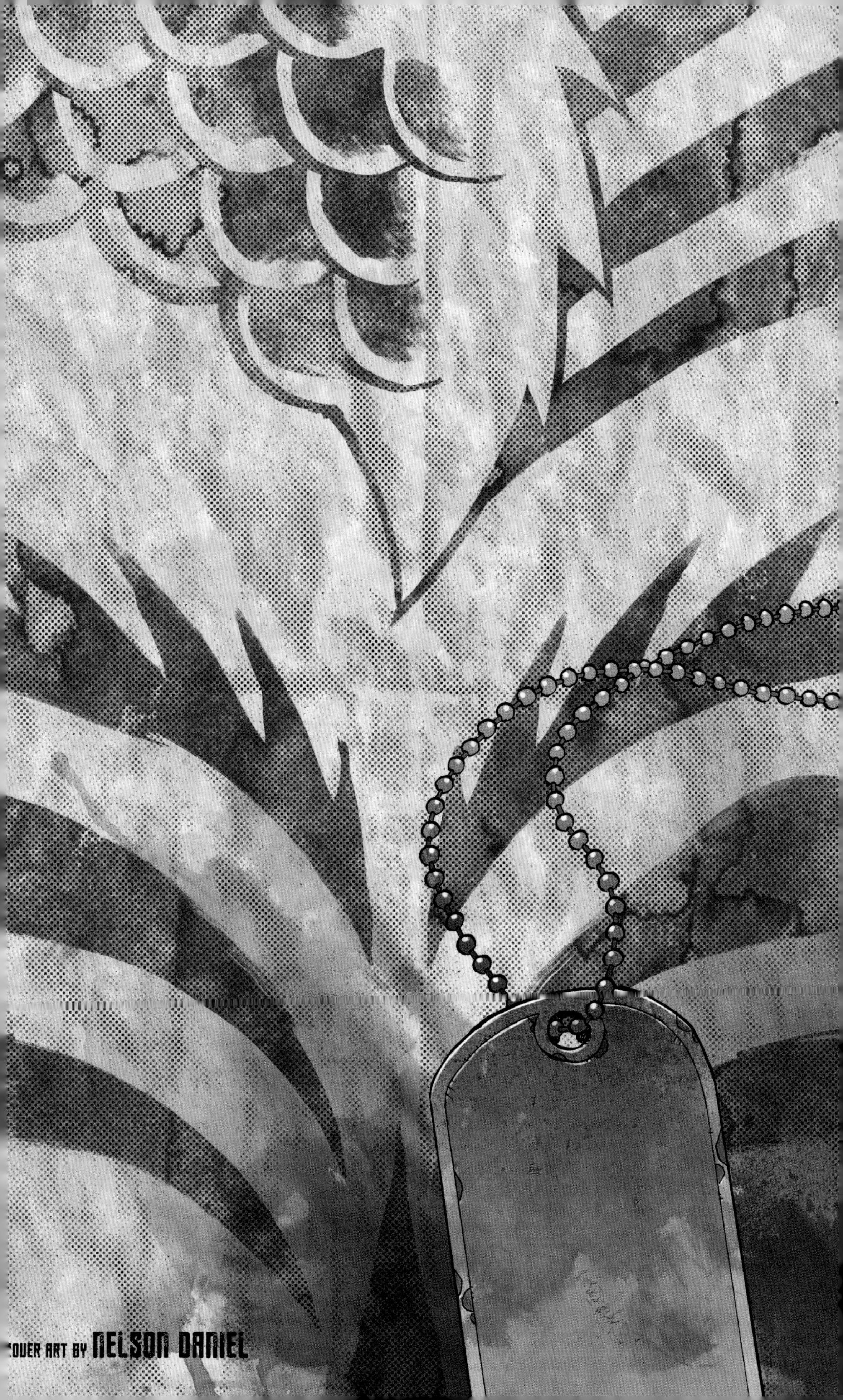
COVER ART BY NELSON DANIEL

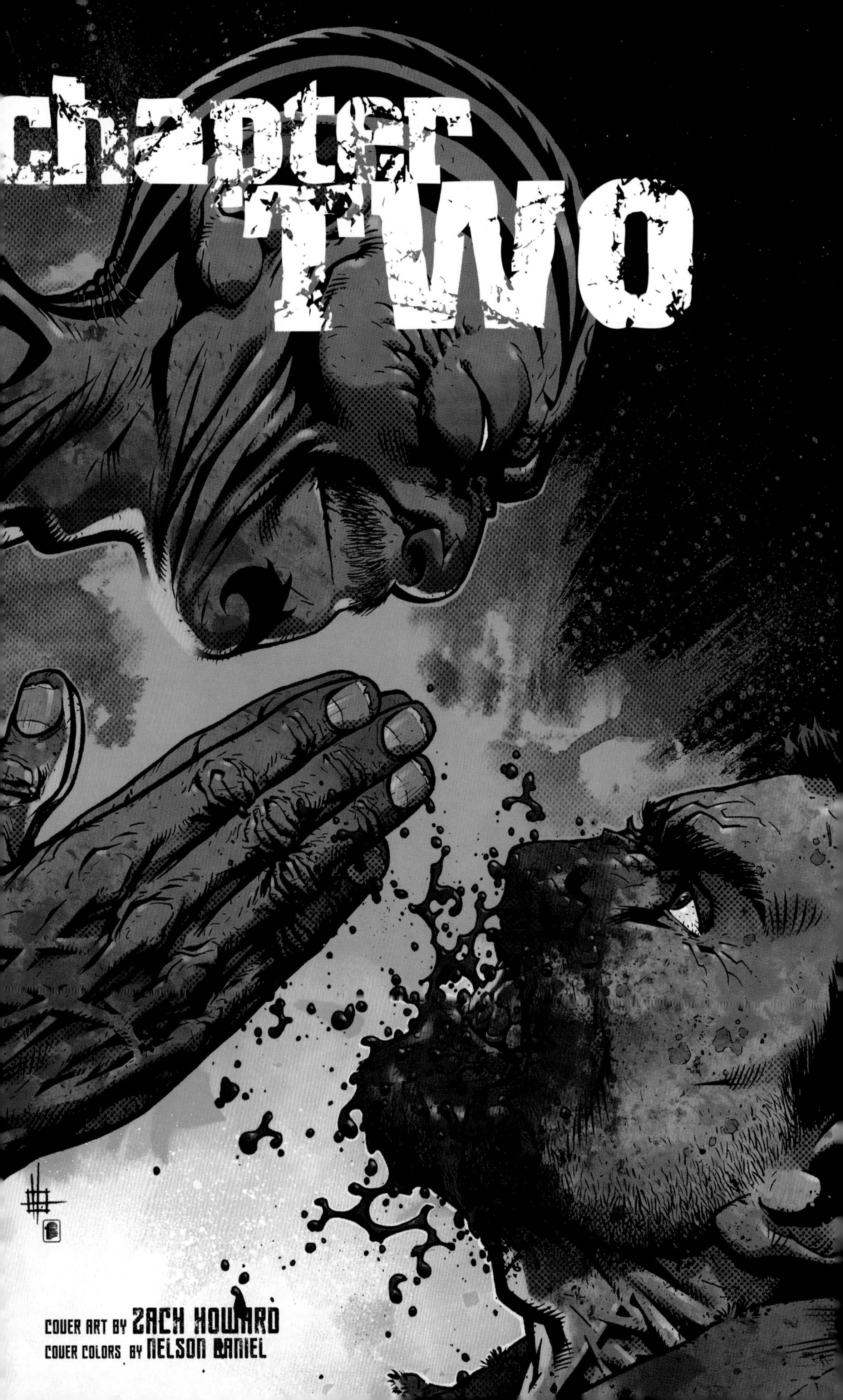
chapter TWO
COVER ART BY ZACH HOWARD
COVER COLORS BY NELSON DANIEL

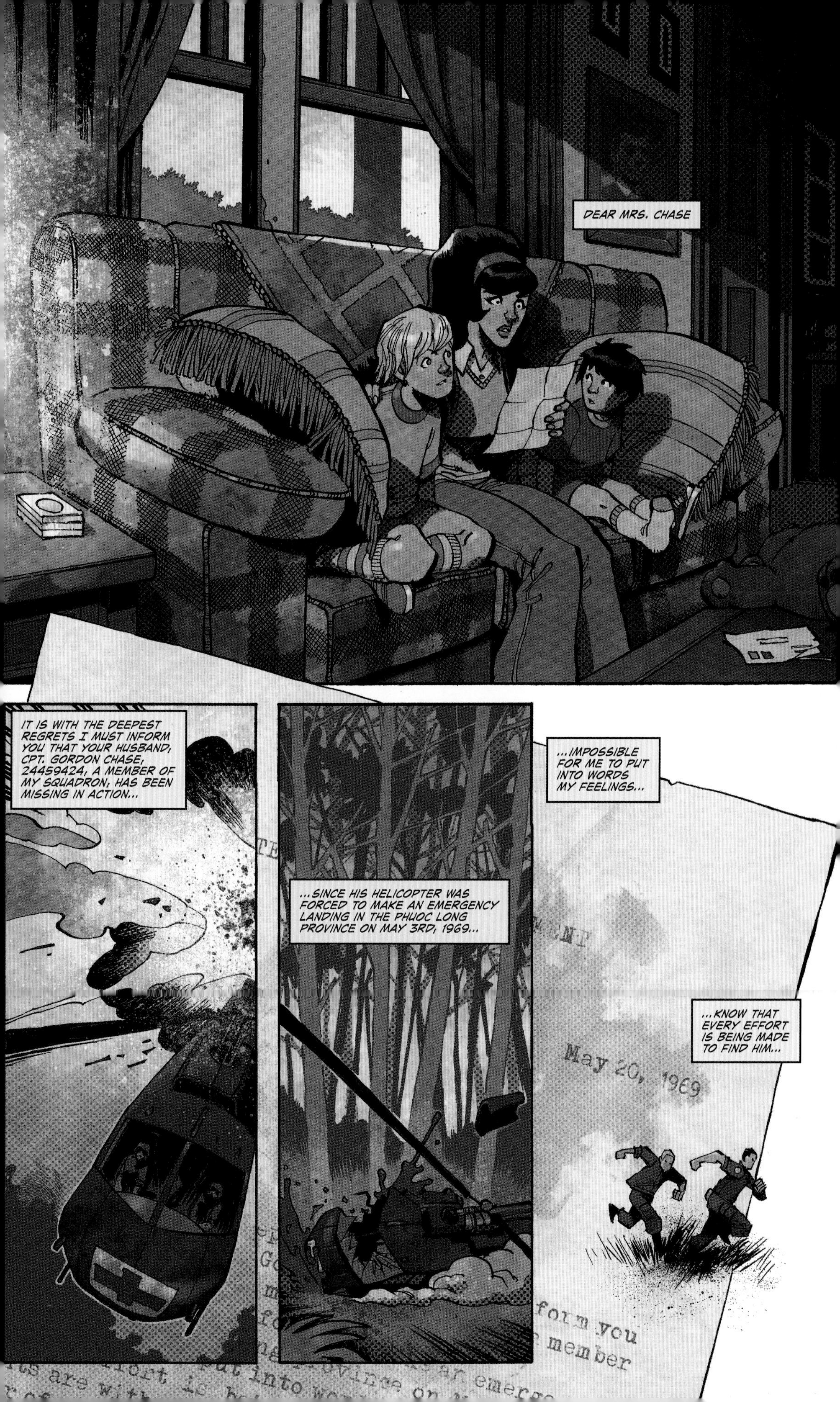
DEAR MRS. CHASE
IT IS WITH THE DEEPEST REGRETS I MUST INFORM YOU THAT YOUR HUSBAND, CPT. GORDON CHASE, 24459424, A MEMBER OF MY SQUADRON, HAS BEEN MISSING IN ACTION...
...SINCE HIS HELICOPTER WAS FORCED TO MAKE AN EMERGENCY LANDING IN THE PHUOC LONG PROVINCE ON MAY 3RD, 1969...
...IMPOSSIBLE FOR ME TO PUT INTO WORDS MY FEELINGS...
...KNOW THAT EVERY EFFORT IS BEING MADE TO FIND HIM...
May 20, 1969

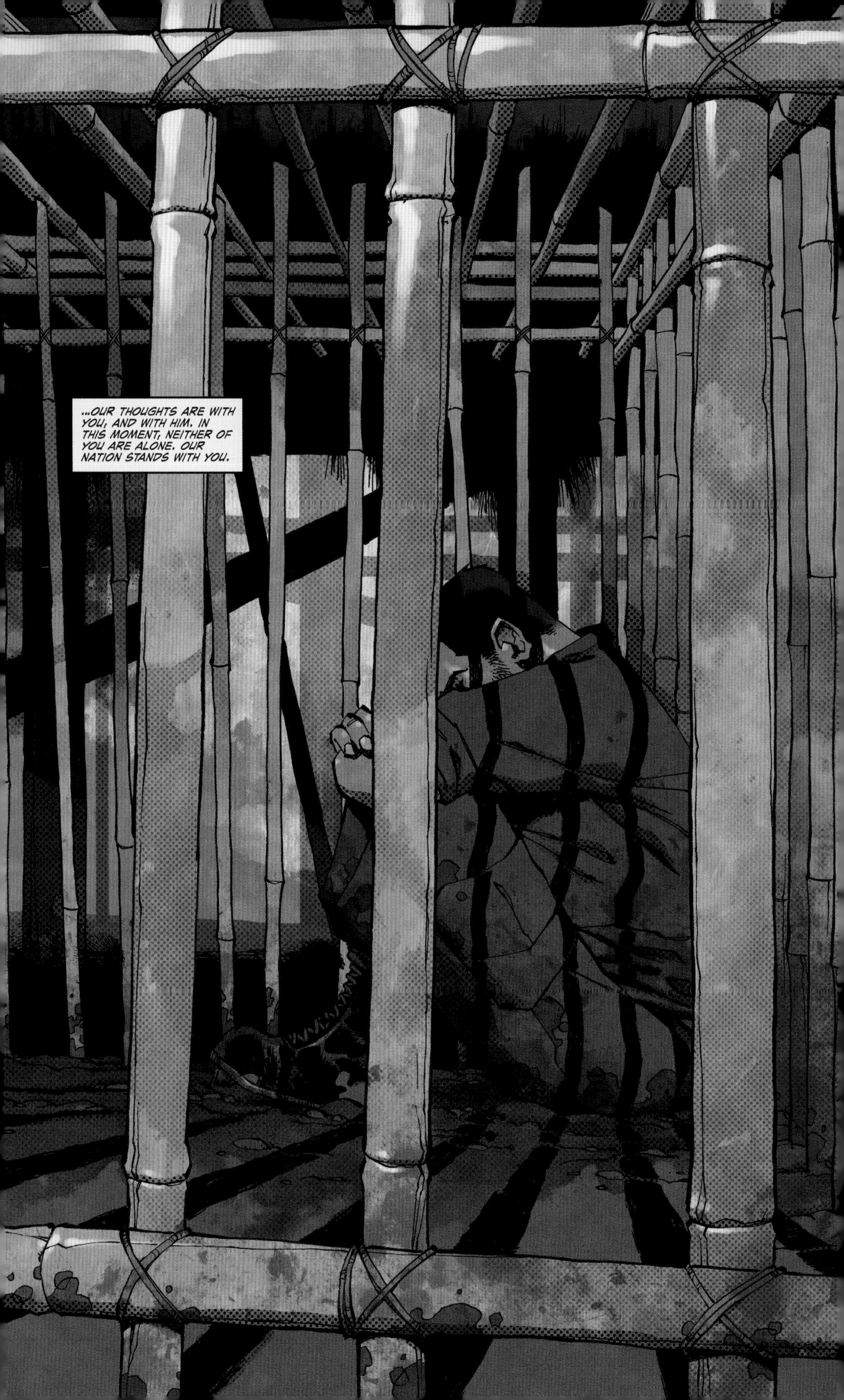
...OUR THOUGHTS ARE WITH YOU, AND WITH HIM. IN THIS MOMENT, NEITHER OF YOU ARE ALONE. OUR NATION STANDS WITH YOU.

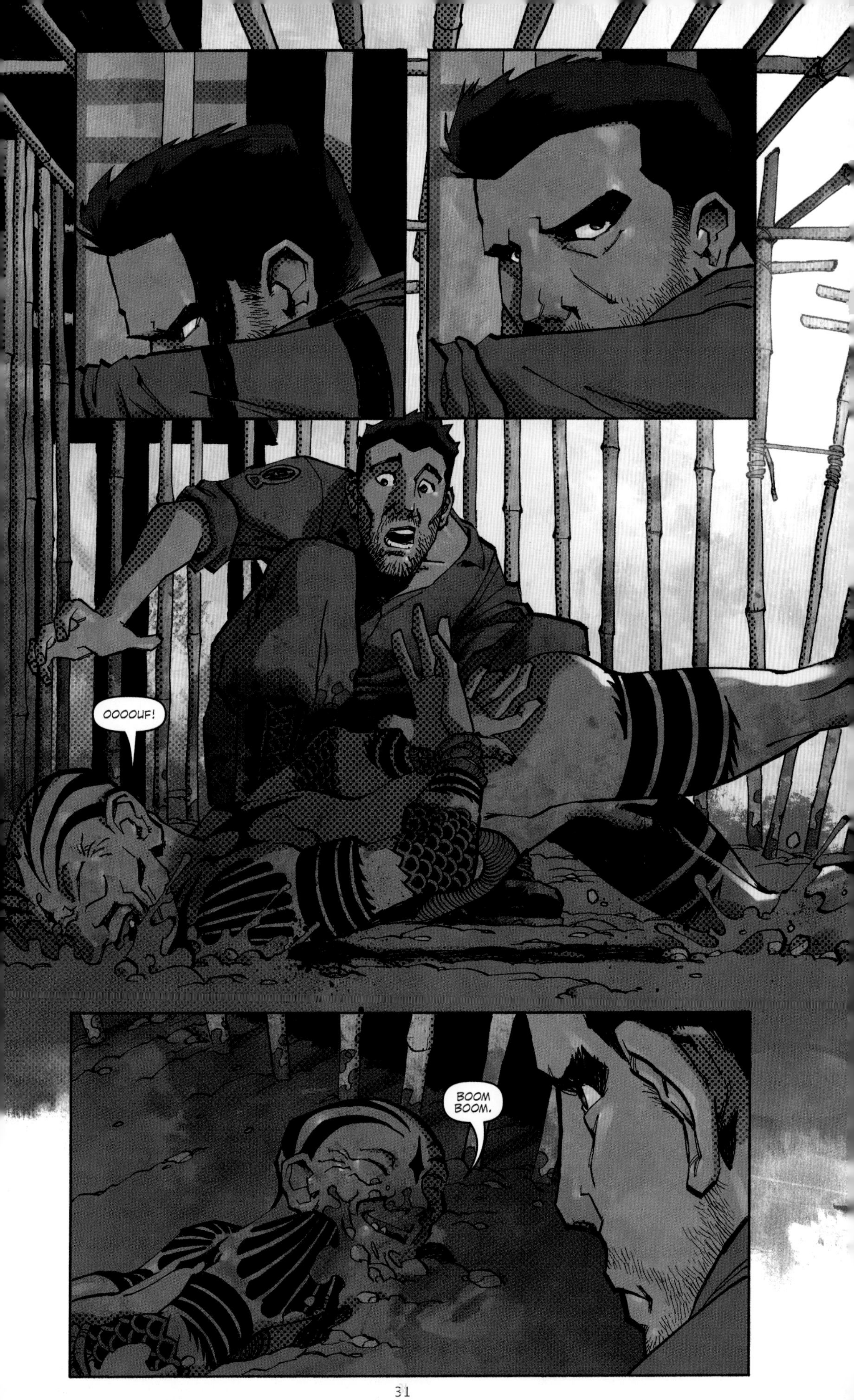
OOOOUF!
BOOM BOOM.

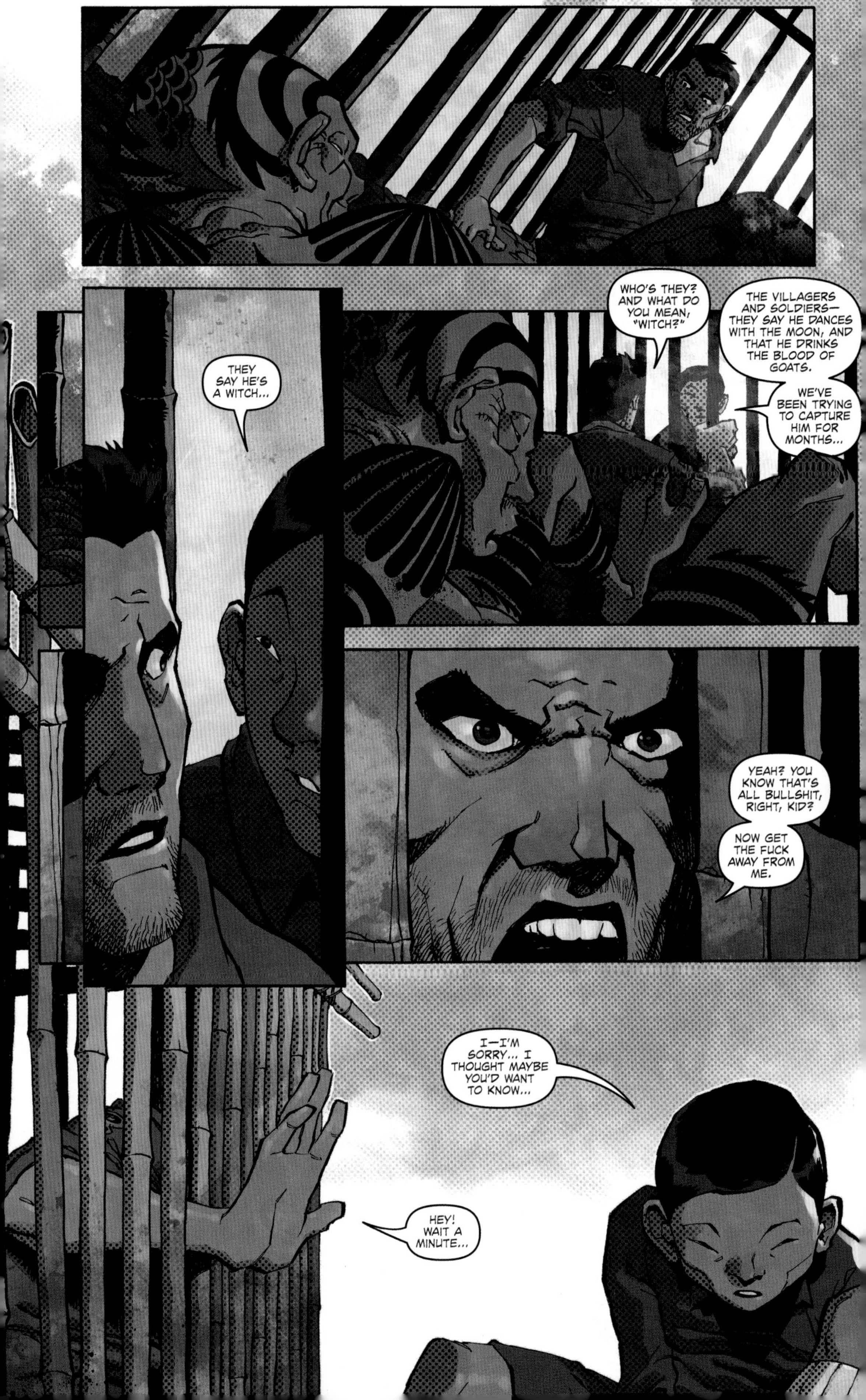
THEY SAY HE'S A WITCH...
WHO'S THEY? AND WHAT DO YOU MEAN, "WITCH?"
THE VILLAGERS AND SOLDIERS— THEY SAY HE DANCES WITH THE MOON, AND THAT HE DRINKS THE BLOOD OF GOATS.
WE'VE BEEN TRYING TO CAPTURE HIM FOR MONTHS...
YEAH? YOU KNOW THAT'S ALL BULLSHIT, RIGHT, KID?
NOW GET THE FUCK AWAY FROM ME.
I—I'M SORRY... I THOUGHT MAYBE YOU'D WANT TO KNOW...
HEY! WAIT A MINUTE...

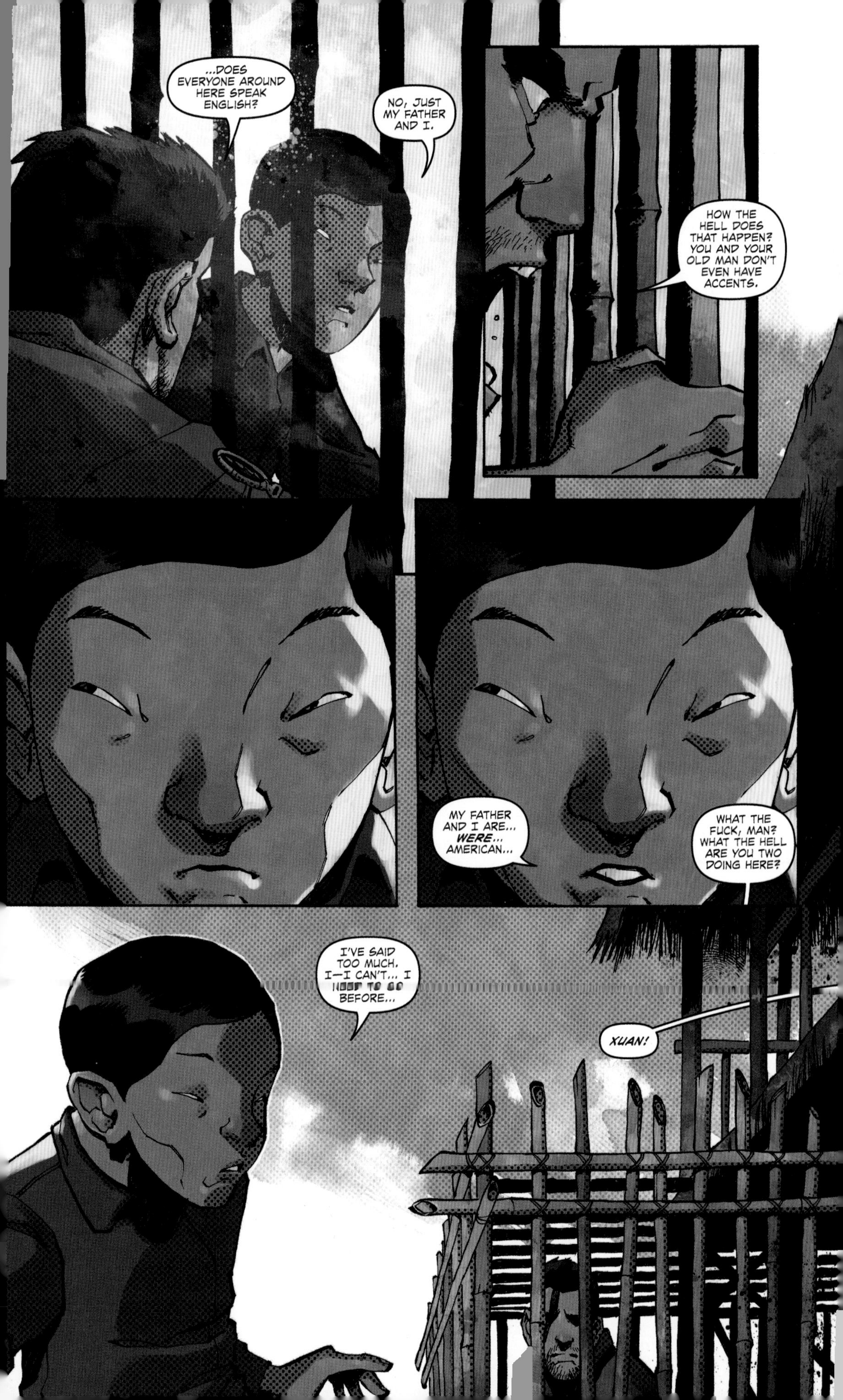
...DOES EVERYONE AROUND HERE SPEAK ENGLISH?
NO, JUST MY FATHER AND I.
HOW THE HELL DOES THAT HAPPEN? YOU AND YOUR OLD MAN DON'T EVEN HAVE ACCENTS.
MY FATHER AND I ARE... *WERE*... AMERICAN...
WHAT THE FUCK, MAN? WHAT THE HELL ARE YOU TWO DOING HERE?
I'VE SAID TOO MUCH. I—I CAN'T... I
BEFORE...
XUAN!

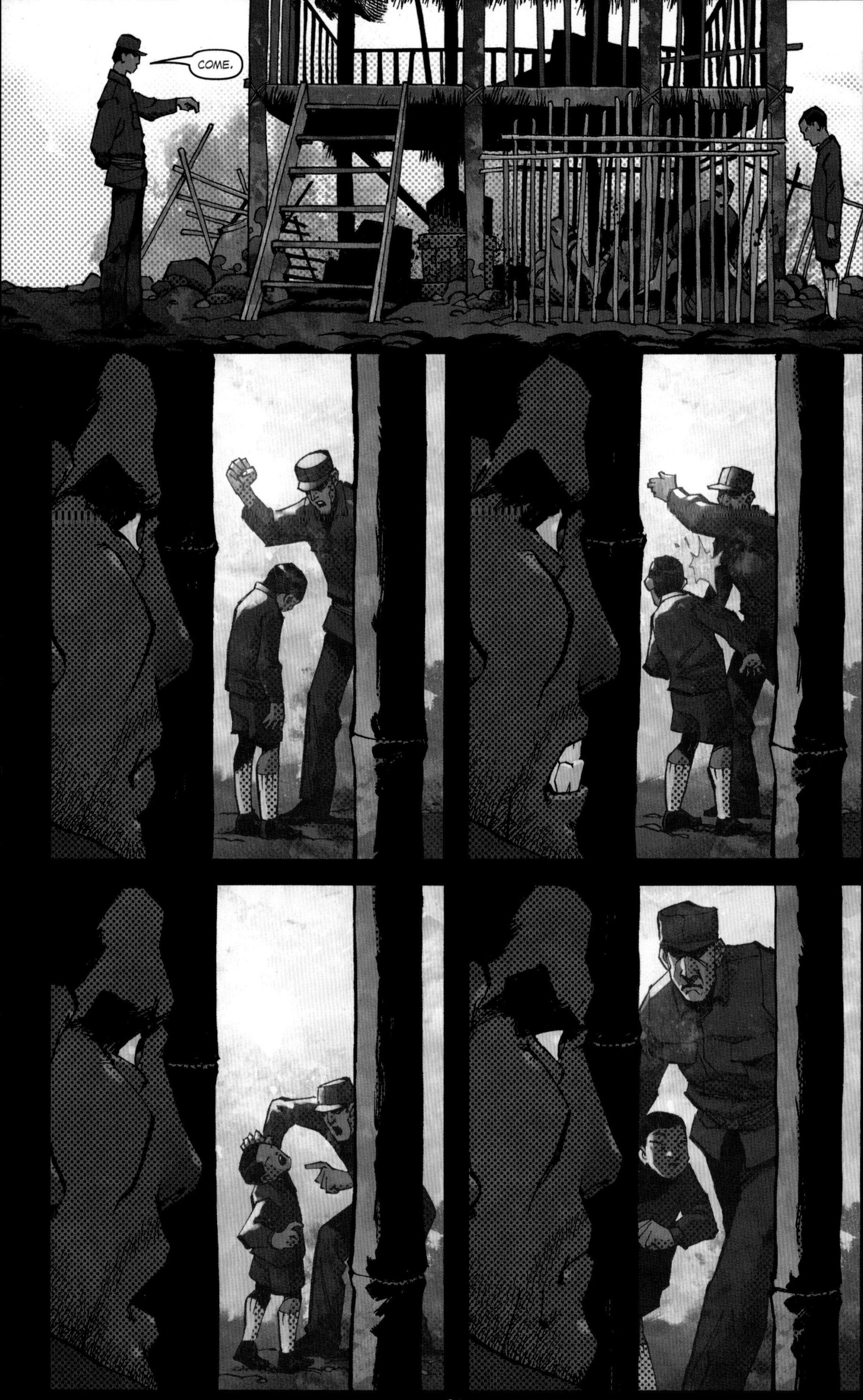
COME.

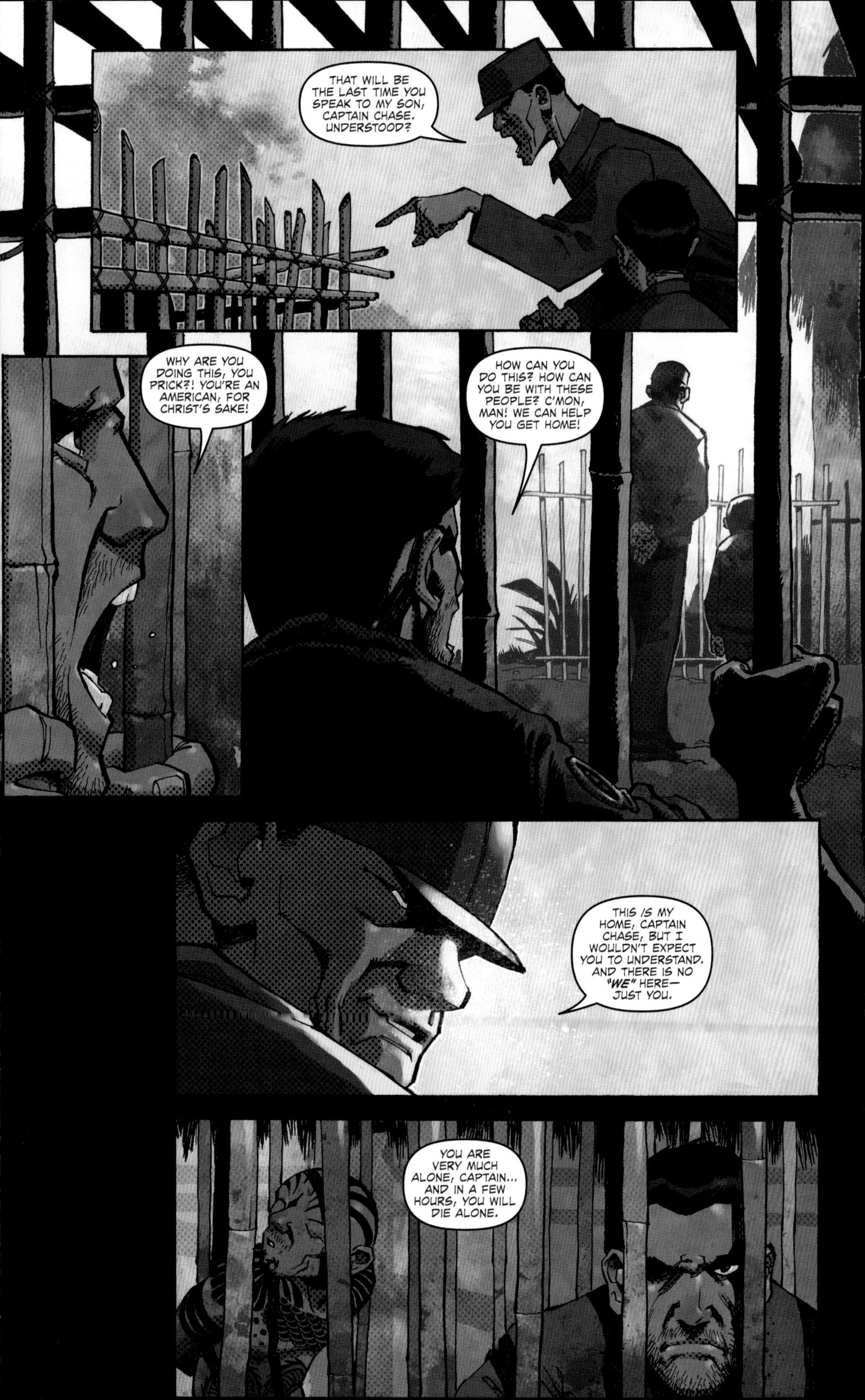
THAT WILL BE THE LAST TIME YOU SPEAK TO MY SON, CAPTAIN CHASE. UNDERSTOOD?
WHY ARE YOU DOING THIS, YOU PRICK?! YOU'RE AN AMERICAN, FOR CHRIST'S SAKE!
HOW CAN YOU DO THIS? HOW CAN YOU BE WITH THESE PEOPLE? C'MON, MAN! WE CAN HELP YOU GET HOME!
THIS *IS* MY HOME, CAPTAIN CHASE, BUT I WOULDN'T EXPECT YOU TO UNDERSTAND. AND THERE IS NO ***"WE"*** HERE— JUST YOU.
YOU ARE VERY MUCH ALONE, CAPTAIN... AND IN A FEW HOURS, YOU WILL DIE ALONE.

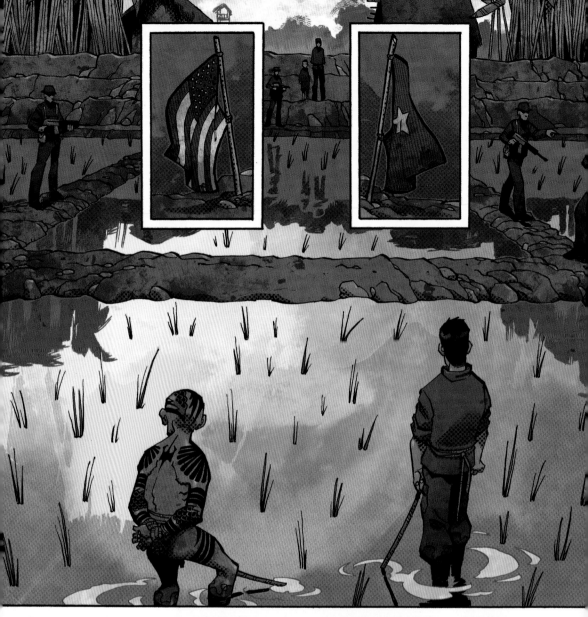

THE RULES ARE SIMPLE, CAPTAIN CHASE—THE FIRST ONE TO GET TO HIS FLAG IS THE WINNER...

AND THE LOSER?

THE LOSER GETS RAPED BY THE ENTIRE CAMP... AND WHEN MY MEN ARE FINISHED WITH HIM...

...I PUT A BULLET IN HIS HEAD AND BURN HIS BODY TO ASH SO THERE IS NOTHING LEFT TO SEND HOME TO HIS FAMILY.

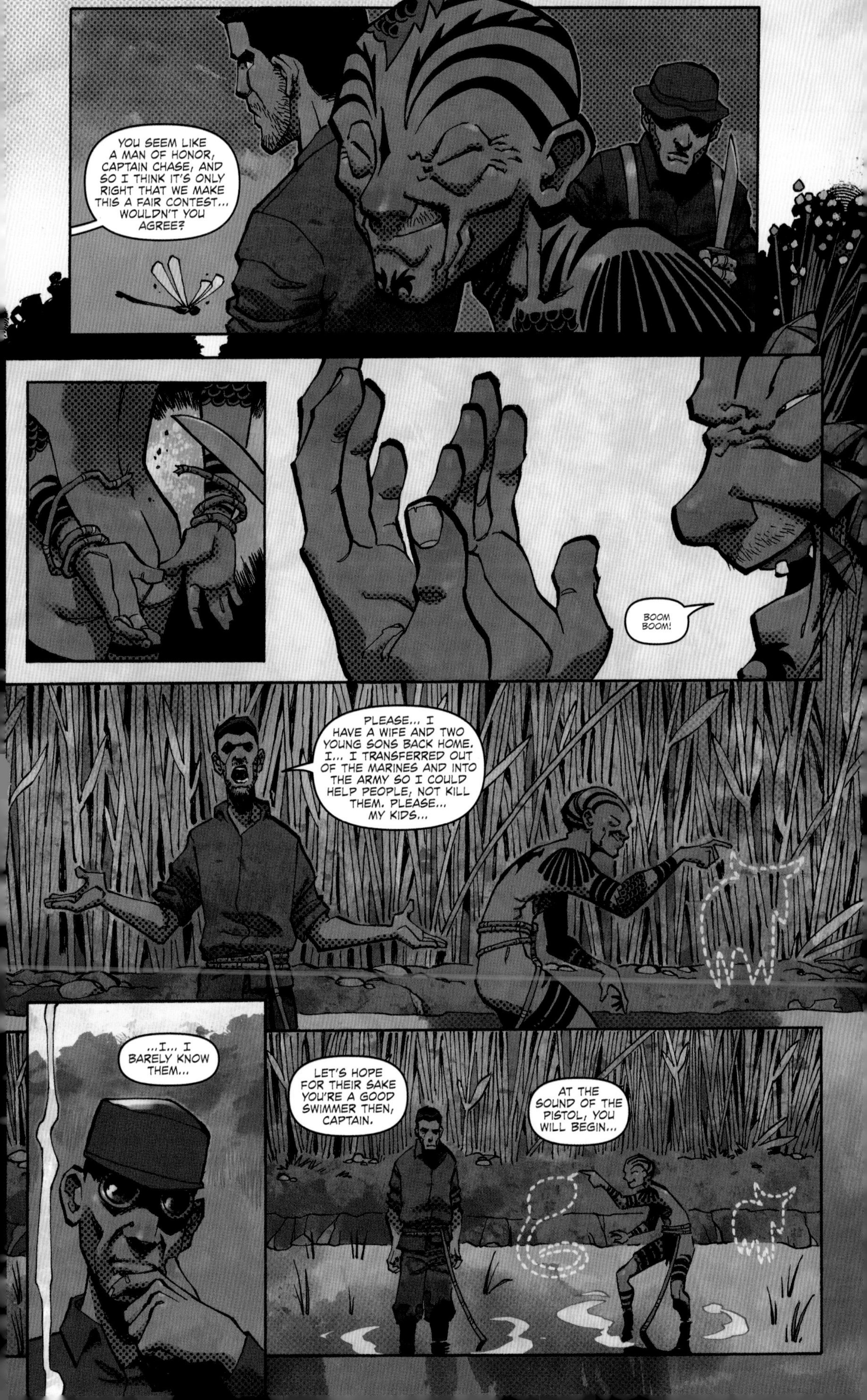
YOU SEEM LIKE A MAN OF HONOR, CAPTAIN CHASE, AND SO I THINK IT'S ONLY RIGHT THAT WE MAKE THIS A FAIR CONTEST... WOULDN'T YOU AGREE?
BOOM BOOM!
PLEASE... I HAVE A WIFE AND TWO YOUNG SONS BACK HOME. I... I TRANSFERRED OUT OF THE MARINES AND INTO THE ARMY SO I COULD HELP PEOPLE, NOT KILL THEM. PLEASE... MY KIDS...
...I... I BARELY KNOW THEM...
LET'S HOPE FOR THEIR SAKE YOU'RE A GOOD SWIMMER THEN, CAPTAIN.
AT THE SOUND OF THE PISTOL, YOU WILL BEGIN...

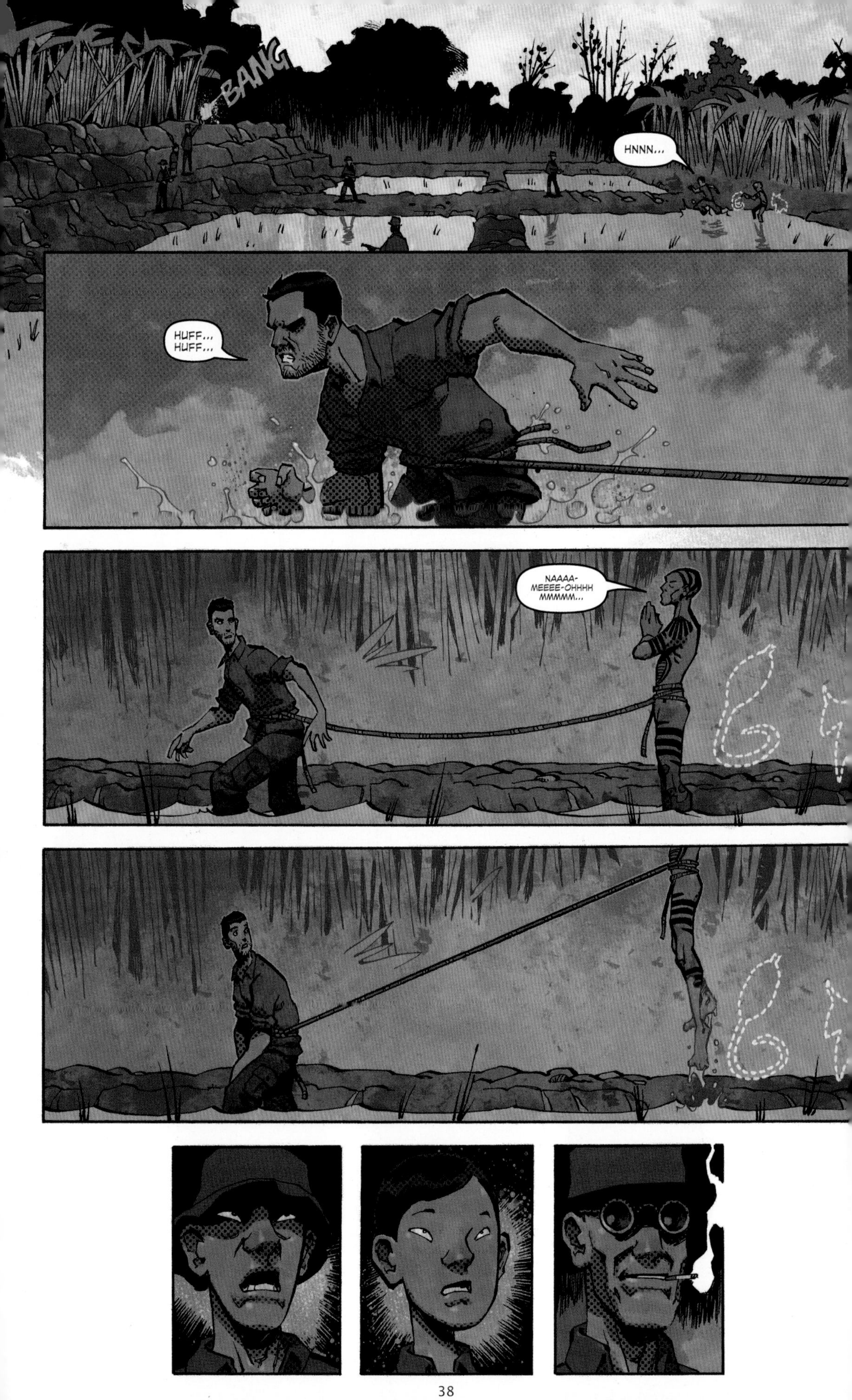
BANG
HNNN...
HUFF... HUFF...
NAAAA-MEEEE-OHHHH MMMMM...

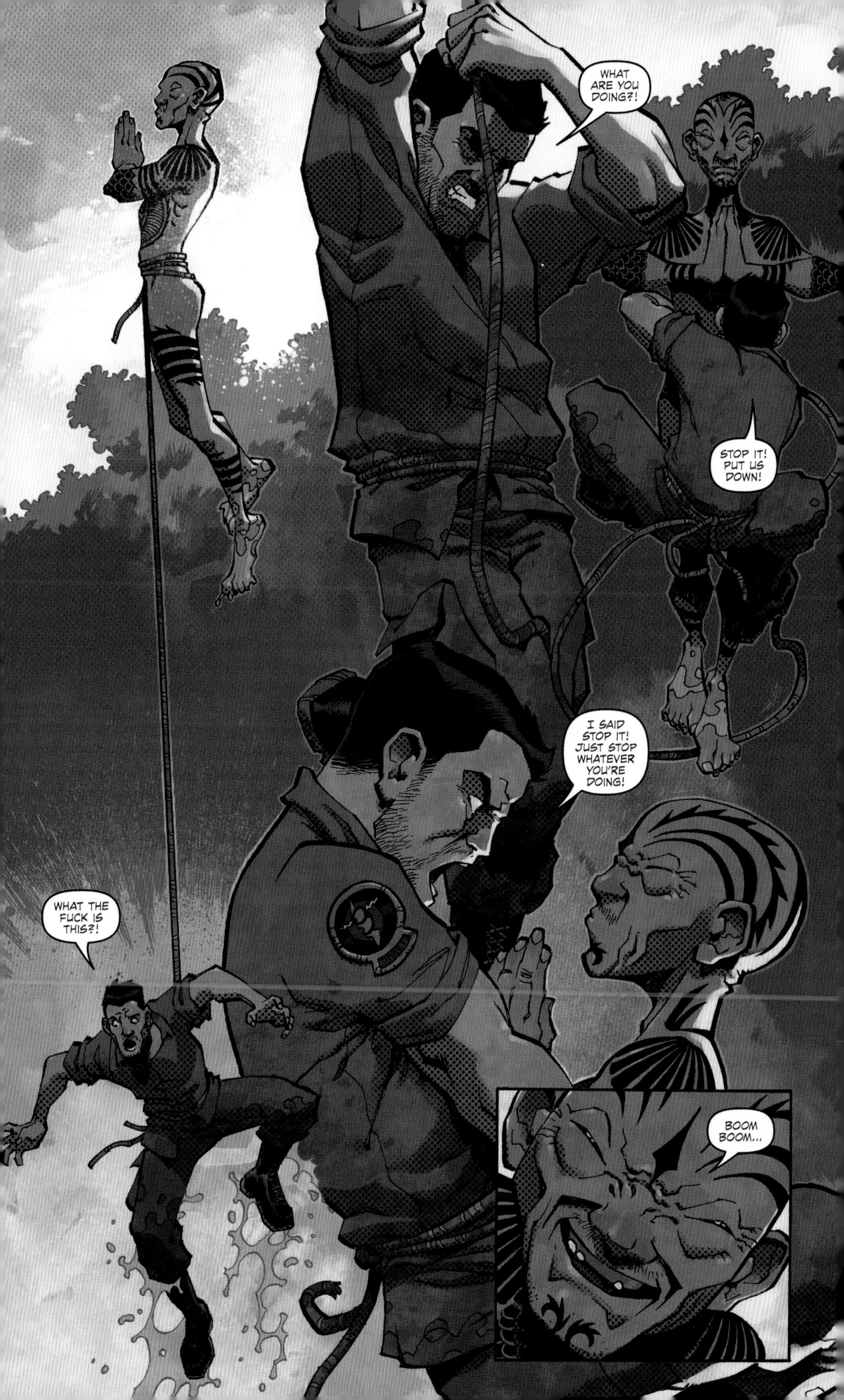
WHAT ARE YOU DOING?!
STOP IT! PUT US DOWN!
I SAID STOP IT! JUST STOP WHATEVER YOU'RE DOING!
WHAT THE FUCK IS THIS?!
BOOM BOOM...

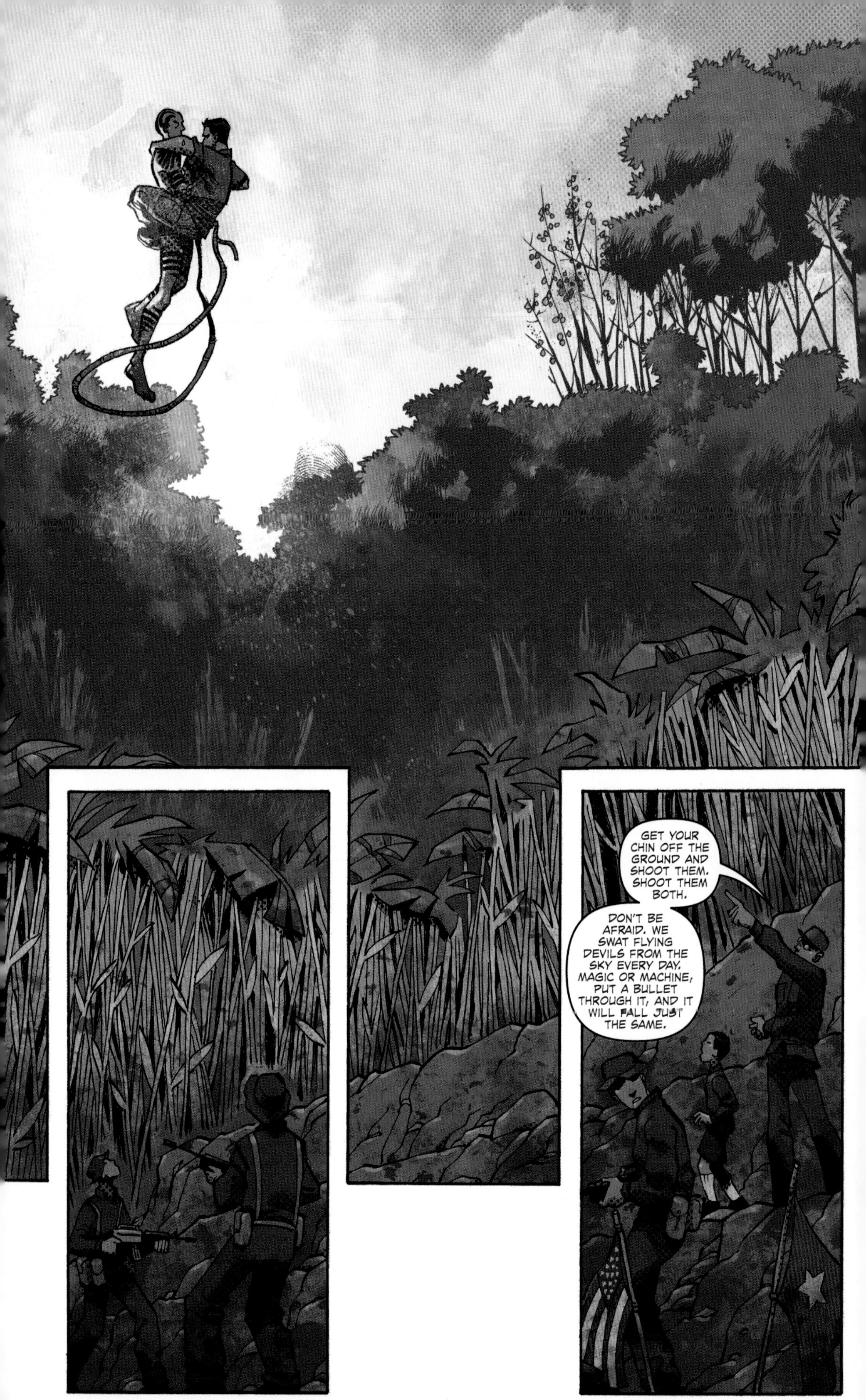
GET YOUR CHIN OFF THE GROUND AND SHOOT THEM. SHOOT THEM BOTH.
DON'T BE AFRAID. WE SWAT FLYING DEVILS FROM THE SKY EVERY DAY. MAGIC OR MACHINE, PUT A BULLET THROUGH IT, AND IT WILL FALL JUST THE SAME.

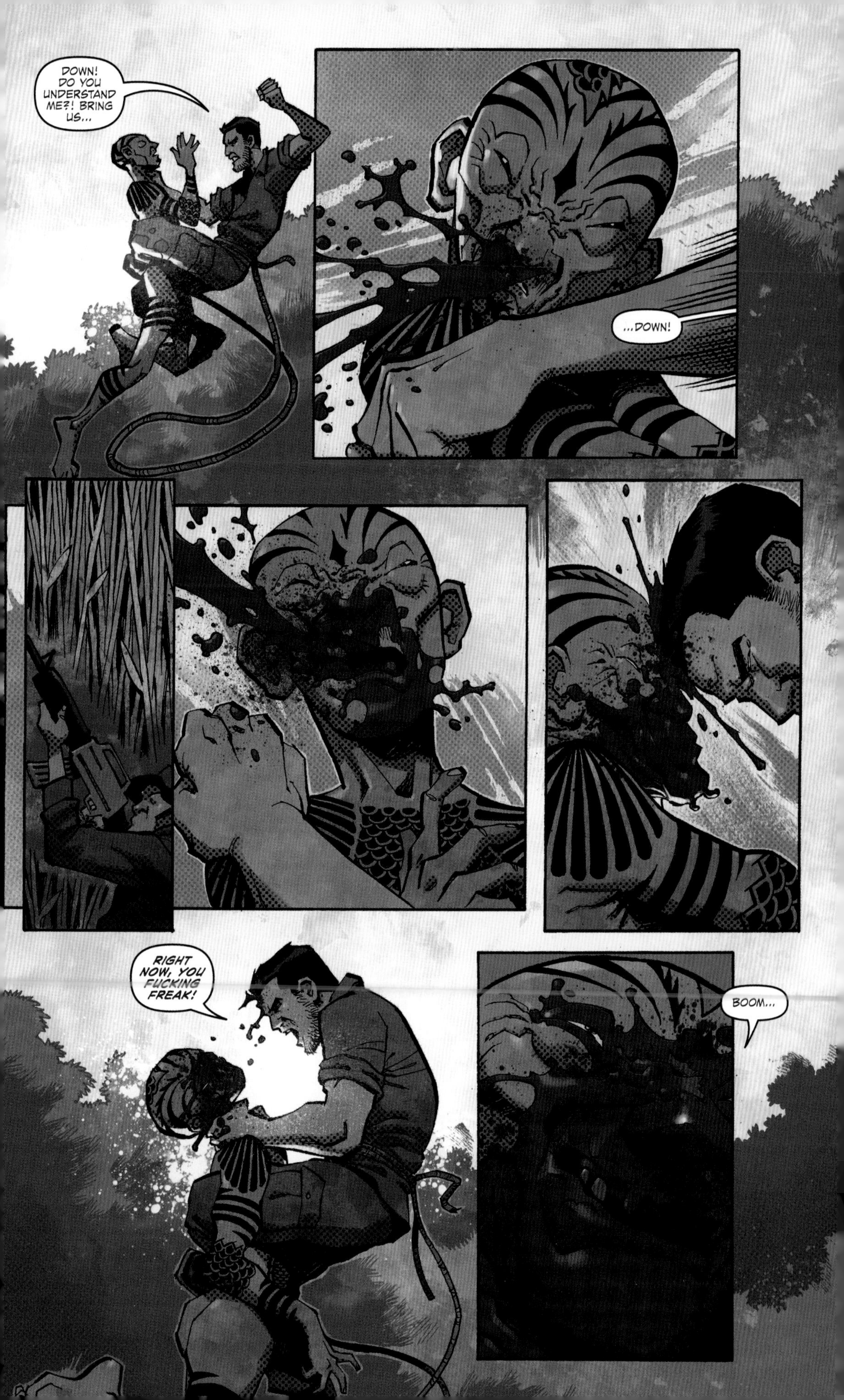
DOWN! DO YOU UNDERSTAND ME?! BRING US...
...DOWN!
RIGHT NOW, YOU FUCKING FREAK!
BOOM...

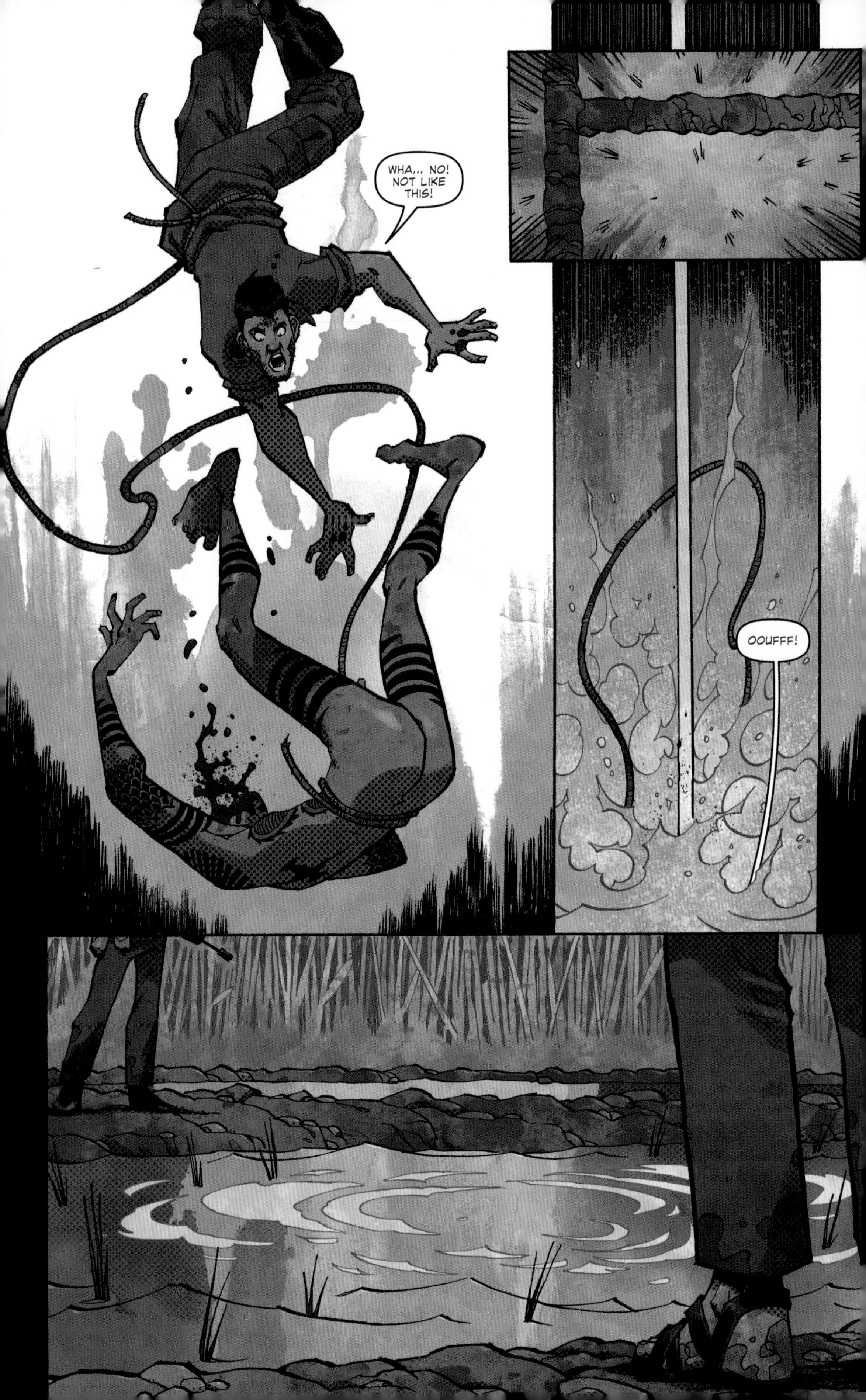
WHA... NO! NOT LIKE THIS!
OOUFFF!

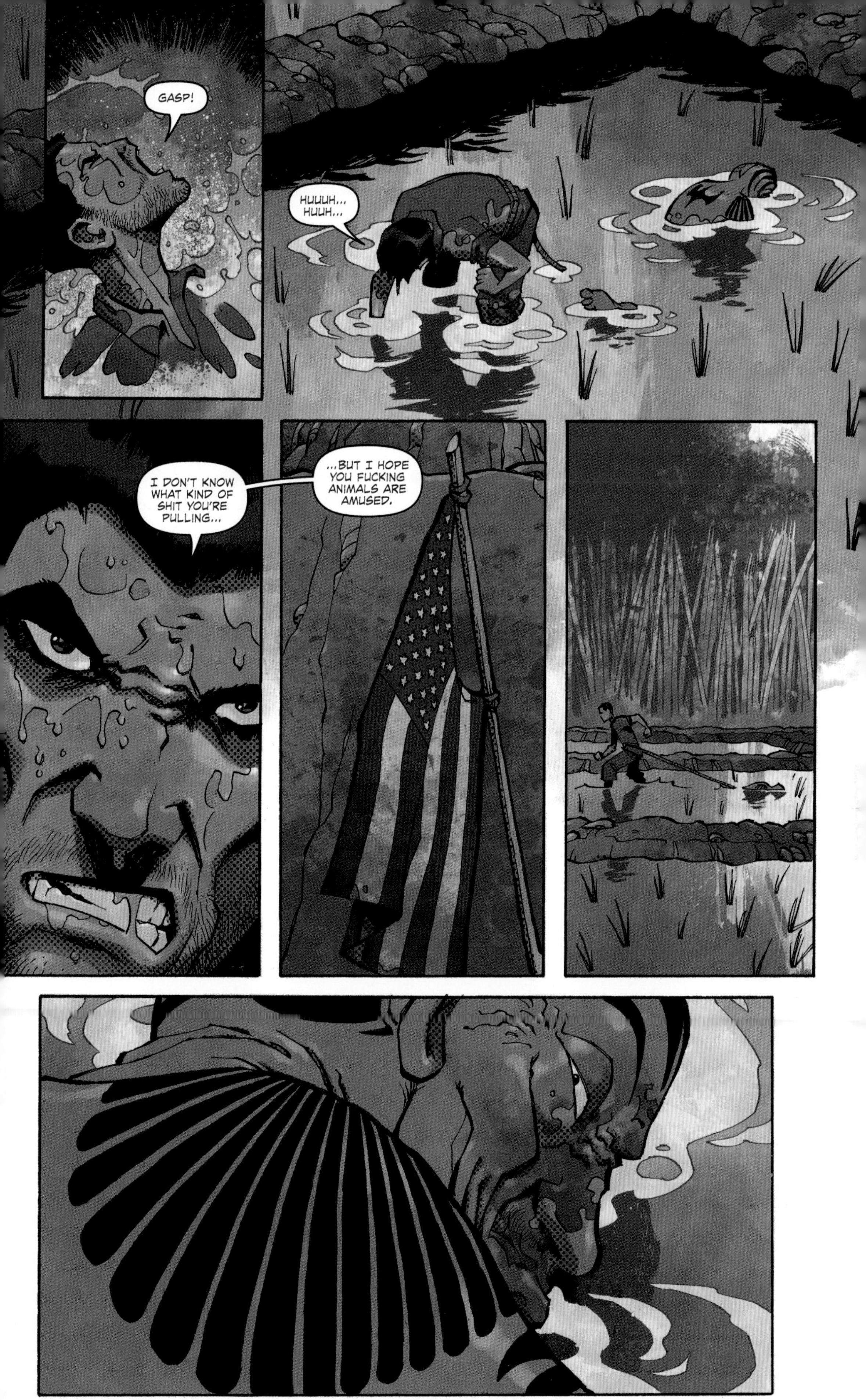
GASP!
HUUUH... HUUH...
I DON'T KNOW WHAT KIND OF SHIT YOU'RE PULLING...
...BUT I HOPE YOU FUCKING ANIMALS ARE AMUSED.

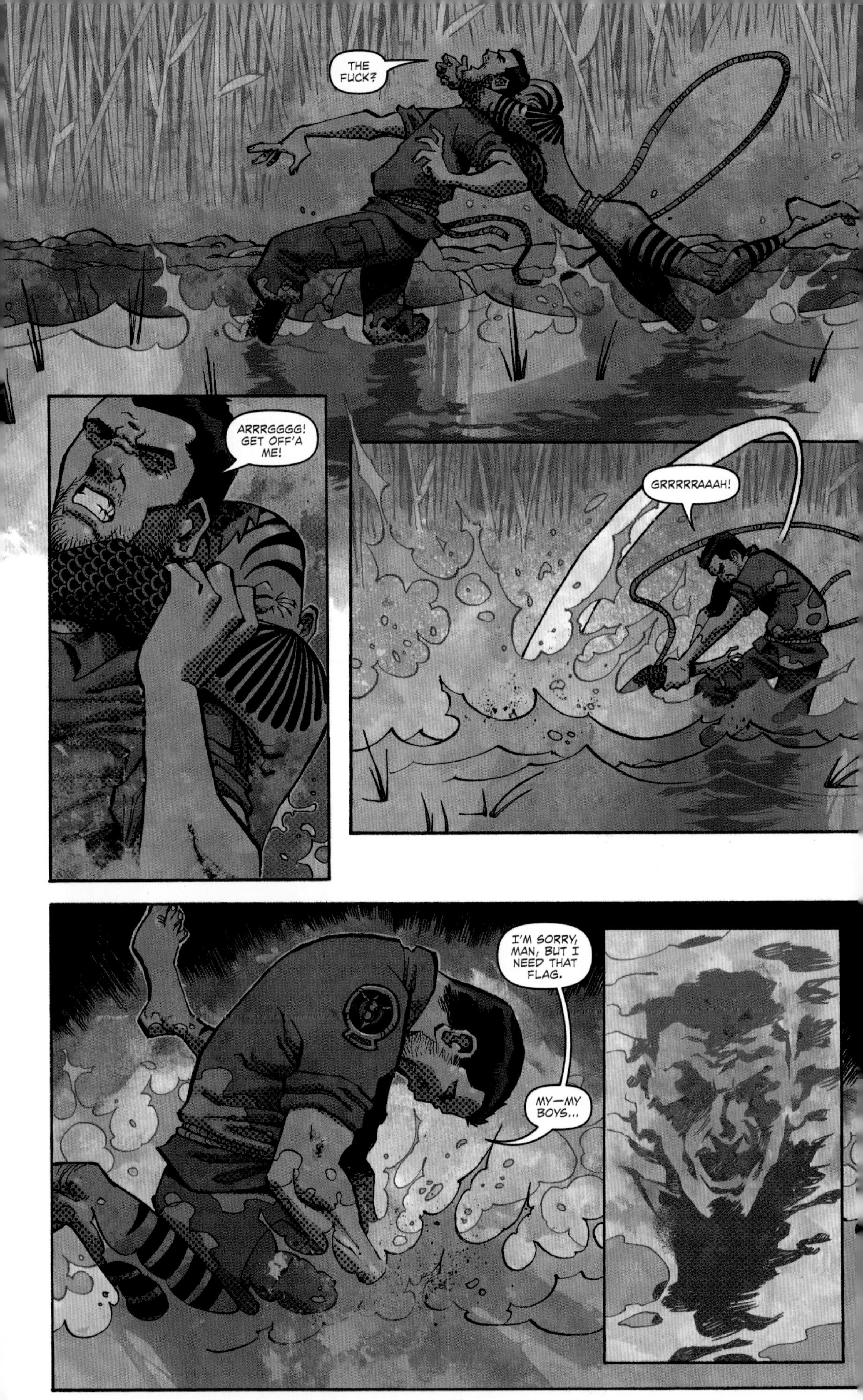
THE FUCK?
ARRRGGGG! GET OFF'A ME!
GRRRRRAAAH!
I'M SORRY, MAN, BUT I NEED THAT FLAG.
MY—MY BOYS...

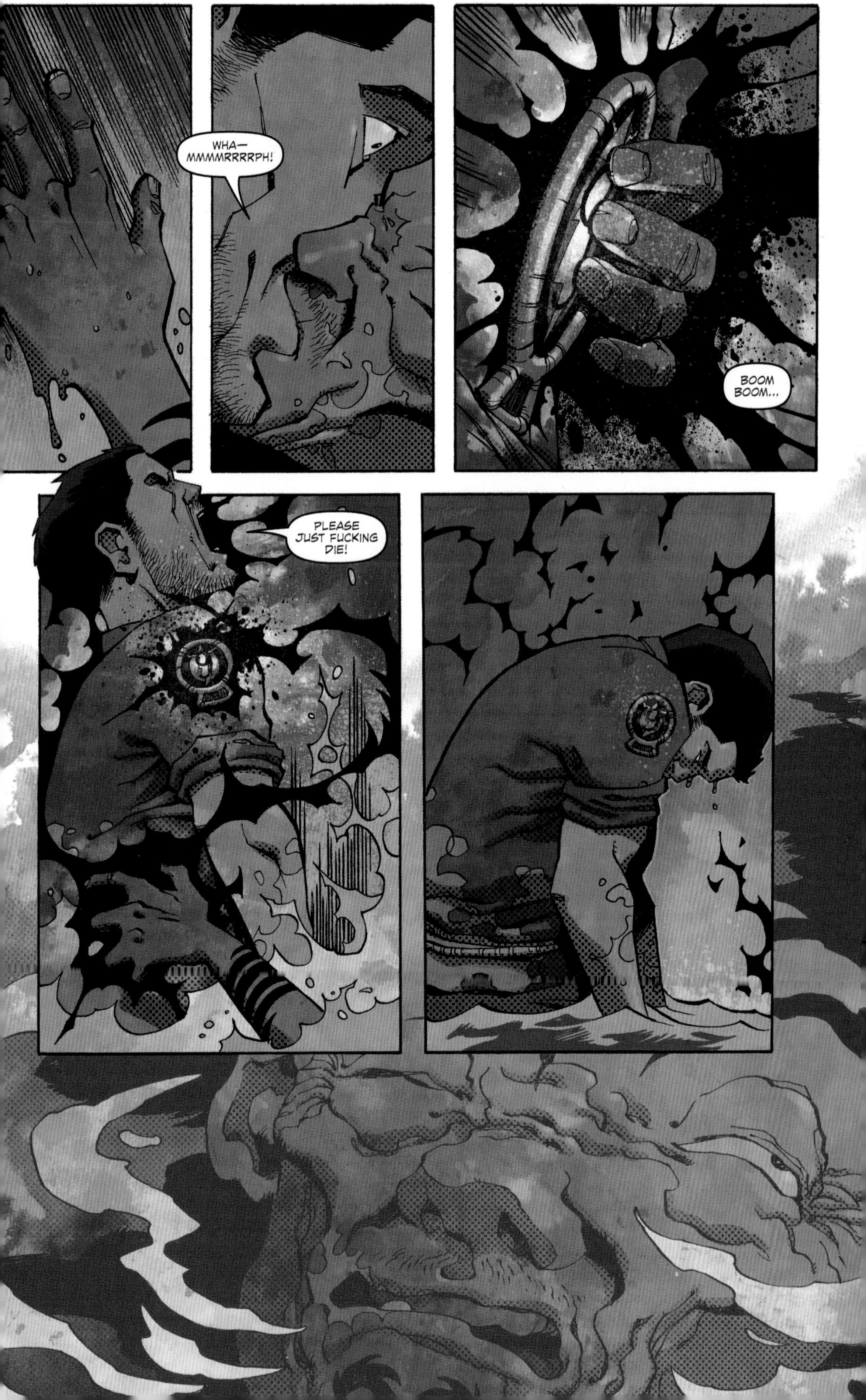
WHA—
MMMMRRRRPH!
BOOM
BOOM...
PLEASE
JUST FUCKING
DIE!

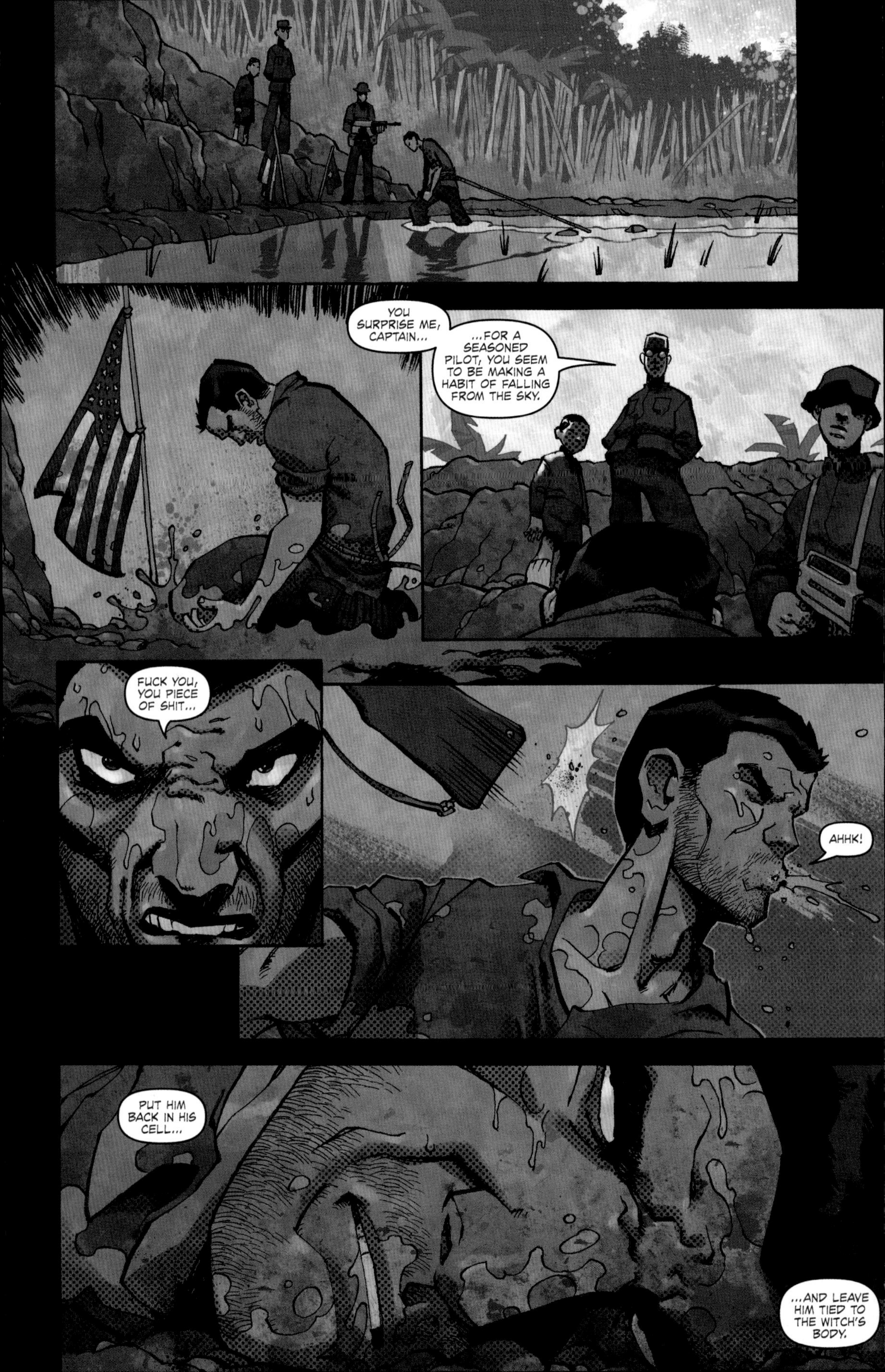
YOU SURPRISE ME, CAPTAIN...
...FOR A SEASONED PILOT, YOU SEEM TO BE MAKING A HABIT OF FALLING FROM THE SKY.
FUCK YOU, YOU PIECE OF SHIT...
AHHK!
PUT HIM BACK IN HIS CELL...
...AND LEAVE HIM TIED TO THE WITCH'S BODY.

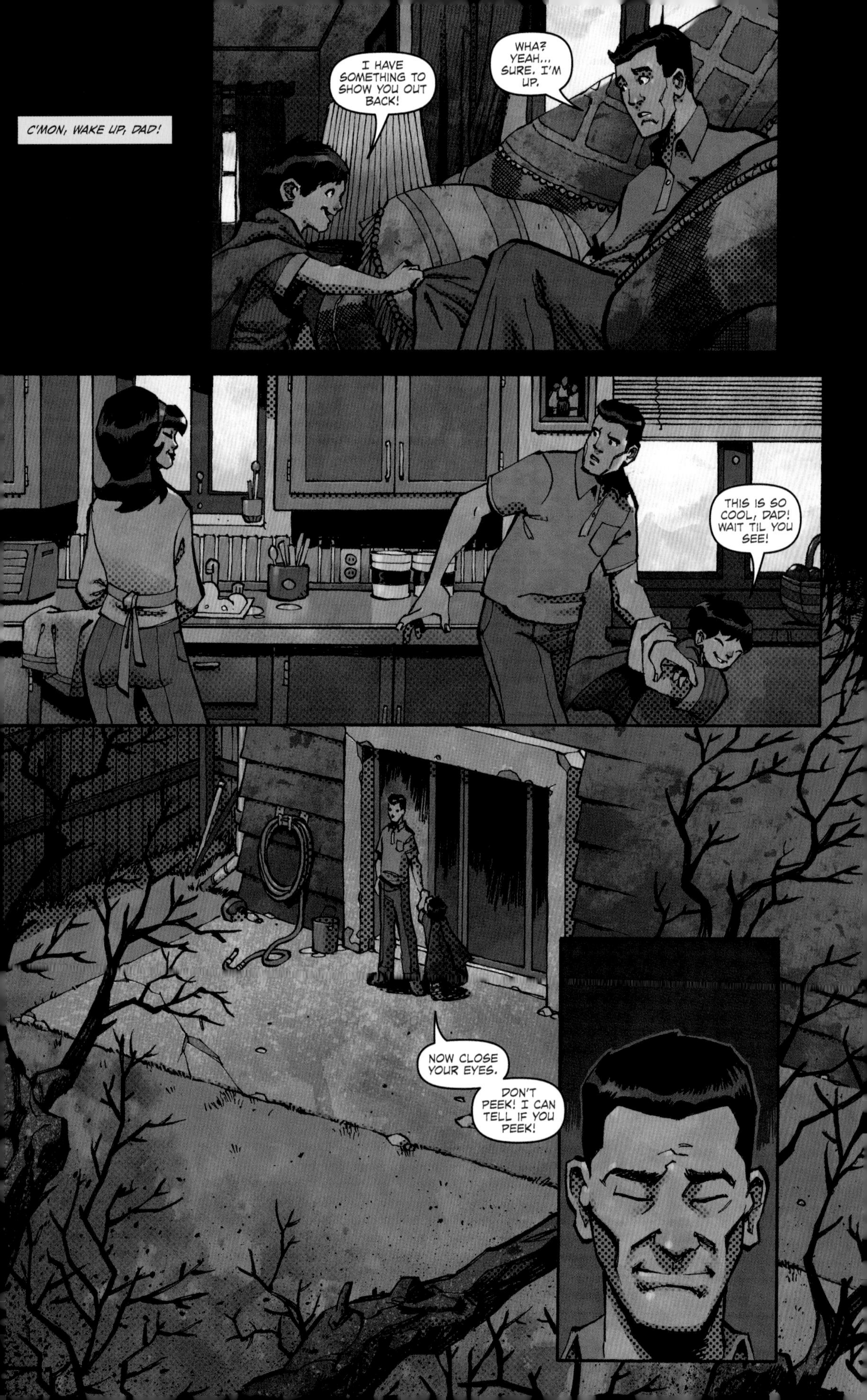
C'MON, WAKE UP, DAD!
I HAVE SOMETHING TO SHOW YOU OUT BACK!
WHA? YEAH... SURE. I'M UP.
THIS IS SO COOL, DAD! WAIT TIL YOU SEE!
NOW CLOSE YOUR EYES.
DON'T PEEK! I CAN TELL IF YOU PEEK!

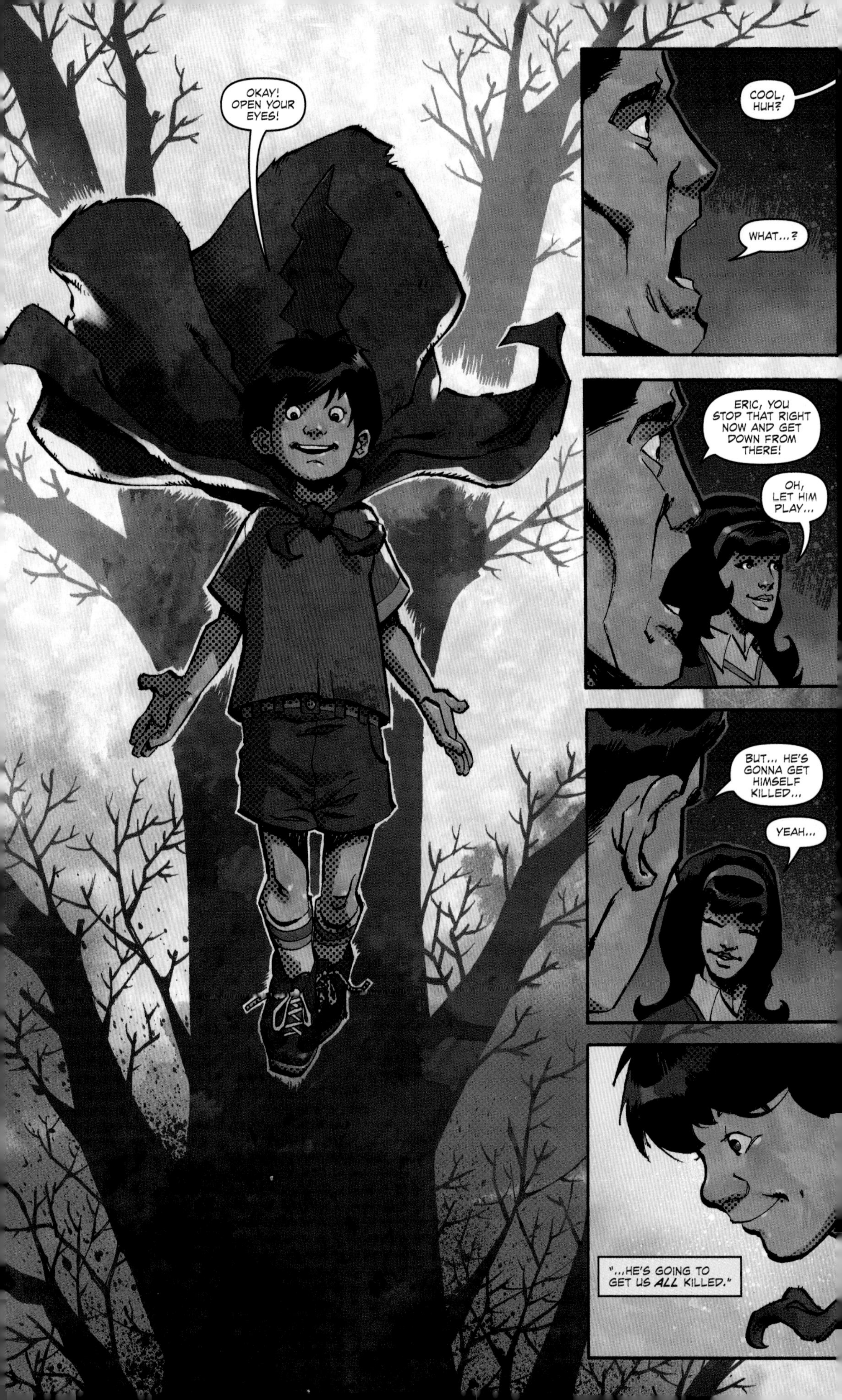
OKAY! OPEN YOUR EYES!
COOL, HUH?
WHAT...?
ERIC, YOU STOP THAT RIGHT NOW AND GET DOWN FROM THERE!
OH, LET HIM PLAY...
BUT... HE'S GONNA GET HIMSELF KILLED...
YEAH...
"...HE'S GOING TO GET US ALL KILLED."

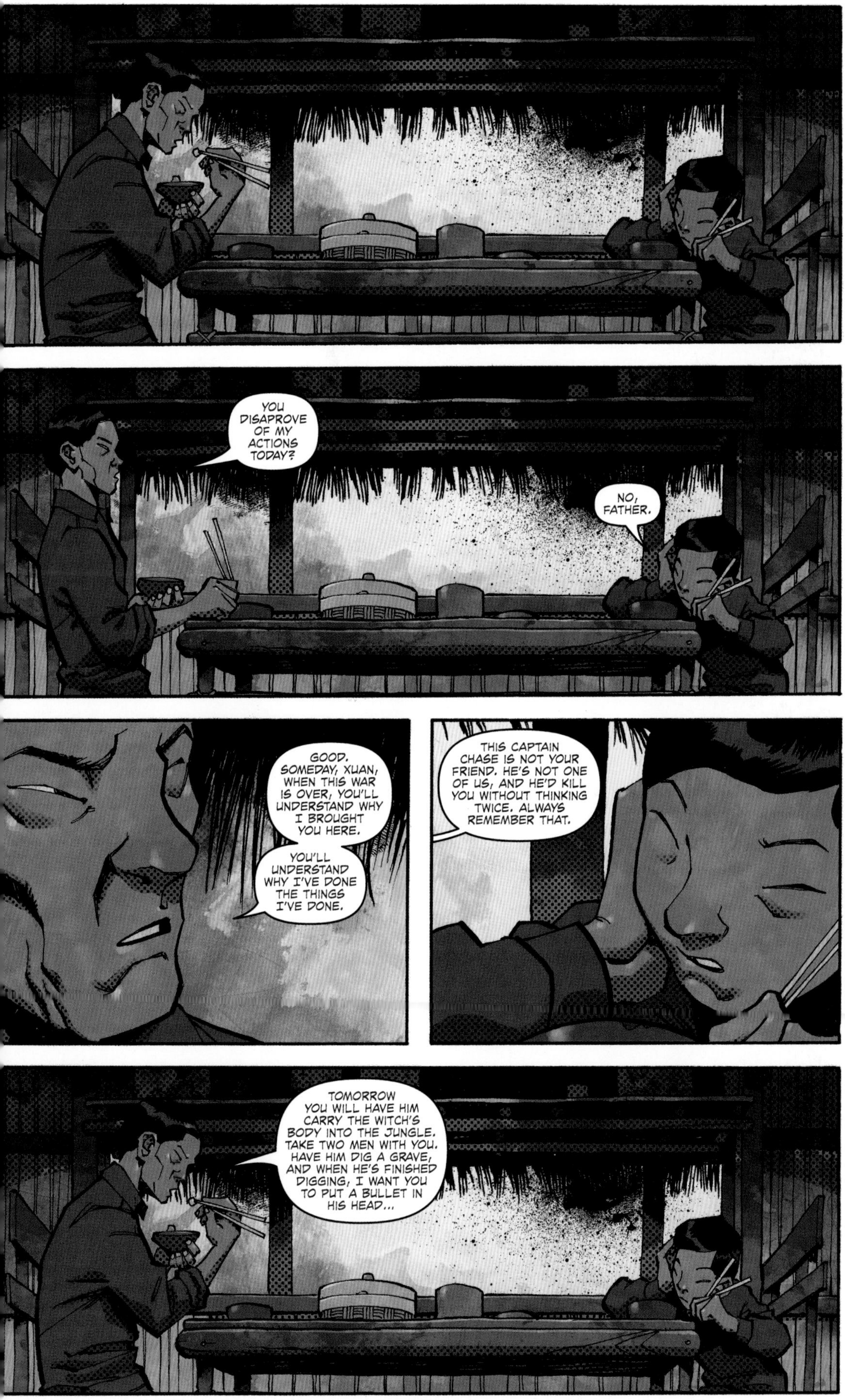
YOU DISAPROVE OF MY ACTIONS TODAY?
NO, FATHER.
GOOD. SOMEDAY, XUAN, WHEN THIS WAR IS OVER, YOU'LL UNDERSTAND WHY I BROUGHT YOU HERE.
YOU'LL UNDERSTAND WHY I'VE DONE THE THINGS I'VE DONE.
THIS CAPTAIN CHASE IS NOT YOUR FRIEND. HE'S NOT ONE OF US, AND HE'D KILL YOU WITHOUT THINKING TWICE. ALWAYS REMEMBER THAT.
TOMORROW YOU WILL HAVE HIM CARRY THE WITCH'S BODY INTO THE JUNGLE. TAKE TWO MEN WITH YOU. HAVE HIM DIG A GRAVE, AND WHEN HE'S FINISHED DIGGING, I WANT YOU TO PUT A BULLET IN HIS HEAD...

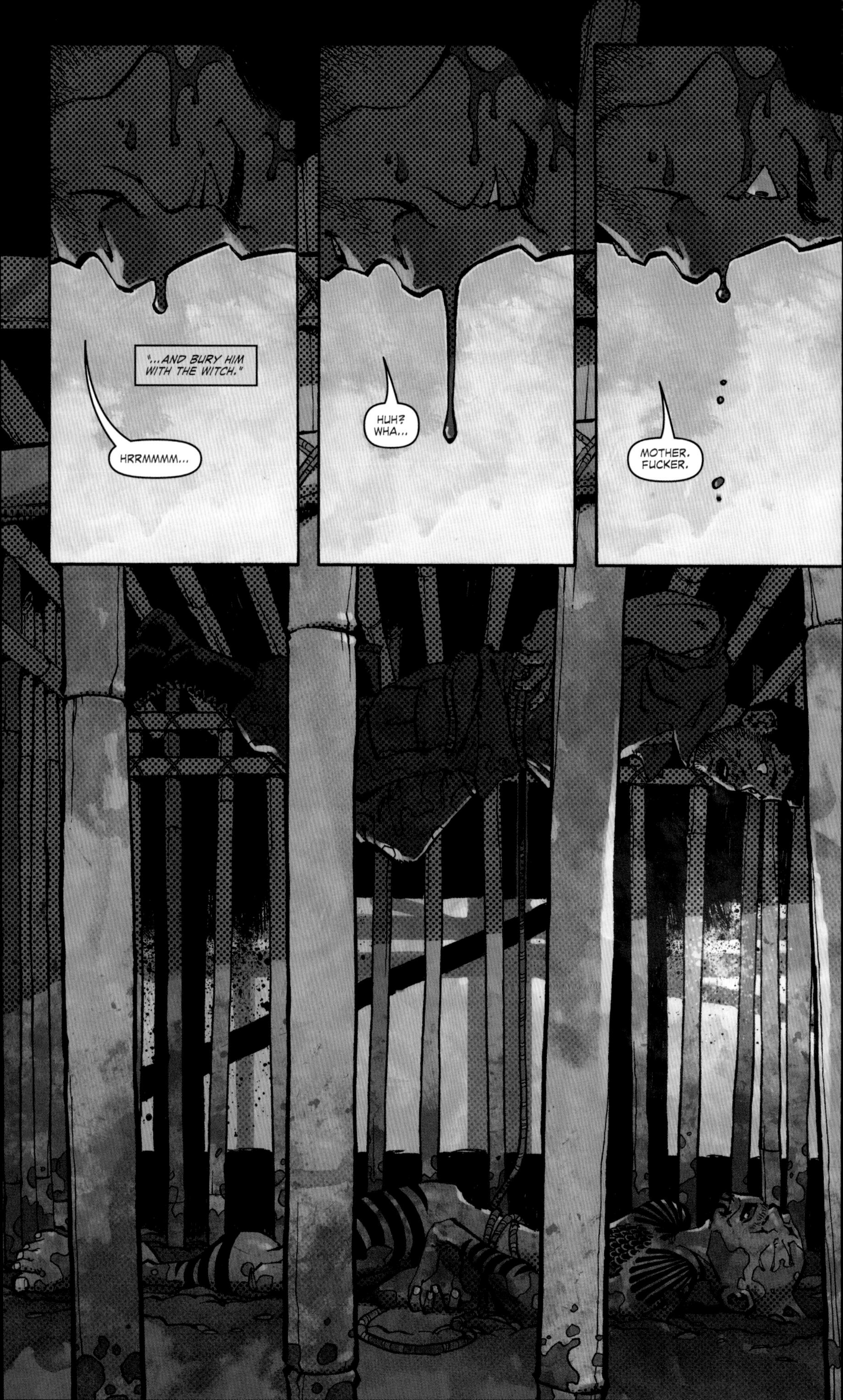
"...AND BURY HIM WITH THE WITCH."
HRRMMMM...
HUH? WHA...
MOTHER. FUCKER.

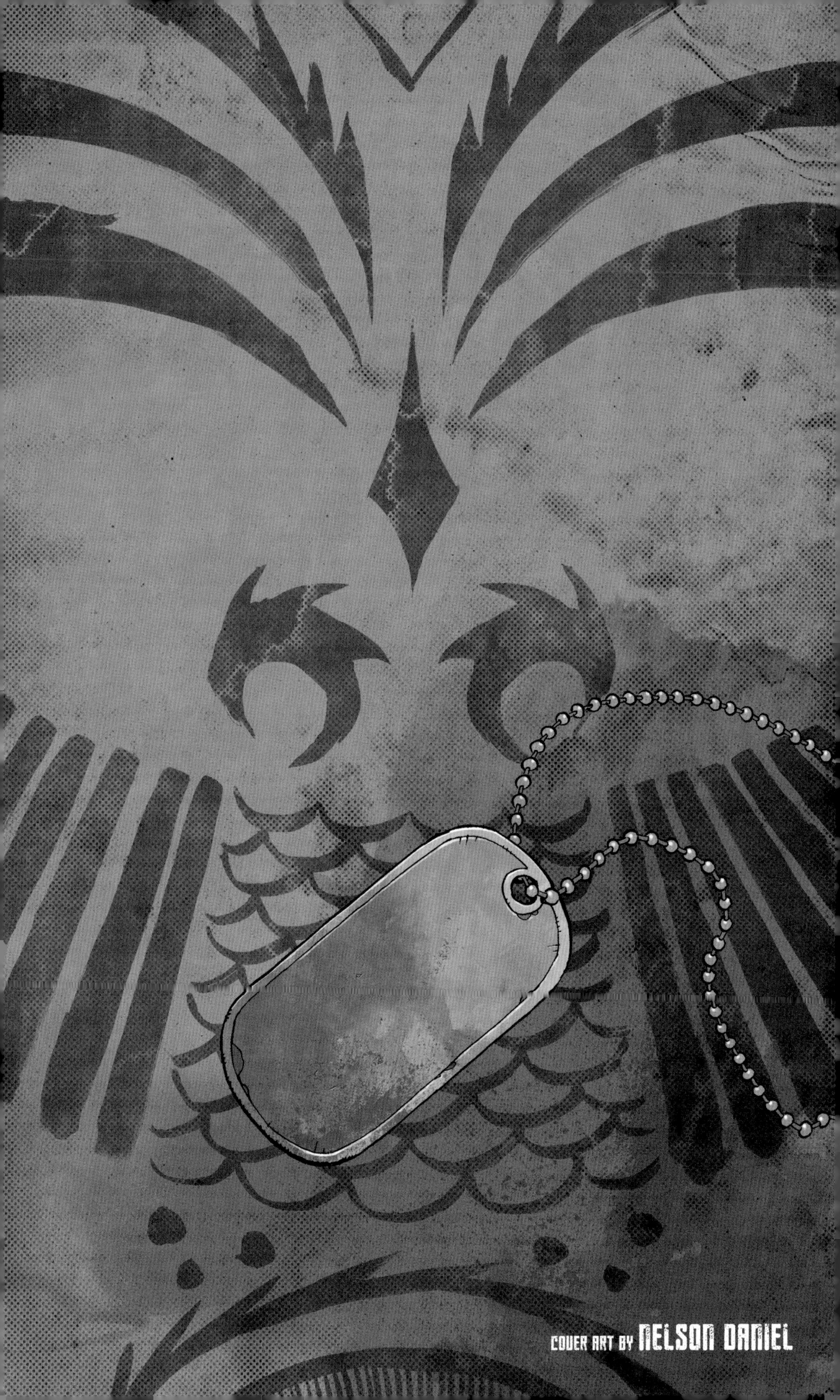
COVER ART BY NELSON DANIEL

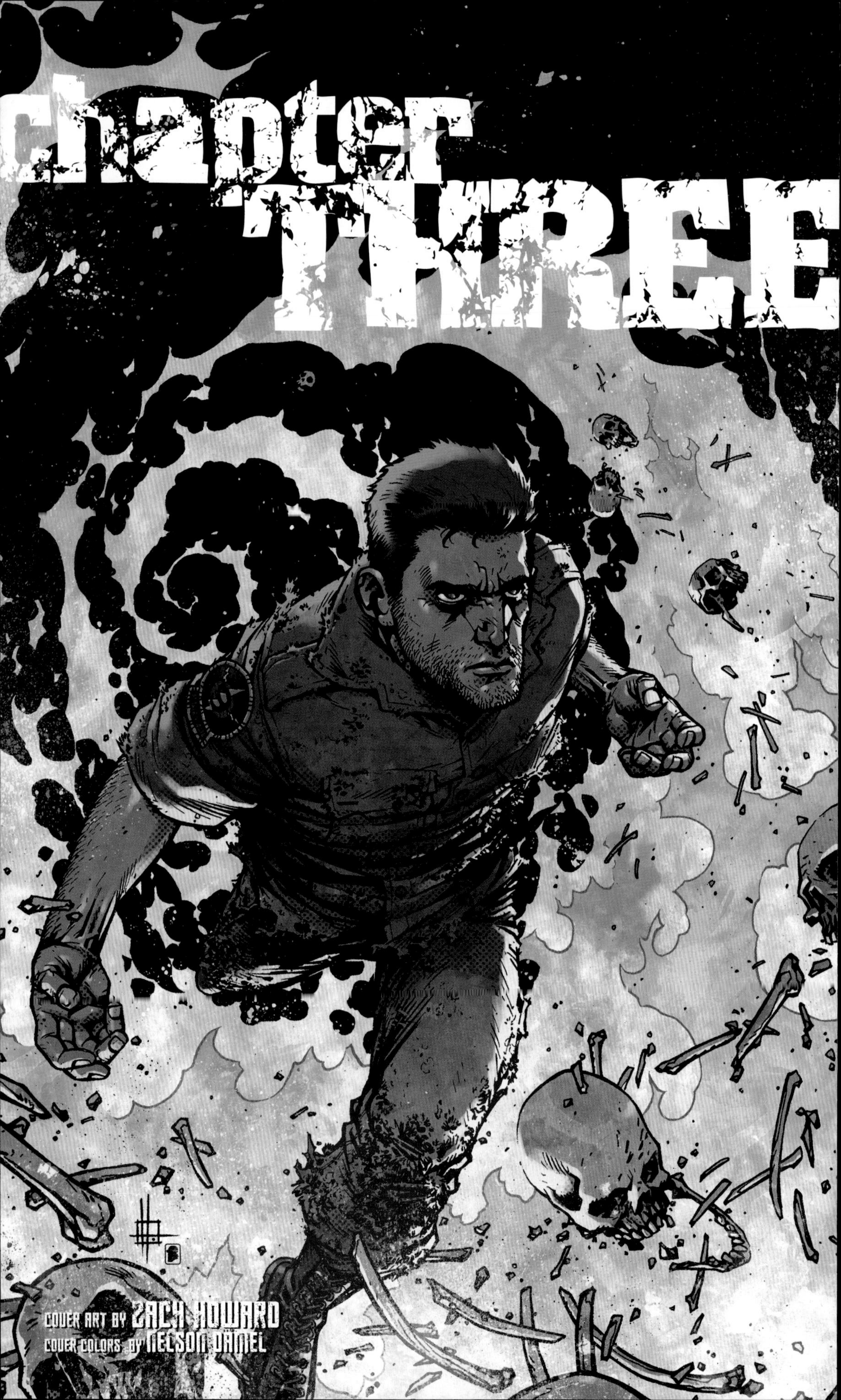

chapter THREE
COVER ART BY ZACH HOWARD
COVER COLORS BY NELSON DANIEL

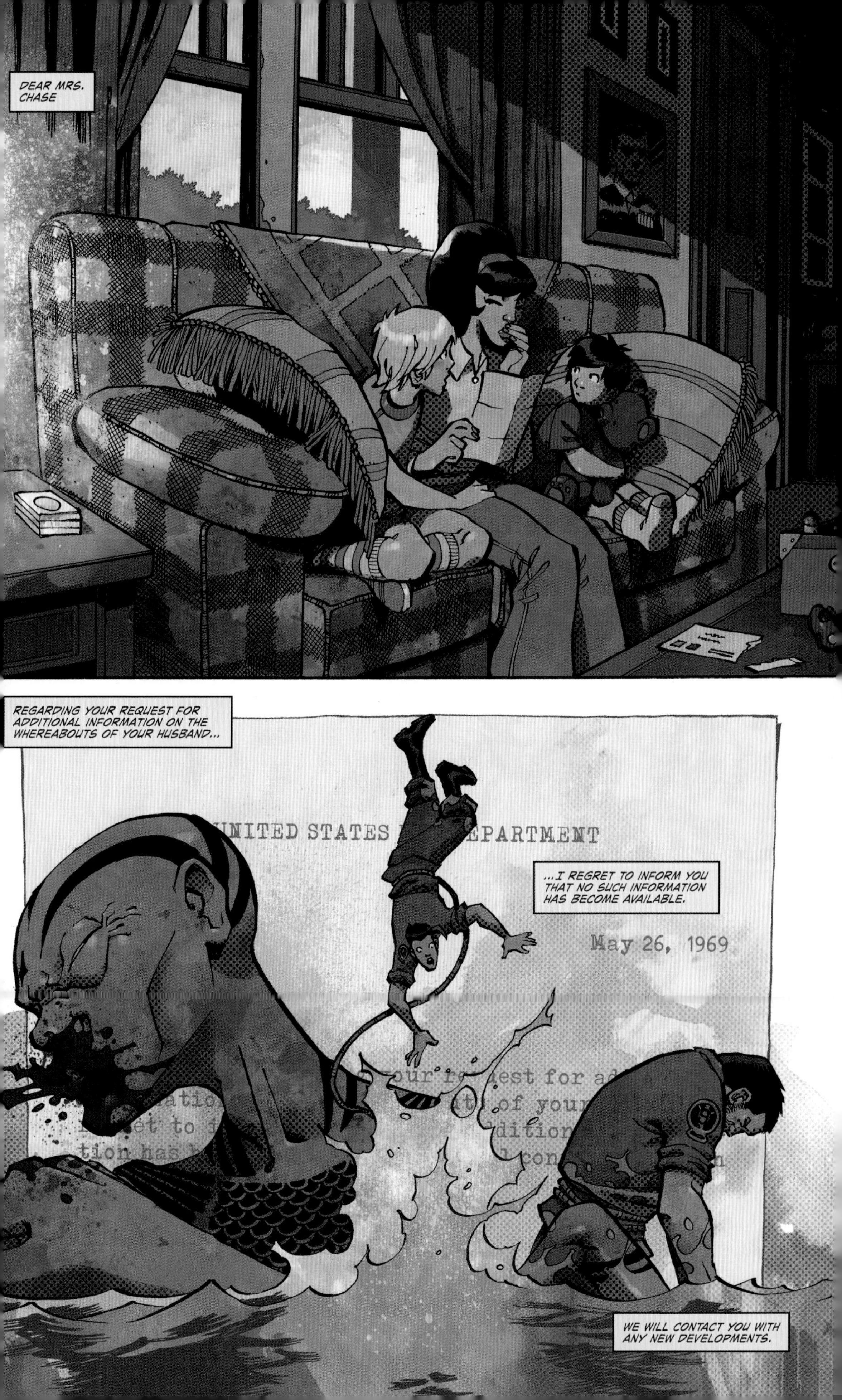

DEAR MRS. CHASE
REGARDING YOUR REQUEST FOR ADDITIONAL INFORMATION ON THE WHEREABOUTS OF YOUR HUSBAND...
...I REGRET TO INFORM YOU THAT NO SUCH INFORMATION HAS BECOME AVAILABLE.
May 26, 1969
WE WILL CONTACT YOU WITH ANY NEW DEVELOPMENTS.

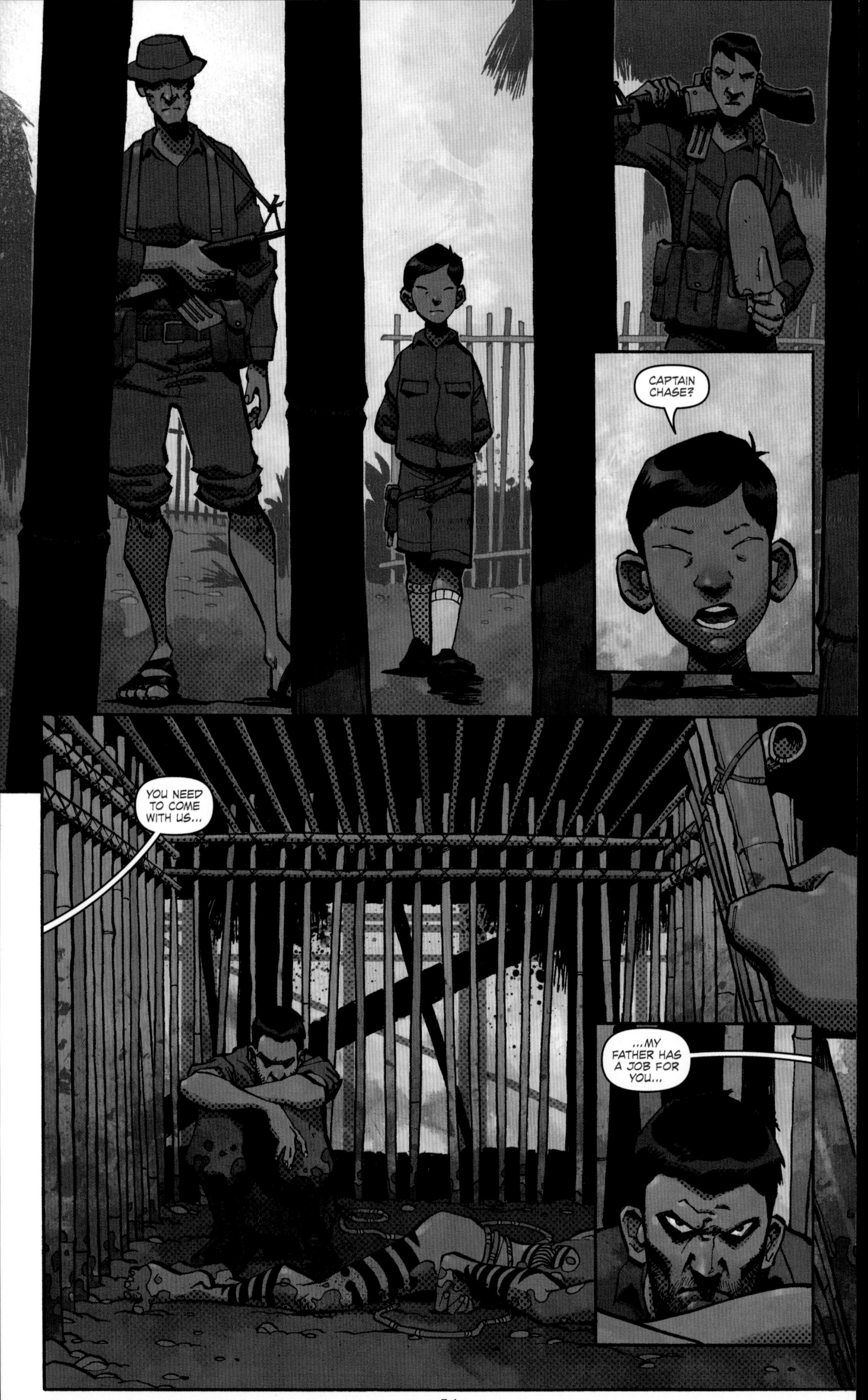
CAPTAIN CHASE?
YOU NEED TO COME WITH US...
...MY FATHER HAS A JOB FOR YOU...

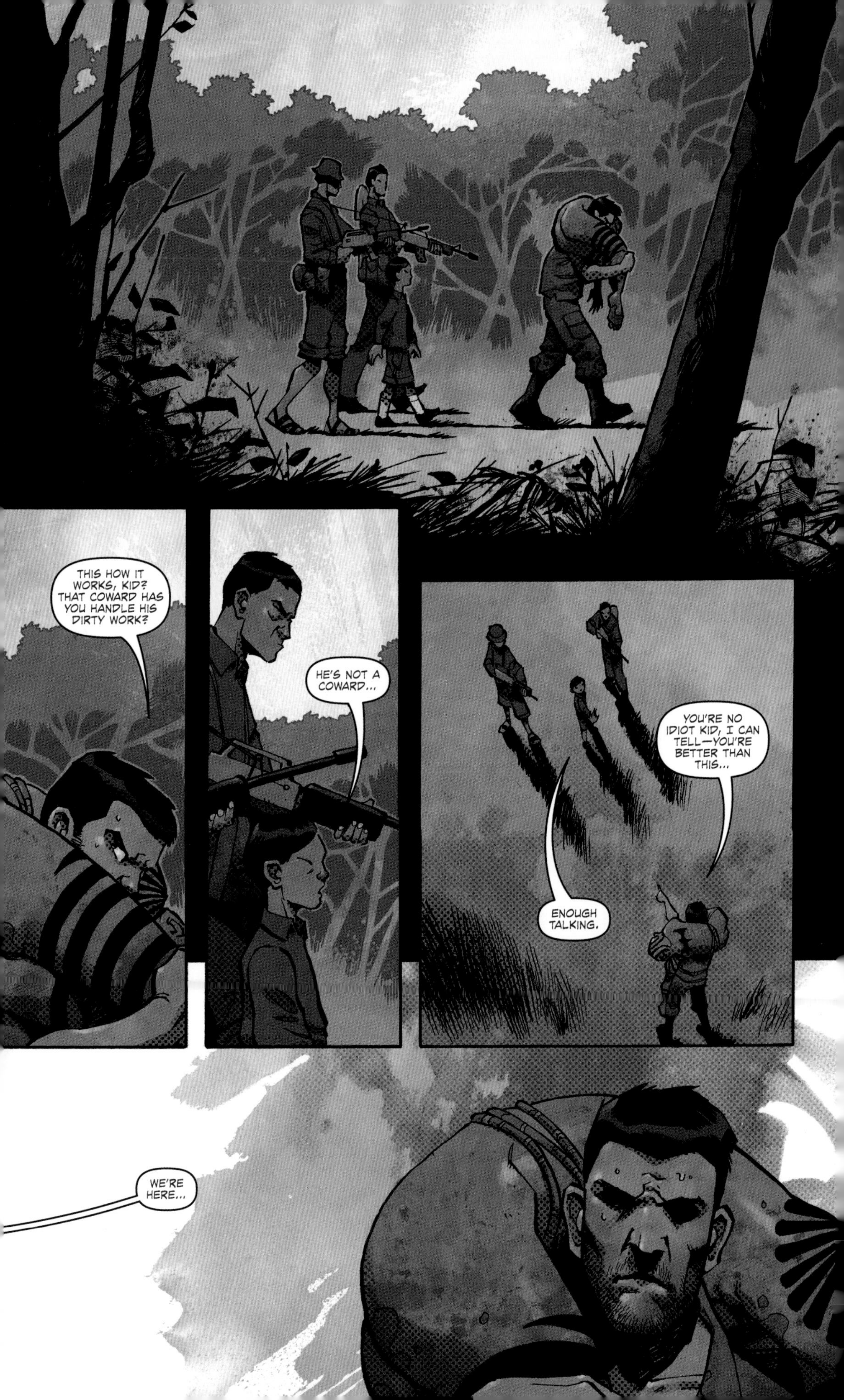
THIS HOW IT WORKS, KID? THAT COWARD HAS YOU HANDLE HIS DIRTY WORK?
HE'S NOT A COWARD...
YOU'RE NO IDIOT KID, I CAN TELL—YOU'RE BETTER THAN THIS...
ENOUGH TALKING.
WE'RE HERE...

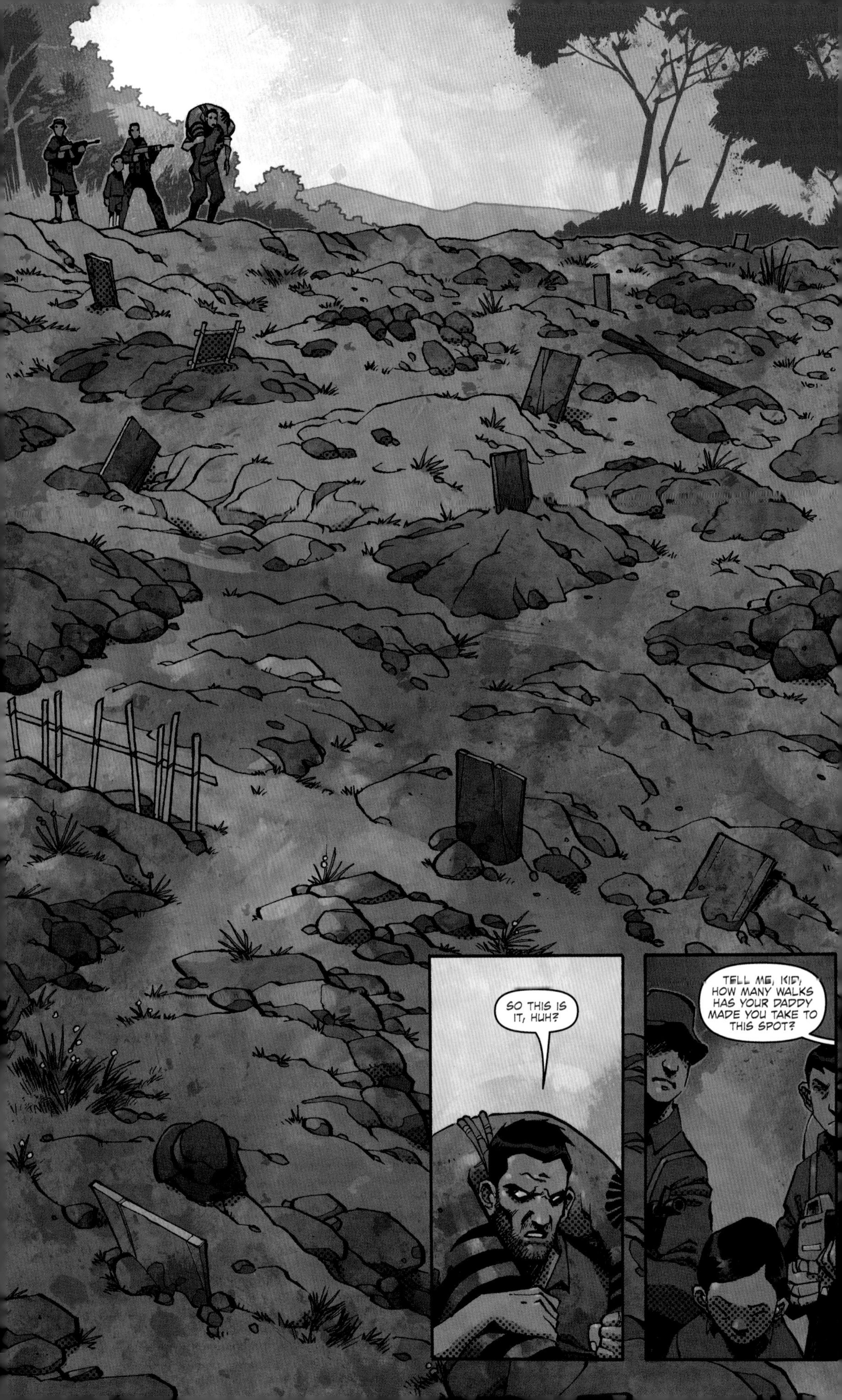
SO THIS IS IT, HUH?
TELL ME, KID, HOW MANY WALKS HAS YOUR DADDY MADE YOU TAKE TO THIS SPOT?

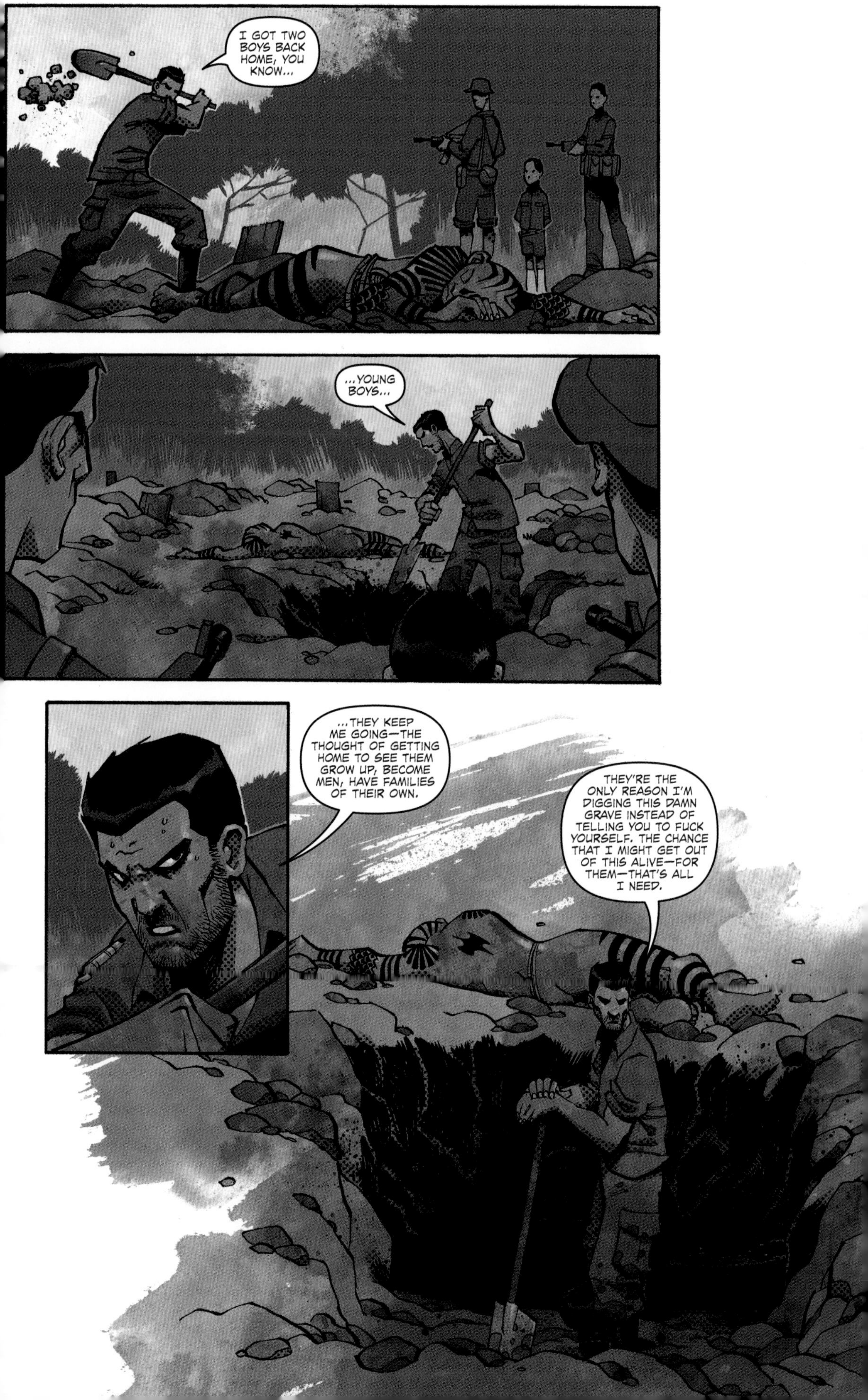

I GOT TWO BOYS BACK HOME, YOU KNOW...
...YOUNG BOYS...
...THEY KEEP ME GOING—THE THOUGHT OF GETTING HOME TO SEE THEM GROW UP, BECOME MEN, HAVE FAMILIES OF THEIR OWN.
THEY'RE THE ONLY REASON I'M DIGGING THIS DAMN GRAVE INSTEAD OF TELLING YOU TO FUCK YOURSELF. THE CHANCE THAT I MIGHT GET OUT OF THIS ALIVE—FOR THEM—THAT'S ALL I NEED.

YOU THINK YOUR DADDY WOULD DO THAT FOR YOU? YOU THINK HE'D HUMILIATE HIMSELF JUST FOR THE CHANCE TO SEE YOU AGAIN?

YOU THINK HE'D STARE INTO AN INNOCENT MAN'S EYES WHILE HE DROWNED JUST FOR THE CHANCE TO HEAR YOUR VOICE ONE MORE TIME?

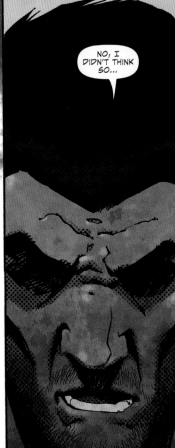

NO, I DIDN'T THINK SO...

...LET ME TELL YOU SOMETHING, KID. IF I CAN KILL AN INNOCENT MAN JUST FOR A *CHANCE* TO SEE MY BOYS AGAIN...

...IMAGINE WHAT I'LL DO TO YOUR DADDY AND HIS MEN...

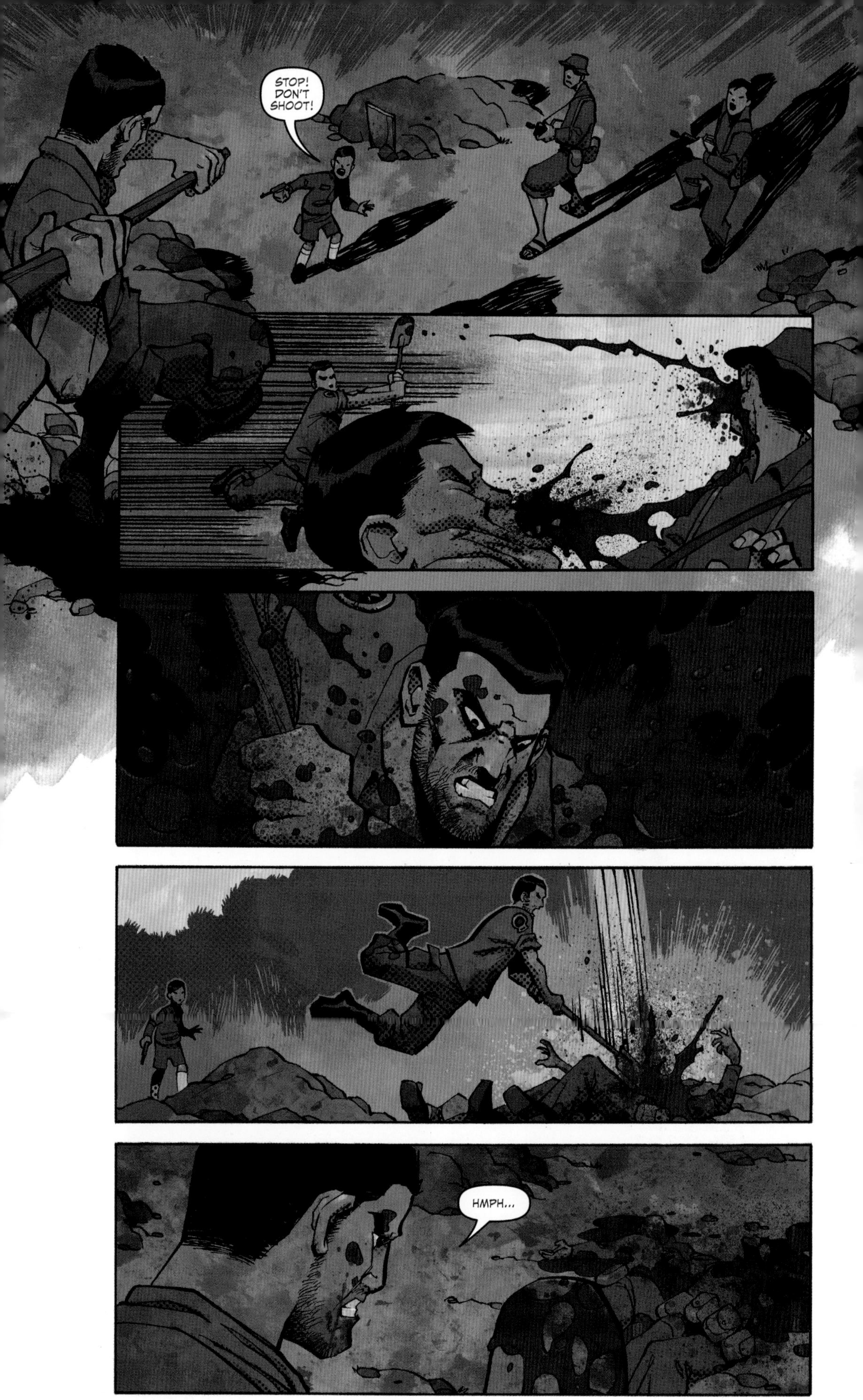
STOP! DON'T SHOOT!
HMPH...

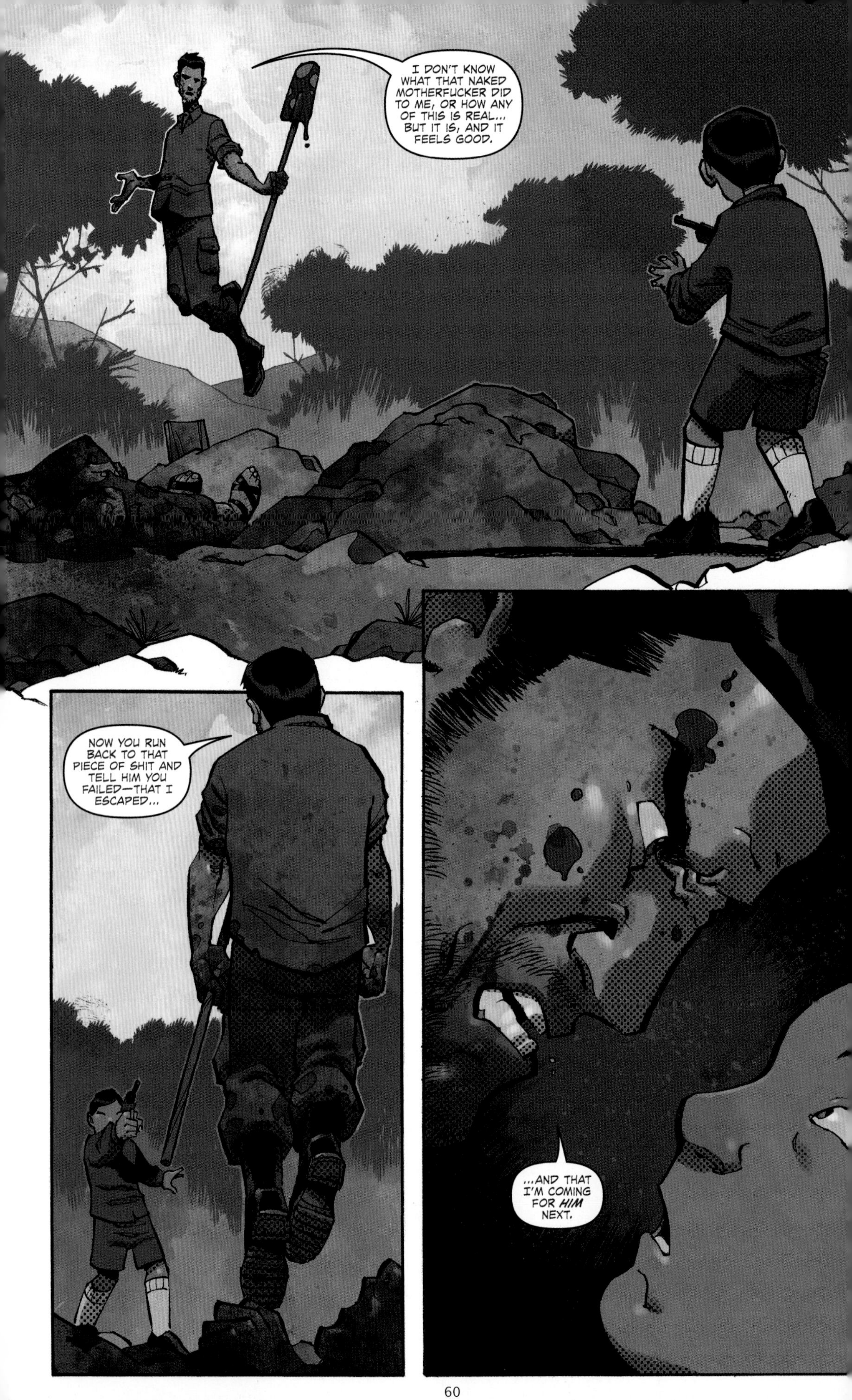
I DON'T KNOW WHAT THAT NAKED MOTHERFUCKER DID TO ME, OR HOW ANY OF THIS IS REAL... BUT IT IS, AND IT FEELS GOOD.
NOW YOU RUN BACK TO THAT PIECE OF SHIT AND TELL HIM YOU FAILED—THAT I ESCAPED...
...AND THAT I'M COMING FOR *HIM* NEXT.

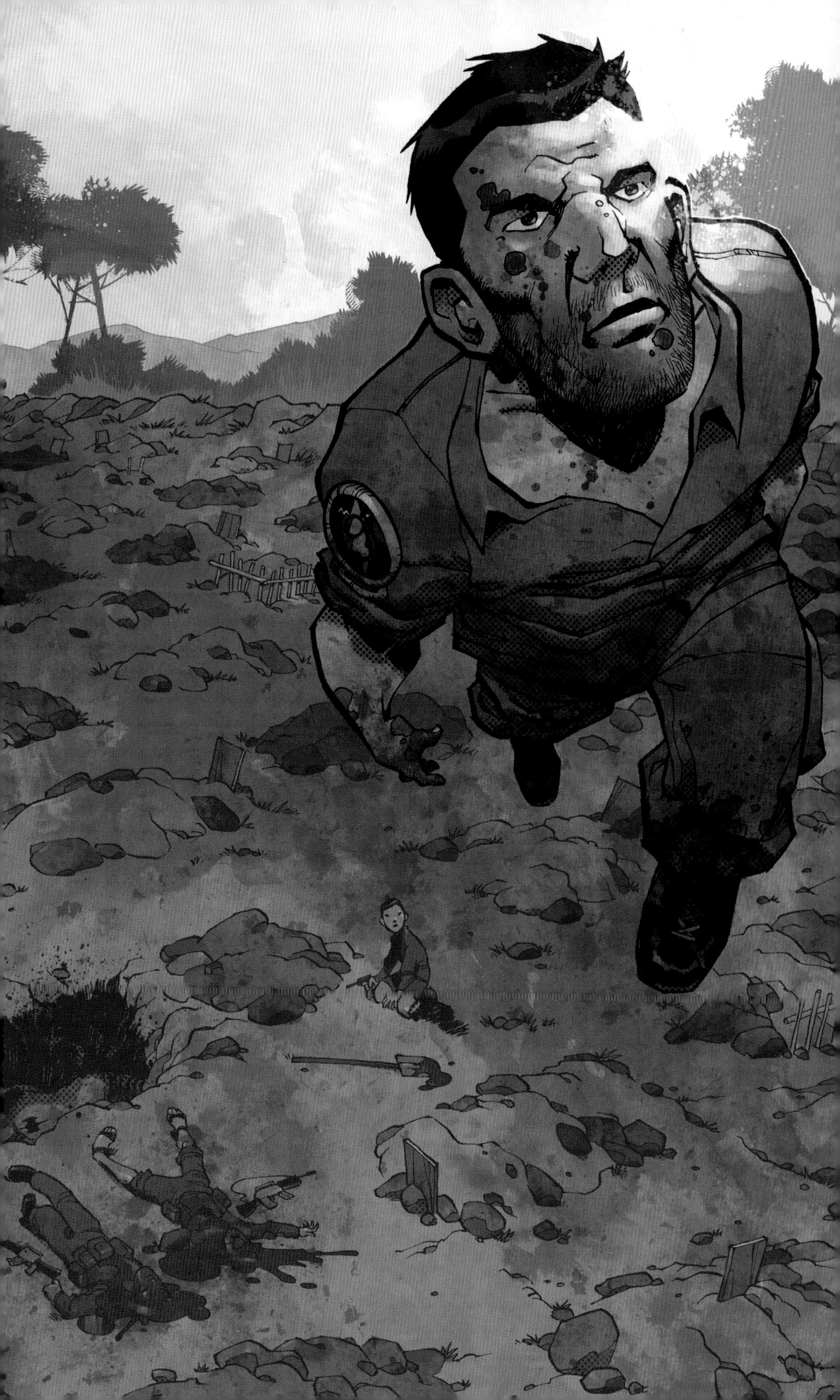

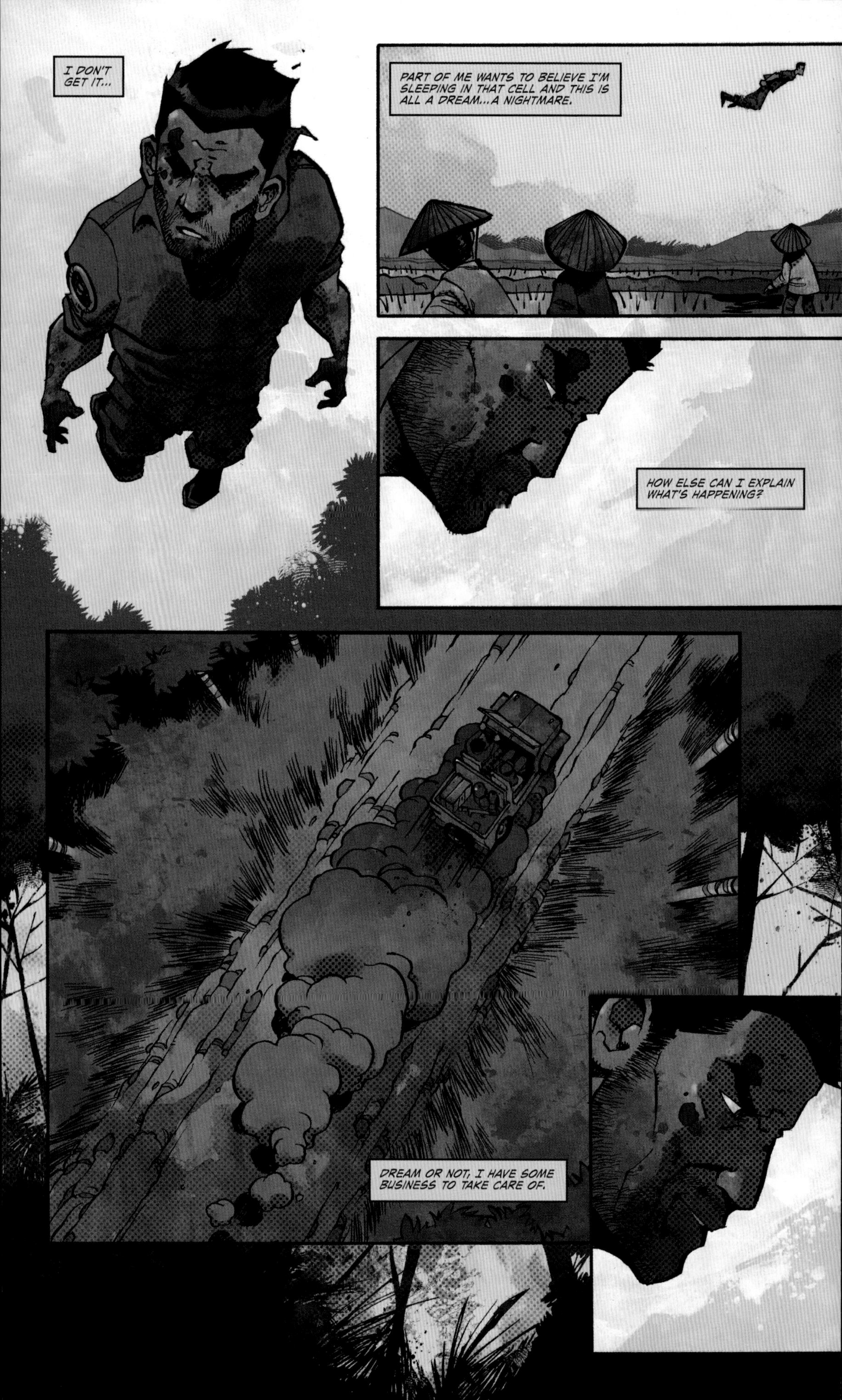
I DON'T GET IT...
PART OF ME WANTS TO BELIEVE I'M SLEEPING IN THAT CELL AND THIS IS ALL A DREAM...A NIGHTMARE.
HOW ELSE CAN I EXPLAIN WHAT'S HAPPENING?
DREAM OR NOT, I HAVE SOME BUSINESS TO TAKE CARE OF.

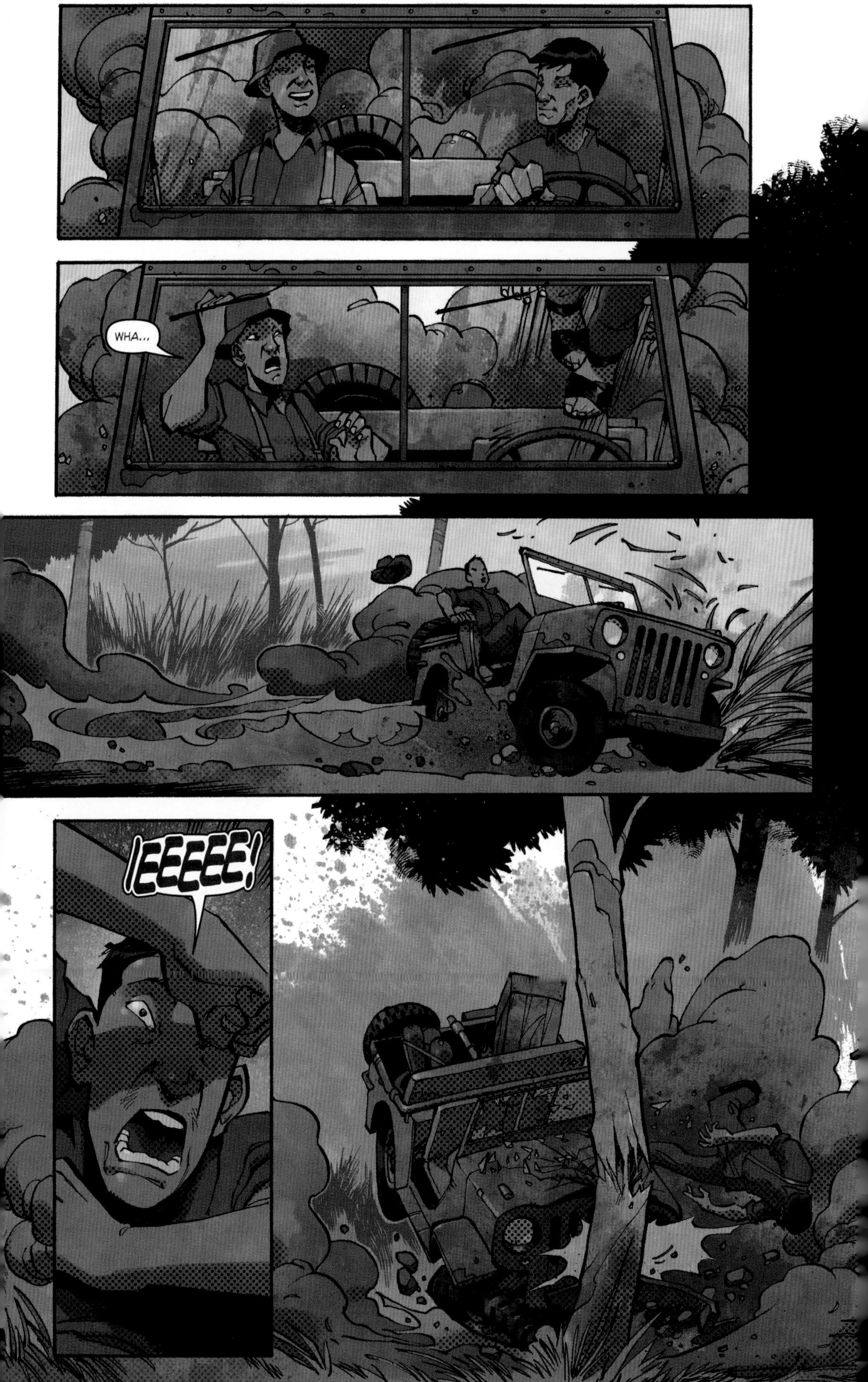
WHA...
EEEEEE!

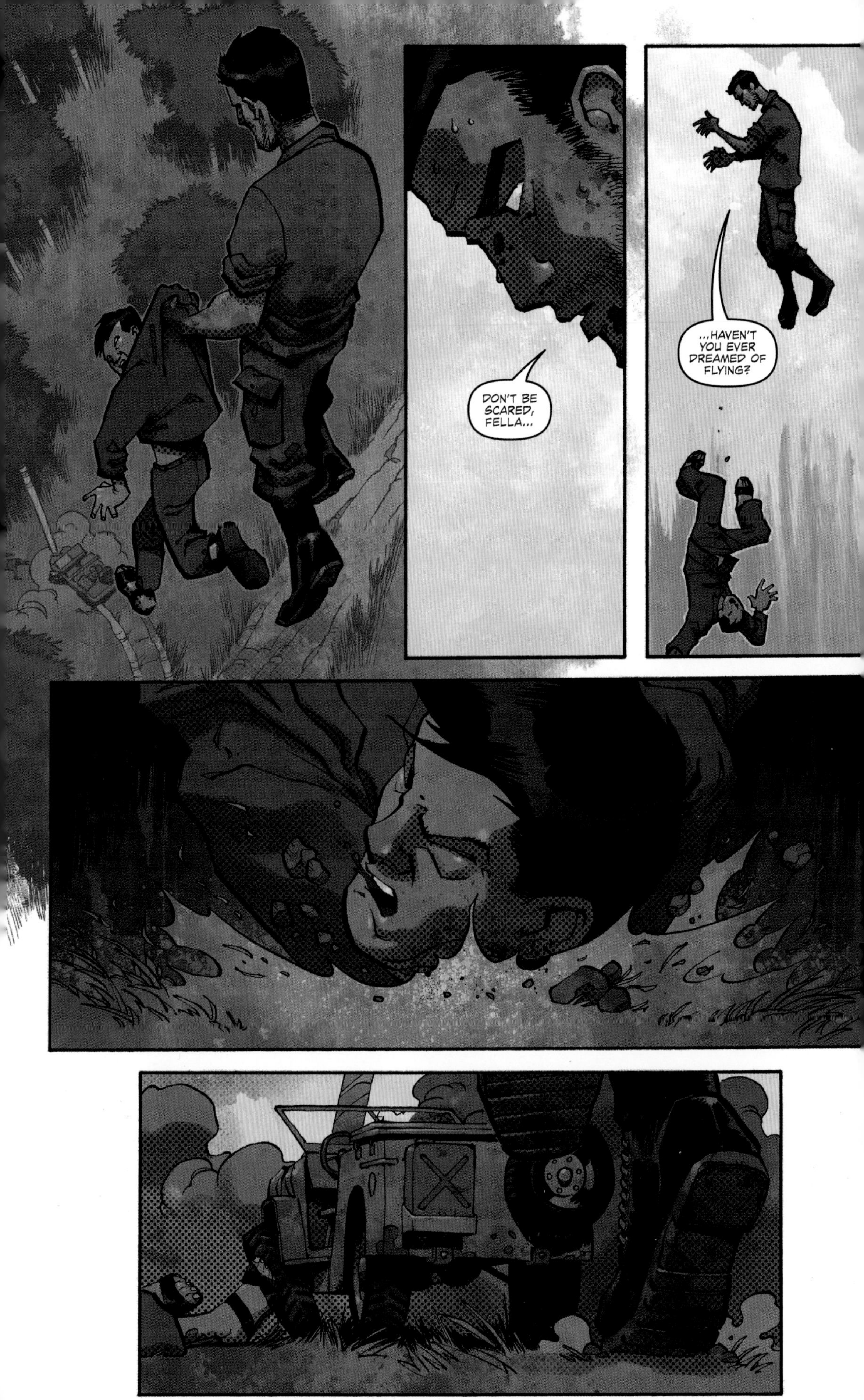
DON'T BE SCARED, FELLA...
...HAVEN'T YOU EVER DREAMED OF FLYING?

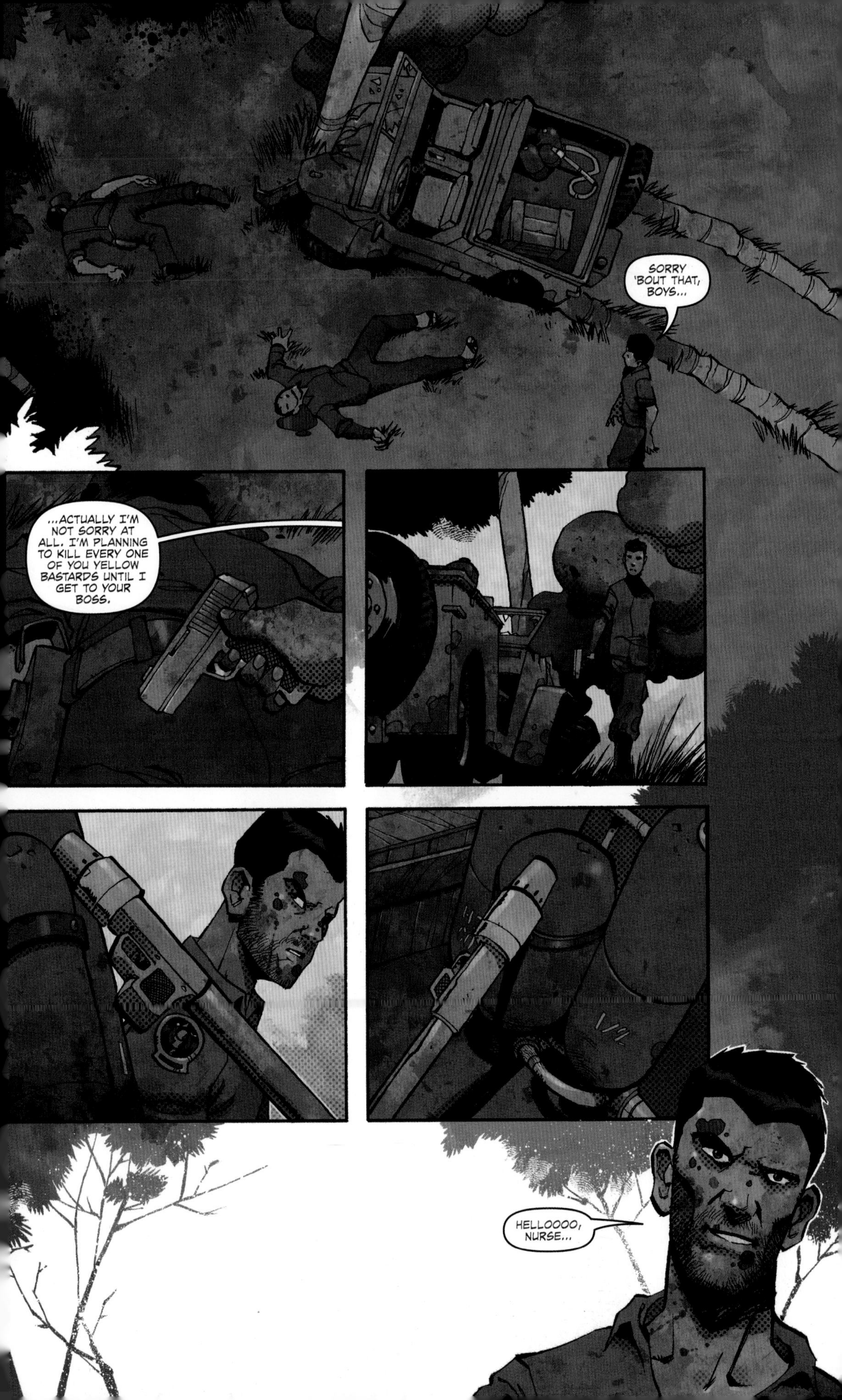
SORRY 'BOUT THAT, BOYS...
...ACTUALLY I'M NOT SORRY AT ALL. I'M PLANNING TO KILL EVERY ONE OF YOU YELLOW BASTARDS UNTIL I GET TO YOUR BOSS.
HELLOOOO, NURSE...

I GIVE YOU A SIMPLE TASK AND YOU MANAGE TO LET ME DOWN YET AGAIN, XUAN. YOU MAKE ME SICK!

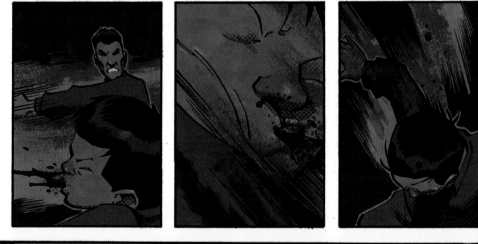

NOW THAT MAN IS OUT THERE AND HE'S LOOKING FOR REVENGE—REVENGE ON ME, YOUR FATHER. YOU'RE NO BETTER THAN A TRAITOR.

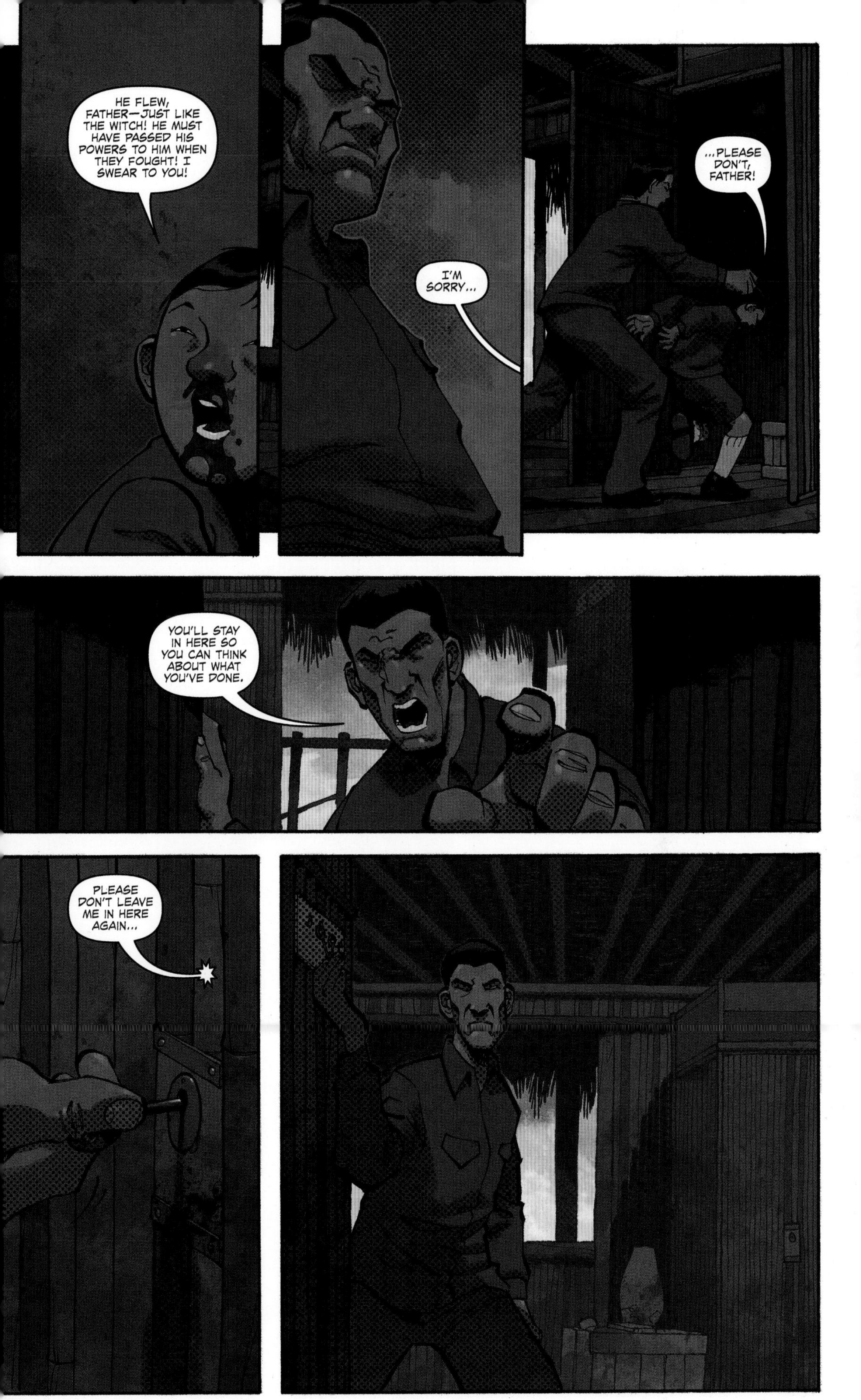
HE FLEW, FATHER—JUST LIKE THE WITCH! HE MUST HAVE PASSED HIS POWERS TO HIM WHEN THEY FOUGHT! I SWEAR TO YOU!
I'M SORRY...
...PLEASE DON'T, FATHER!
YOU'LL STAY IN HERE SO YOU CAN THINK ABOUT WHAT YOU'VE DONE.
PLEASE DON'T LEAVE ME IN HERE AGAIN...

ONE OF THE MOST IMPORTANT SKILLS A DOCTOR CAN LEARN IS TO LET GO OF HIS FEELINGS.

WE SEE A LOT OF TERRIBLE THINGS, AND YOU CAN'T ALLOW YOUR PERSONAL FEELINGS TO GET IN THE WAY OF YOUR WORK.

YOU HAVE TO TREAT EACH SITUATION WITH A LEVEL HEAD AND MOVE ON, NO MATTER THE OUTCOME.

I WAS GOOD AT THAT. I COULD WATCH A KID DIE OF CANCER AND FIVE MINUTES LATER HAVE A COFFEE AND THINK ABOUT WHAT I WAS GOING TO HAVE FOR DINNER. I TRAINED MYSELF NOT TO FEEL ANYTHING, NO MATTER HOW BAD THINGS WERE. NO SADNESS, OR ANGER, OR GUILT—NOTHING. BUT THIS... THIS IS A FEELING I NEVER TRAINED MYSELF TO DEAL WITH...

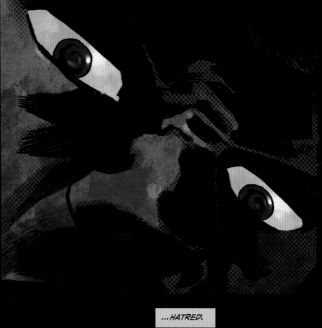

...HATRED.

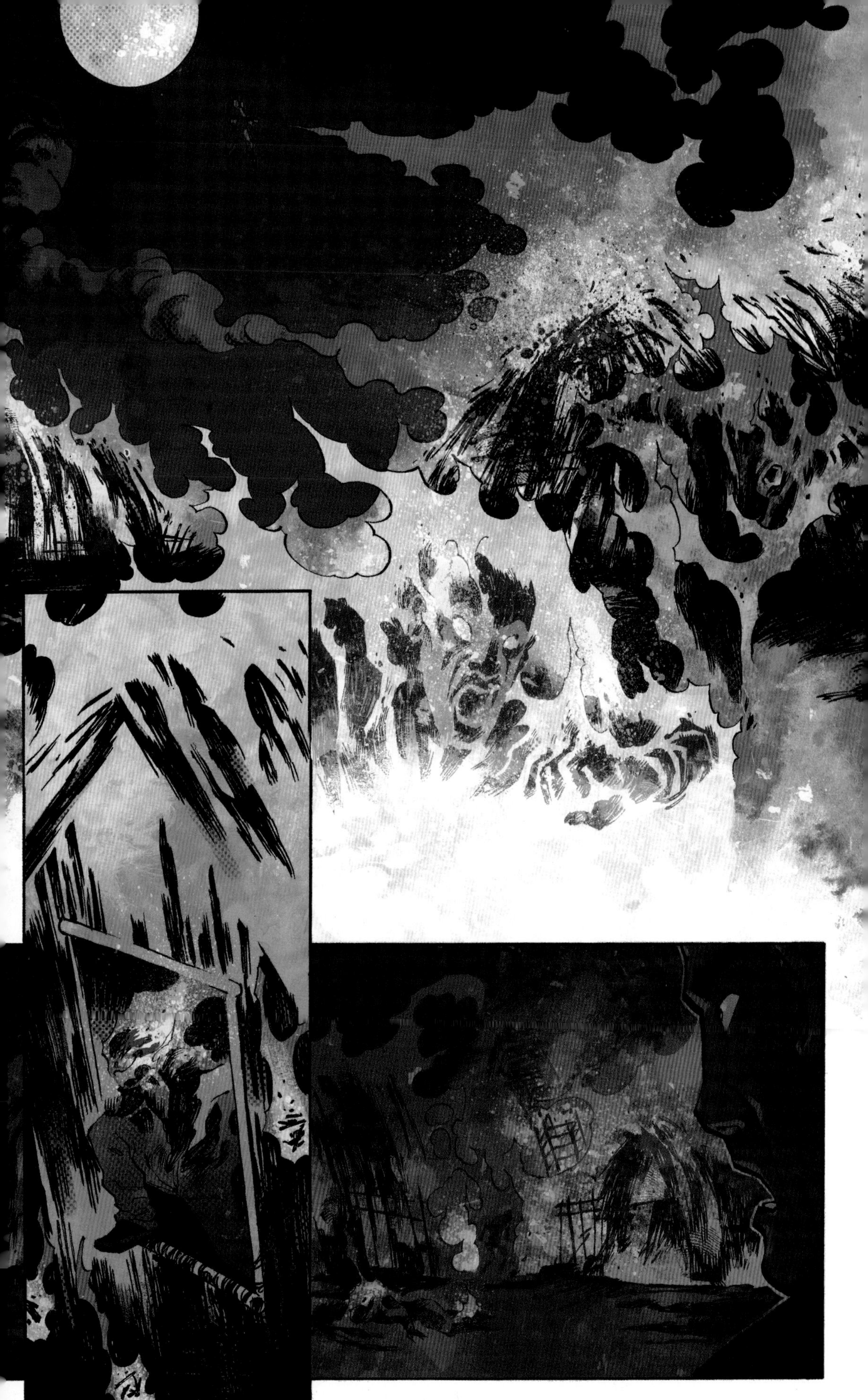

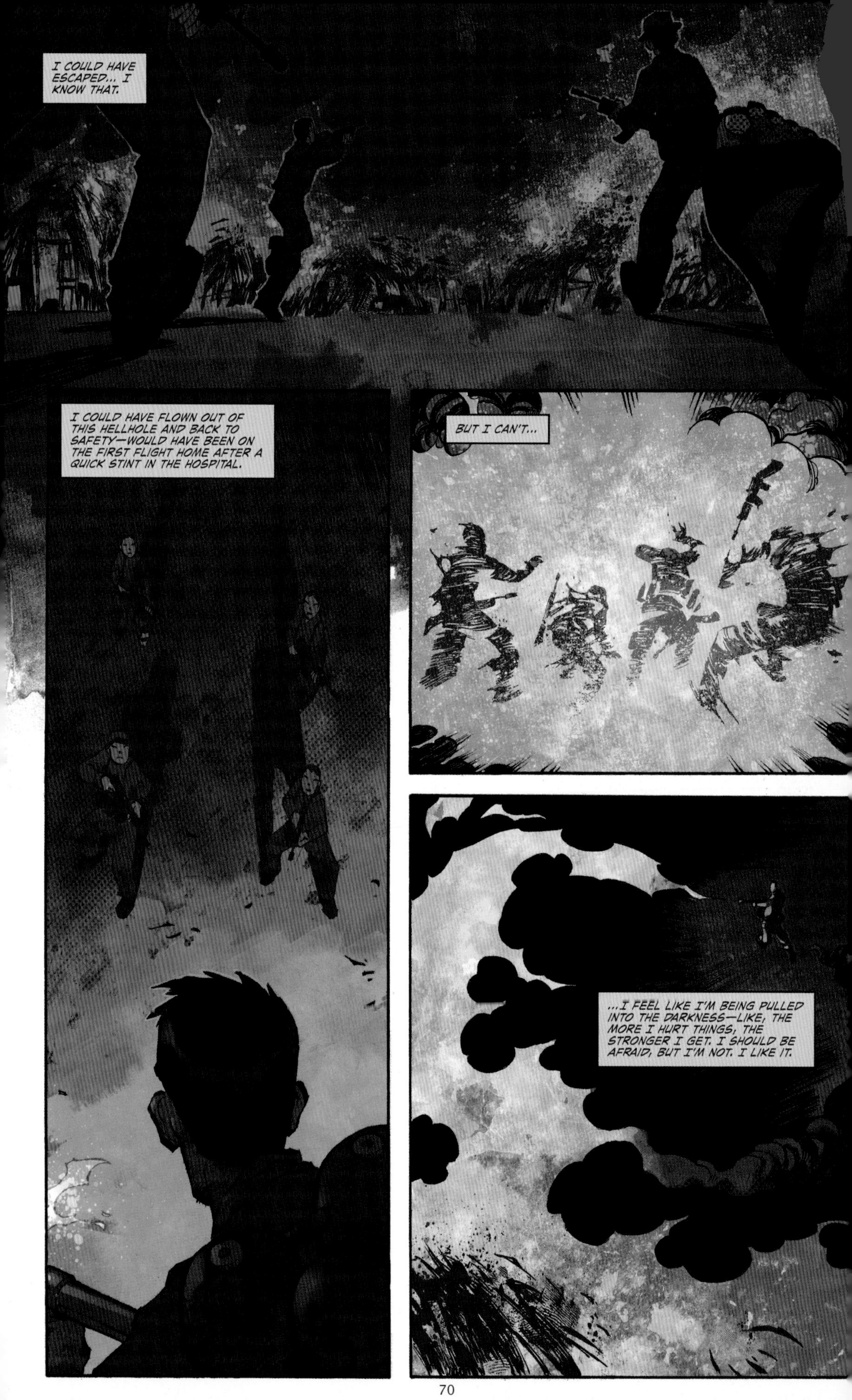
I COULD HAVE ESCAPED... I KNOW THAT.
I COULD HAVE FLOWN OUT OF THIS HELLHOLE AND BACK TO SAFETY—WOULD HAVE BEEN ON THE FIRST FLIGHT HOME AFTER A QUICK STINT IN THE HOSPITAL.
BUT I CAN'T...
...I FEEL LIKE I'M BEING PULLED INTO THE DARKNESS—LIKE, THE MORE I HURT THINGS, THE STRONGER I GET. I SHOULD BE AFRAID, BUT I'M NOT. I LIKE IT.

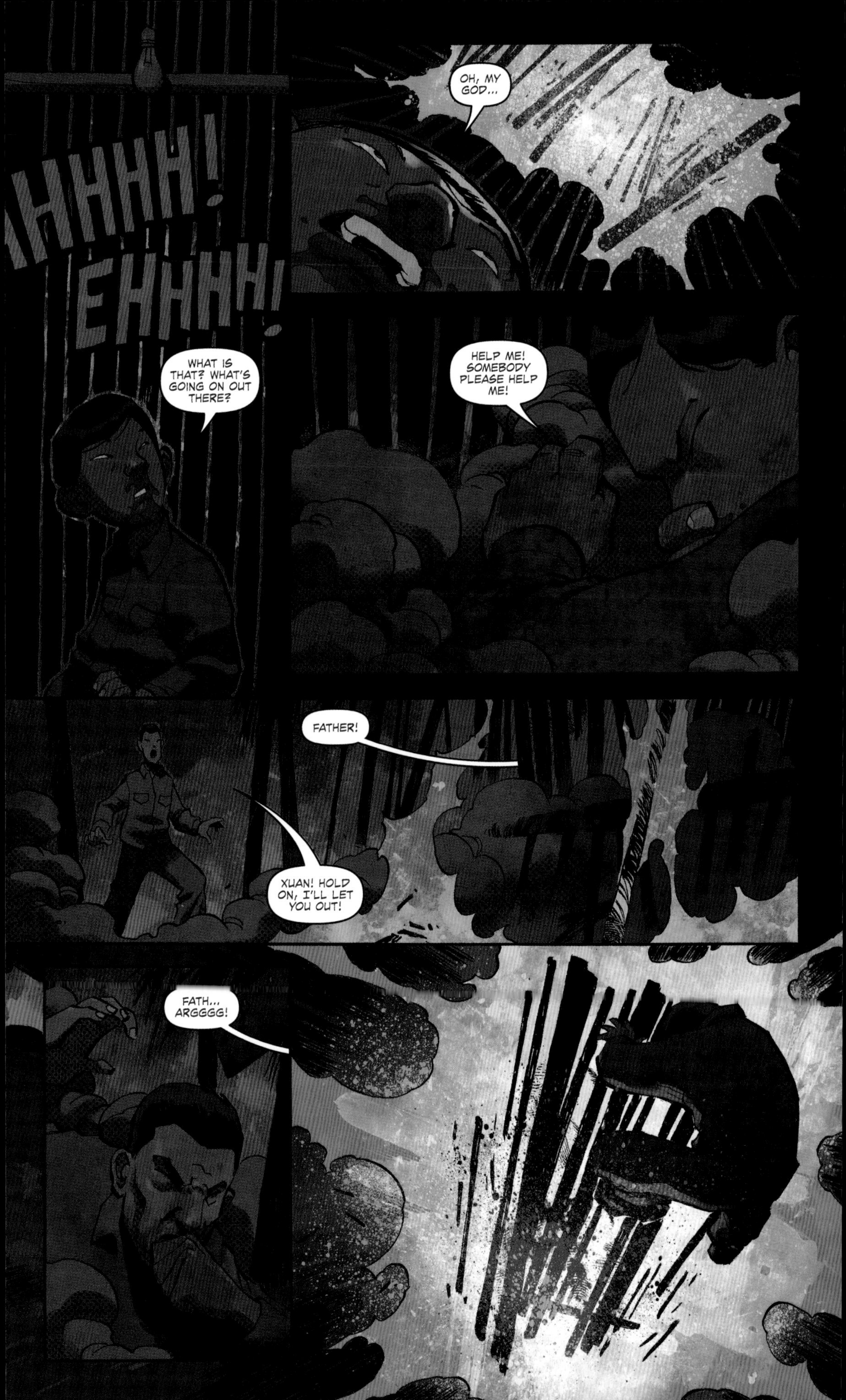
HHHH! EHHHH!
OH, MY GOD...
WHAT IS THAT? WHAT'S GOING ON OUT THERE?
HELP ME! SOMEBODY PLEASE HELP ME!
FATHER!
XUAN! HOLD ON, I'LL LET YOU OUT!
FATH... ARGGGG!

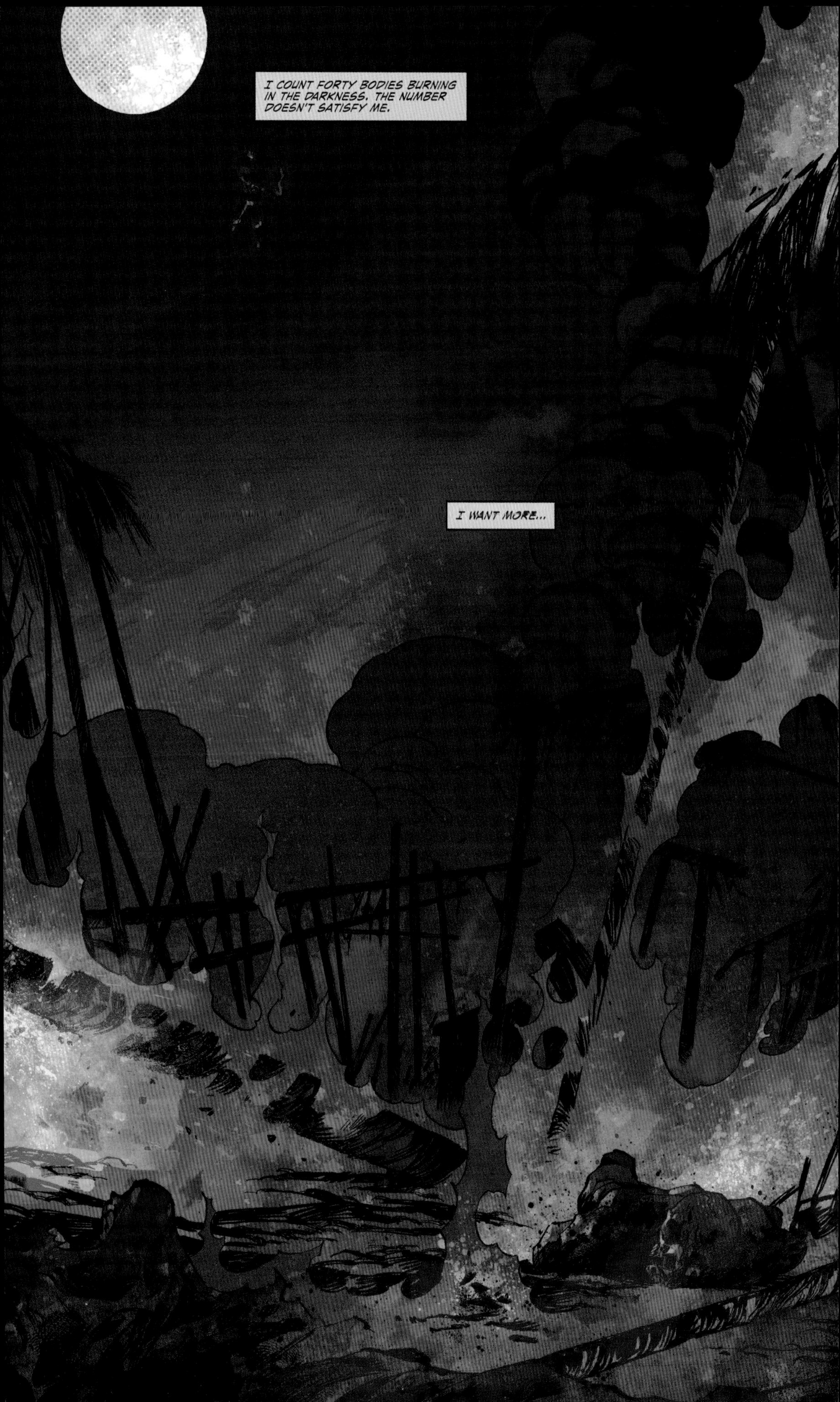
I COUNT FORTY BODIES BURNING IN THE DARKNESS. THE NUMBER DOESN'T SATISFY ME.
I WANT MORE...

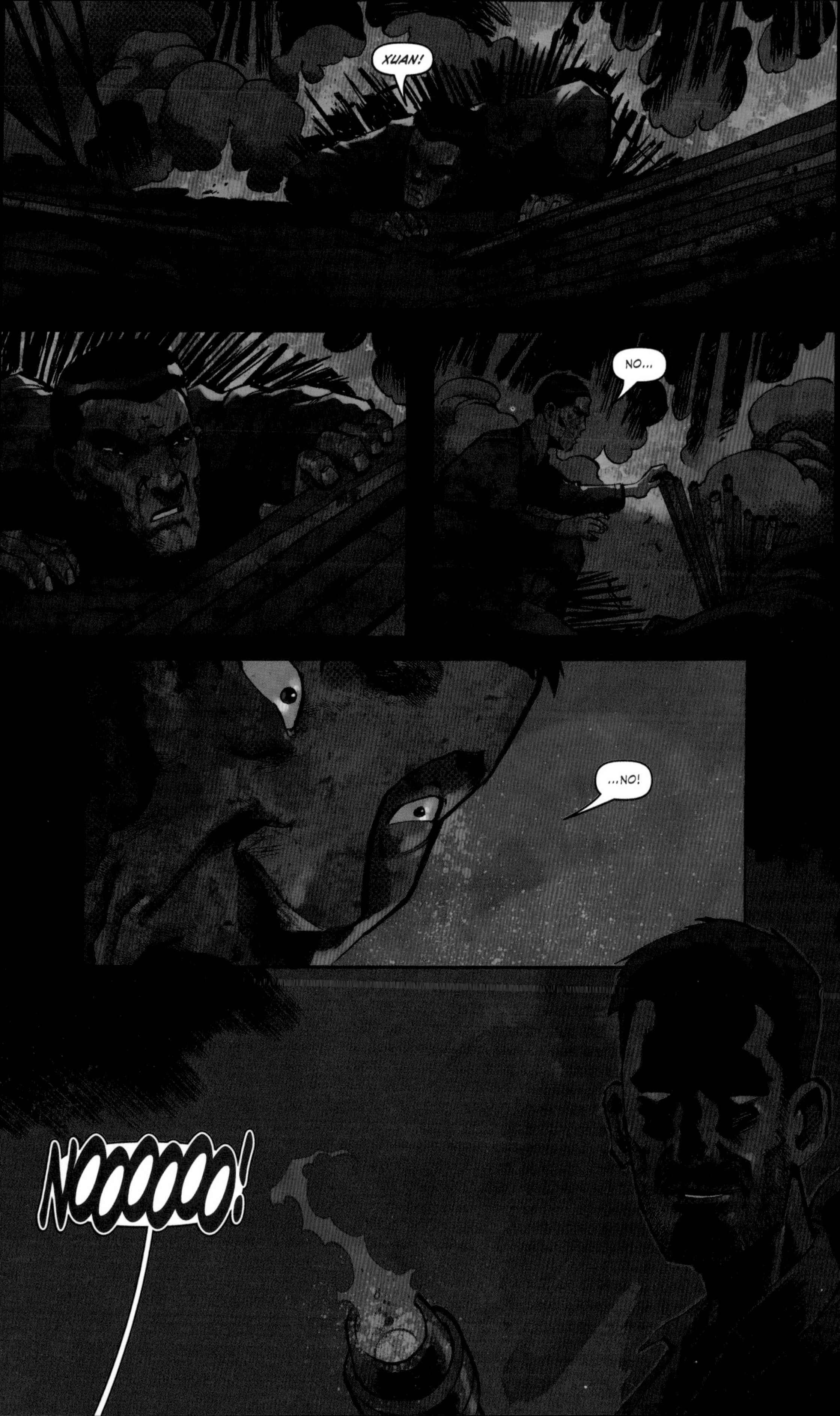
XUAN!
NO...
...NO!
NOOOOOO!

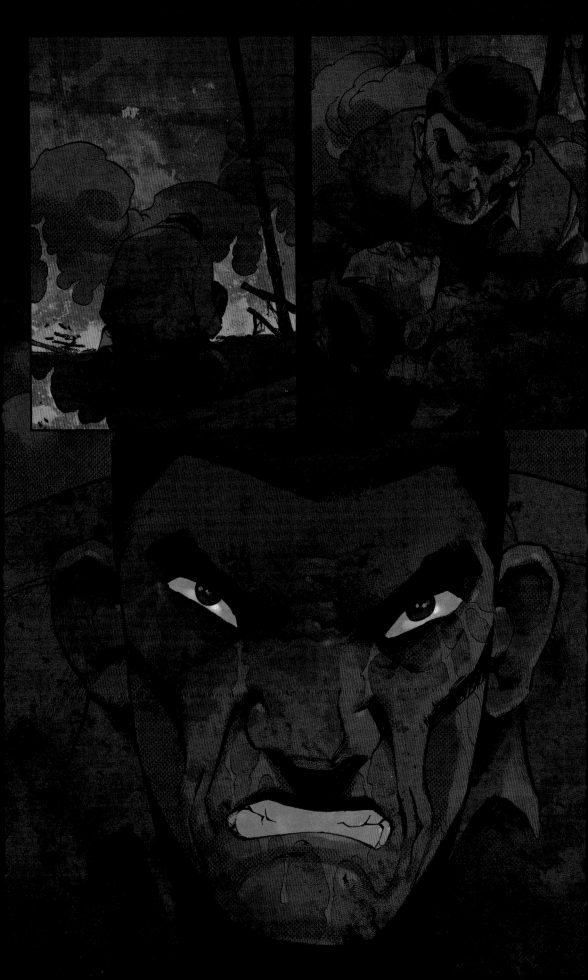

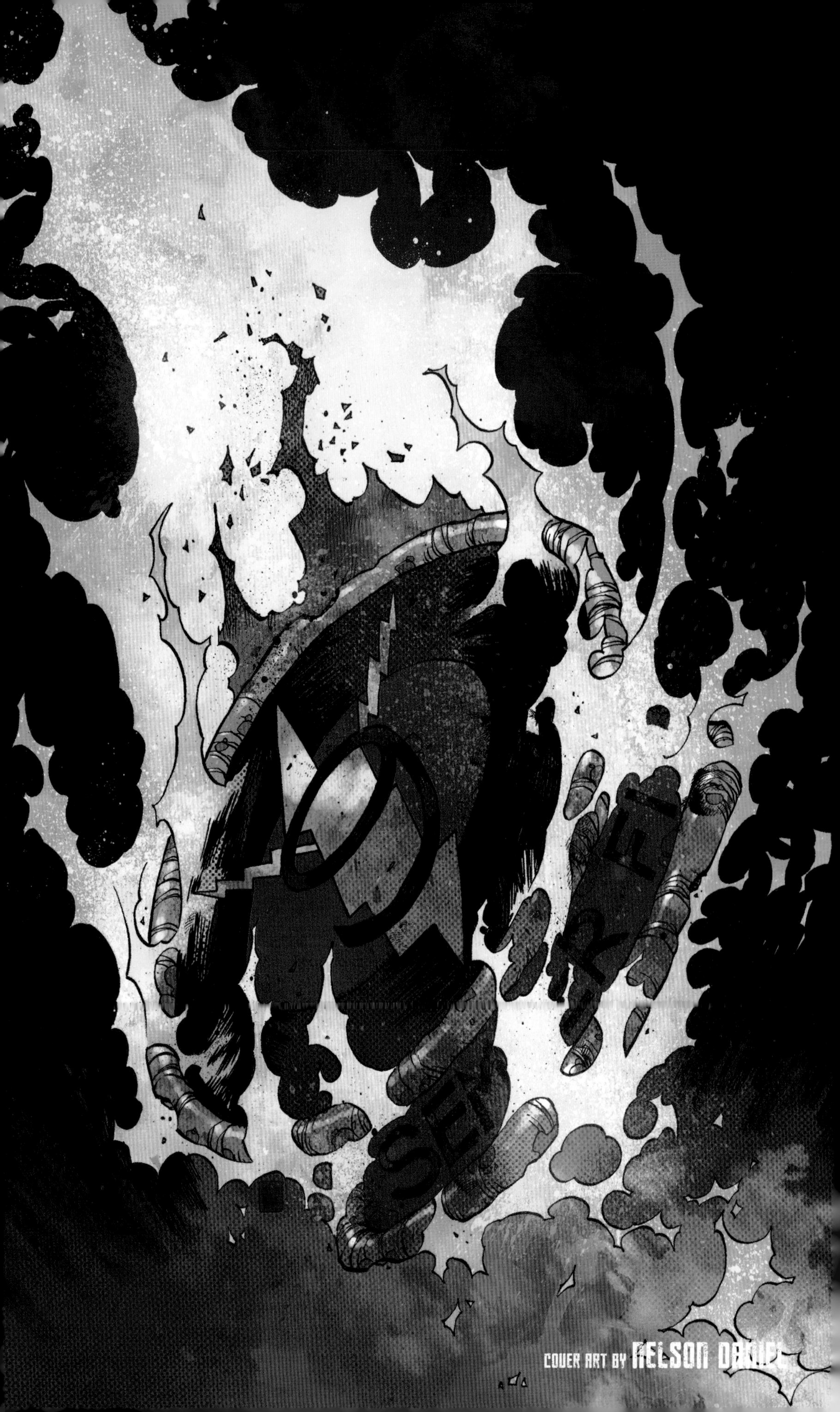

COVER ART BY NELSON DANIEL

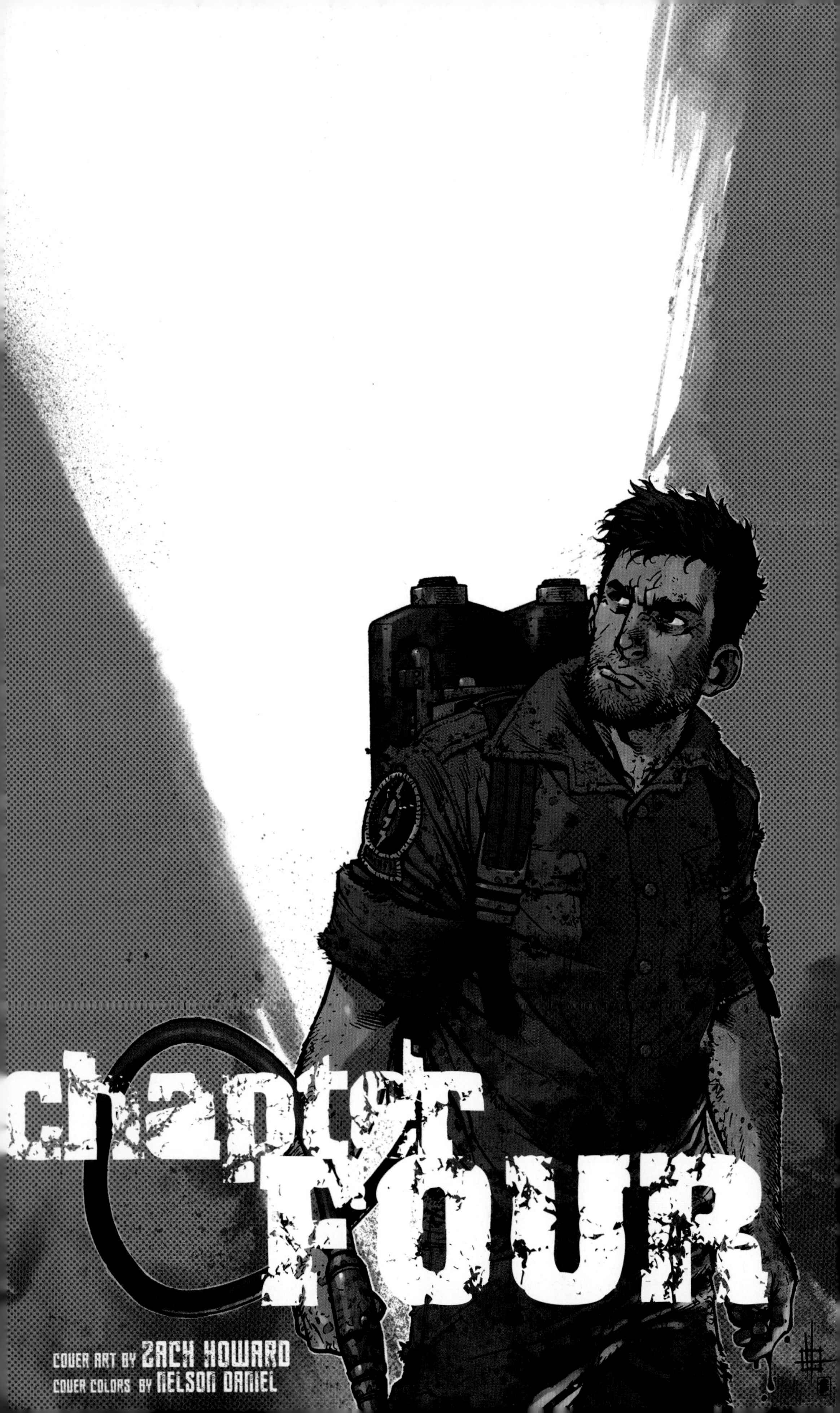
chapter
FOUR
COVER ART BY ZACH HOWARD
COVER COLORS BY NELSON DANIEL

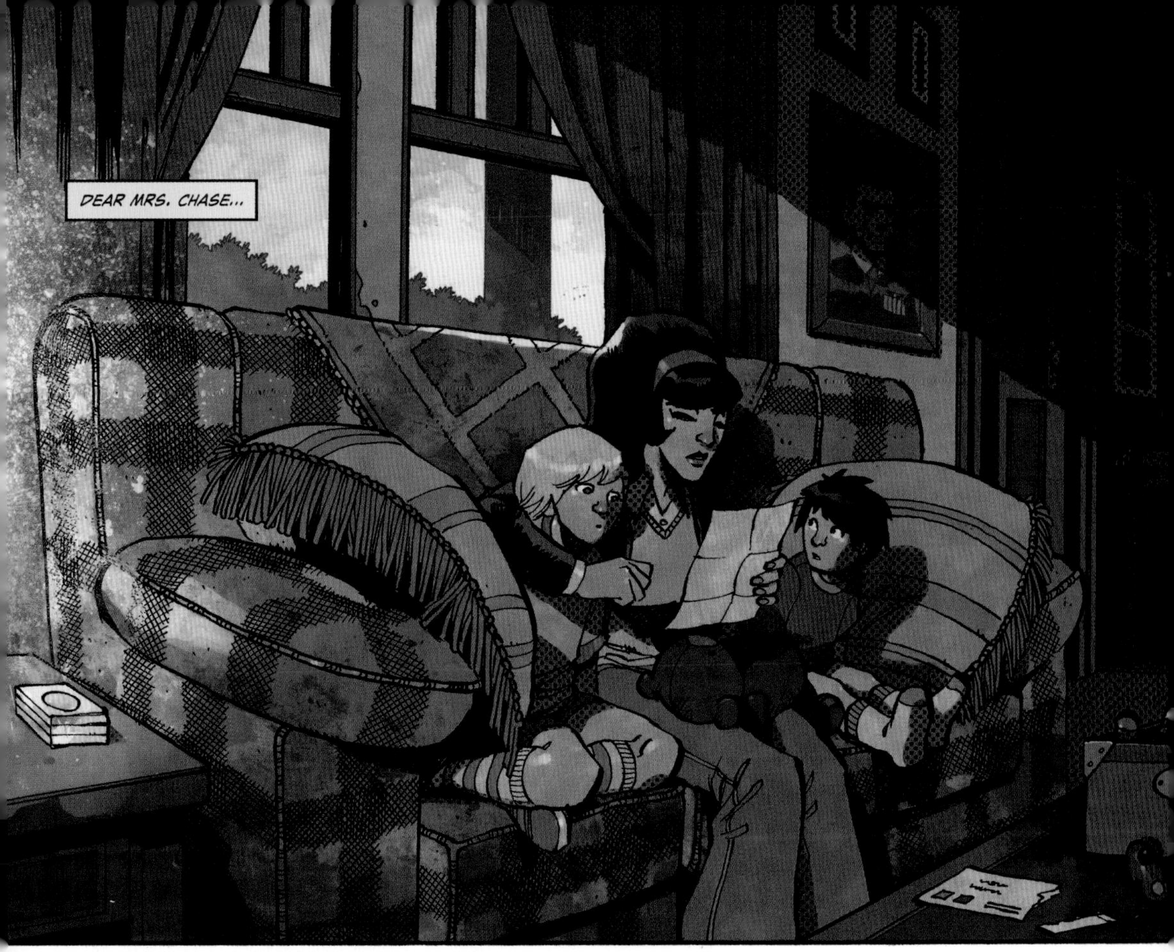
DEAR MRS. CHASE...

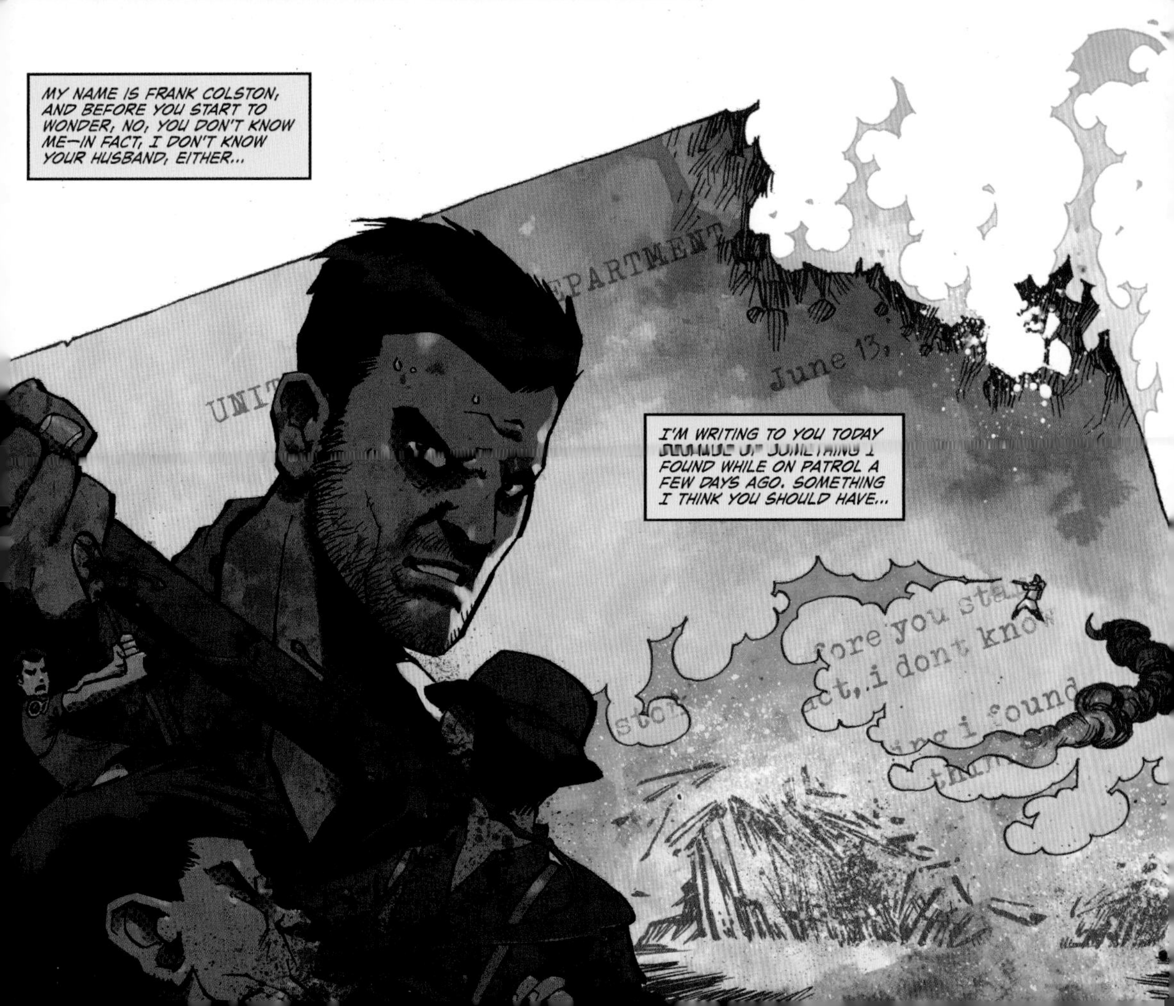
MY NAME IS FRANK COLSTON, AND BEFORE YOU START TO WONDER, NO, YOU DON'T KNOW ME—IN FACT, I DON'T KNOW YOUR HUSBAND, EITHER...
June 13,
I'M WRITING TO YOU TODAY
SOMETHING I
FOUND WHILE ON PATROL A
FEW DAYS AGO. SOMETHING
I THINK YOU SHOULD HAVE...

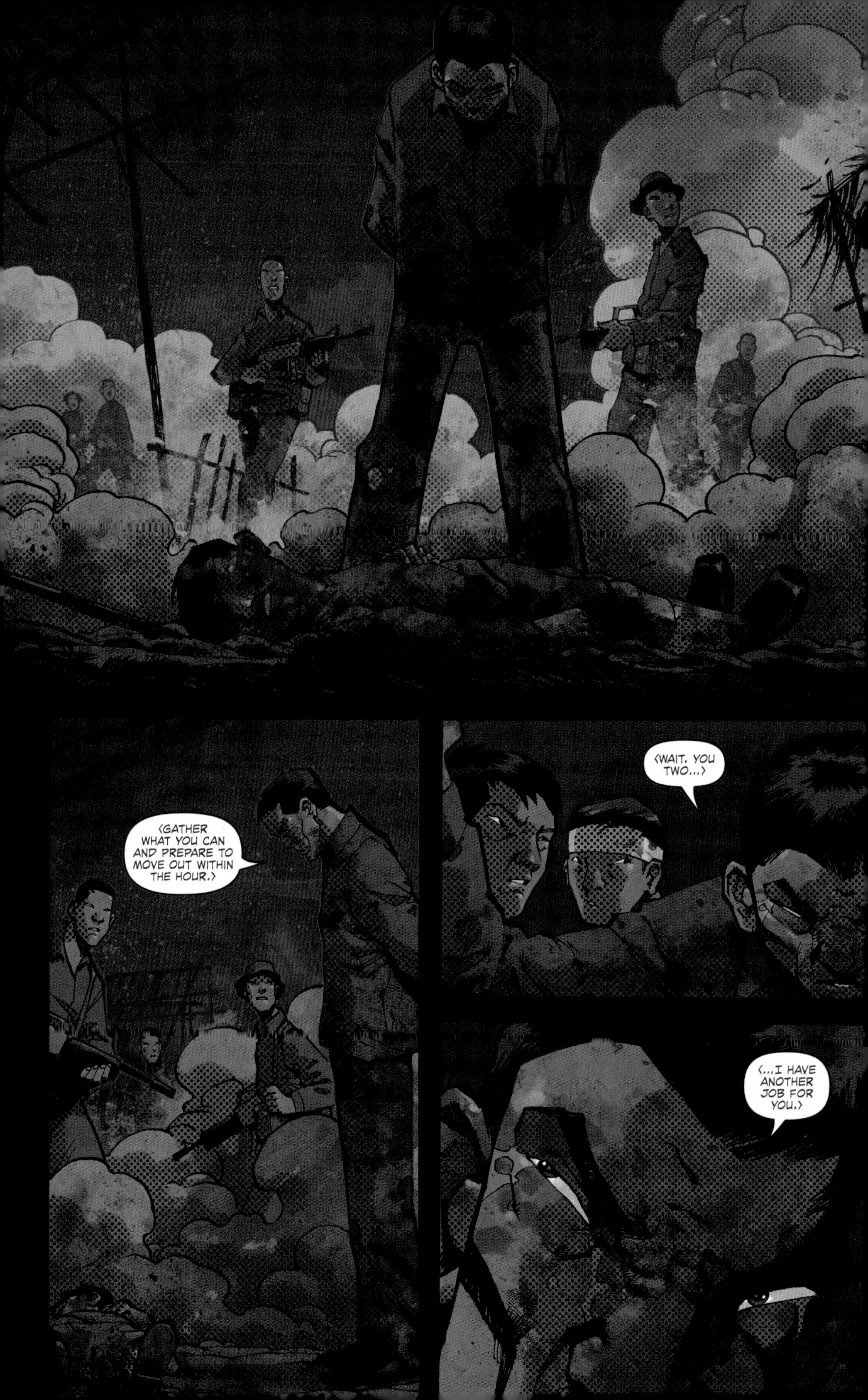
‹GATHER WHAT YOU CAN AND PREPARE TO MOVE OUT WITHIN THE HOUR.›
‹WAIT. YOU TWO...›
‹...I HAVE ANOTHER JOB FOR YOU.›

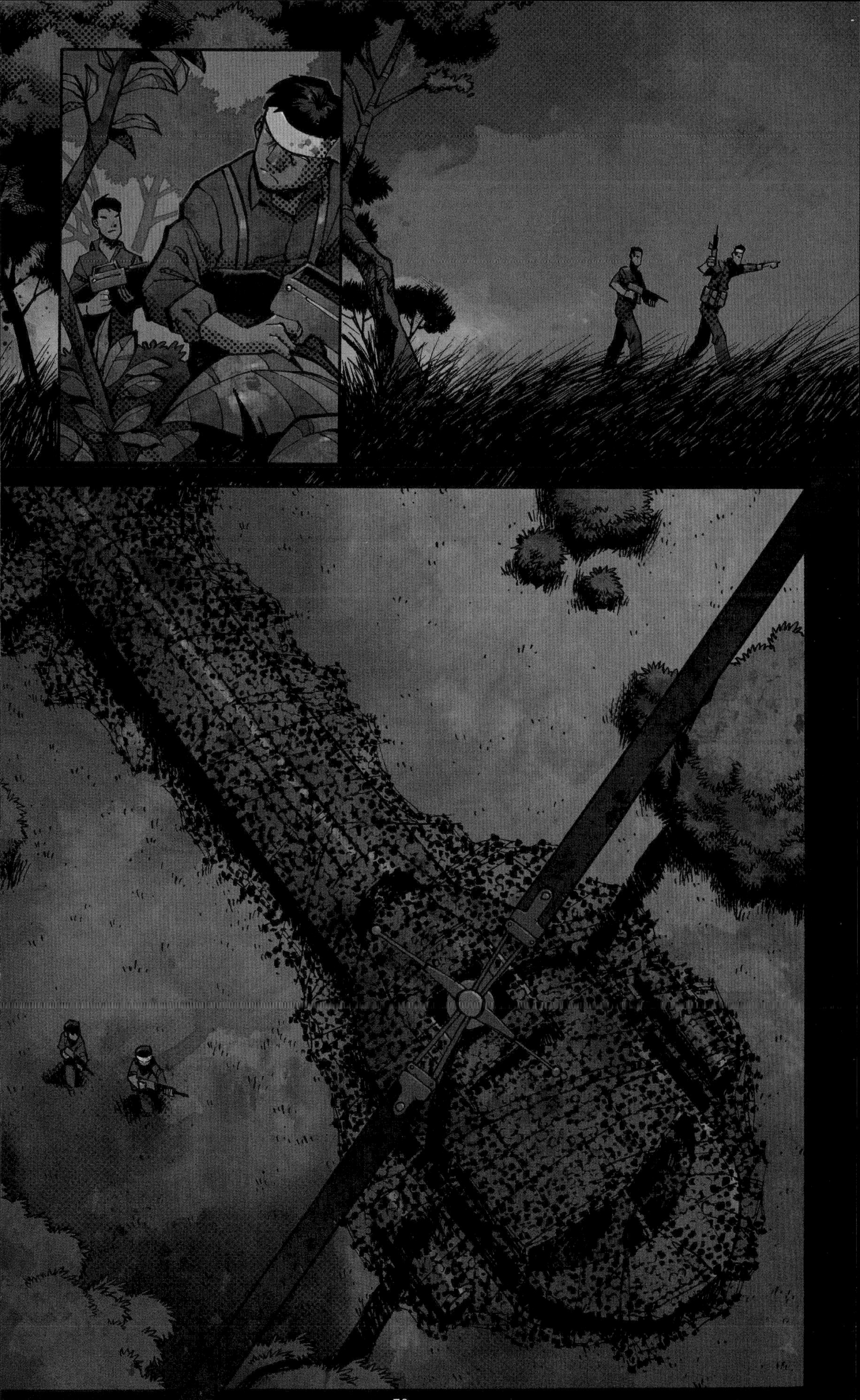

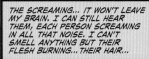

THE SCREAMING... IT WON'T LEAVE MY BRAIN. I CAN STILL HEAR THEM, EACH PERSON SCREAMING IN ALL THAT NOISE. I CAN'T SMELL ANYTHING BUT THEIR FLESH BURNING...THEIR HAIR...

...I CAN HEAR THEIR EYEBALLS CRACKLING IN THEIR SOCKETS, COOKING... COOKING AND SCREAMING AND SMOKING...

...THEY'RE DEAD... YOU'RE ALL DEAD.

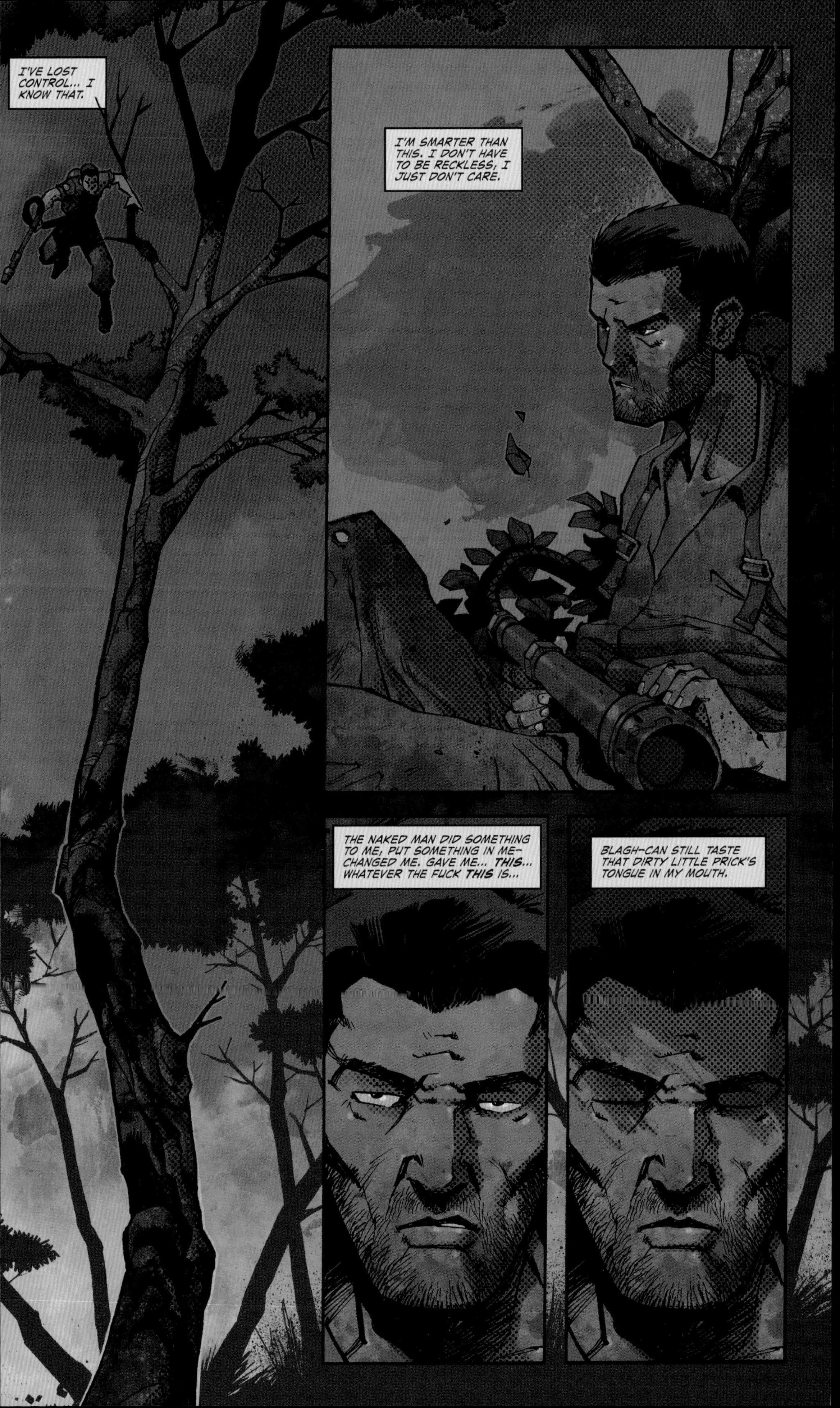
I'VE LOST CONTROL... I KNOW THAT.
I'M SMARTER THAN THIS. I DON'T HAVE TO BE RECKLESS, I JUST DON'T CARE.
THE NAKED MAN DID SOMETHING TO ME, PUT SOMETHING IN ME-CHANGED ME. GAVE ME... THIS... WHATEVER THE FUCK THIS IS...
BLAGH-CAN STILL TASTE THAT DIRTY LITTLE PRICK'S TONGUE IN MY MOUTH.

MAGIC, CURSES—
HOW THE HELL IS
THIS REAL?

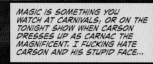

MAGIC IS SOMETHING YOU
WATCH AT CARNIVALS, OR ON THE
TONIGHT SHOW WHEN CARSON
DRESSES UP AS CARNAC THE
MAGNIFICENT. I FUCKING HATE
CARSON AND HIS STUPID FACE...

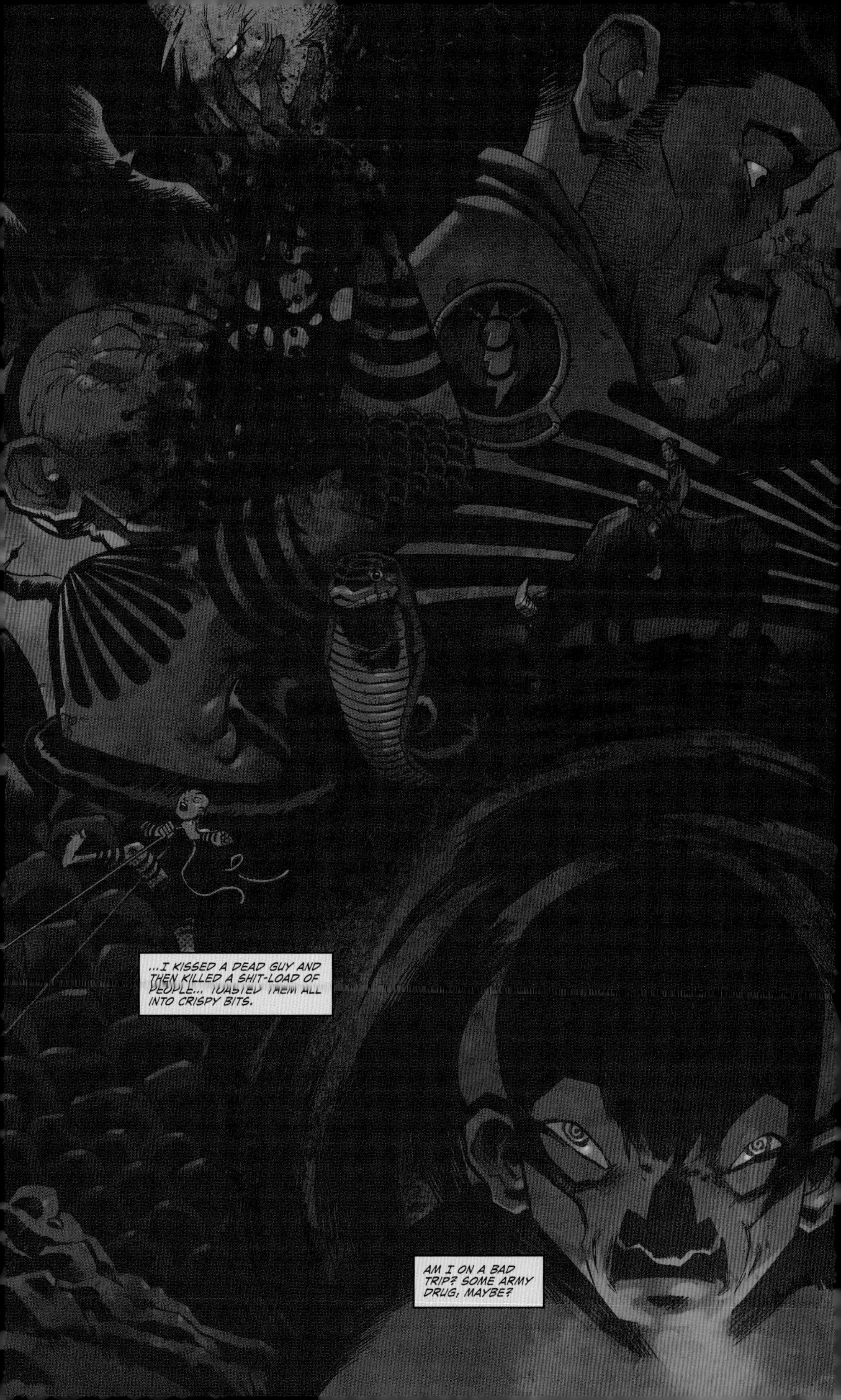
...I KISSED A DEAD GUY AND THEN KILLED A SHIT-LOAD OF PEOPLE... TOASTED THEM ALL INTO CRISPY BITS.
AM I ON A BAD TRIP? SOME ARMY DRUG, MAYBE?

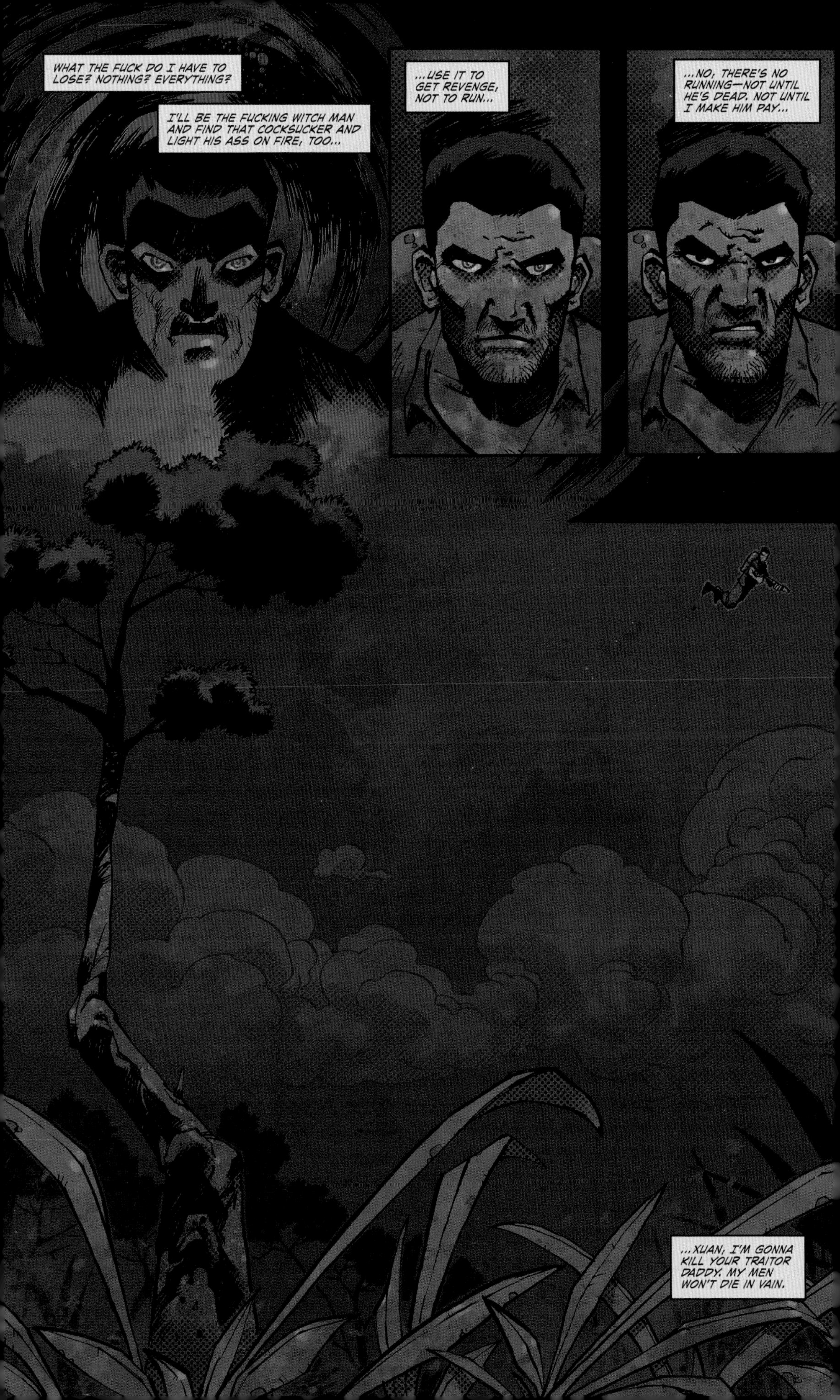
WHAT THE FUCK DO I HAVE TO LOSE? NOTHING? EVERYTHING?
I'LL BE THE FUCKING WITCH MAN AND FIND THAT COCKSUCKER AND LIGHT HIS ASS ON FIRE, TOO...
...USE IT TO GET REVENGE, NOT TO RUN...
...NO, THERE'S NO RUNNING—NOT UNTIL HE'S DEAD. NOT UNTIL I MAKE HIM PAY...
...XUAN, I'M GONNA KILL YOUR TRAITOR DADDY. MY MEN WON'T DIE IN VAIN.

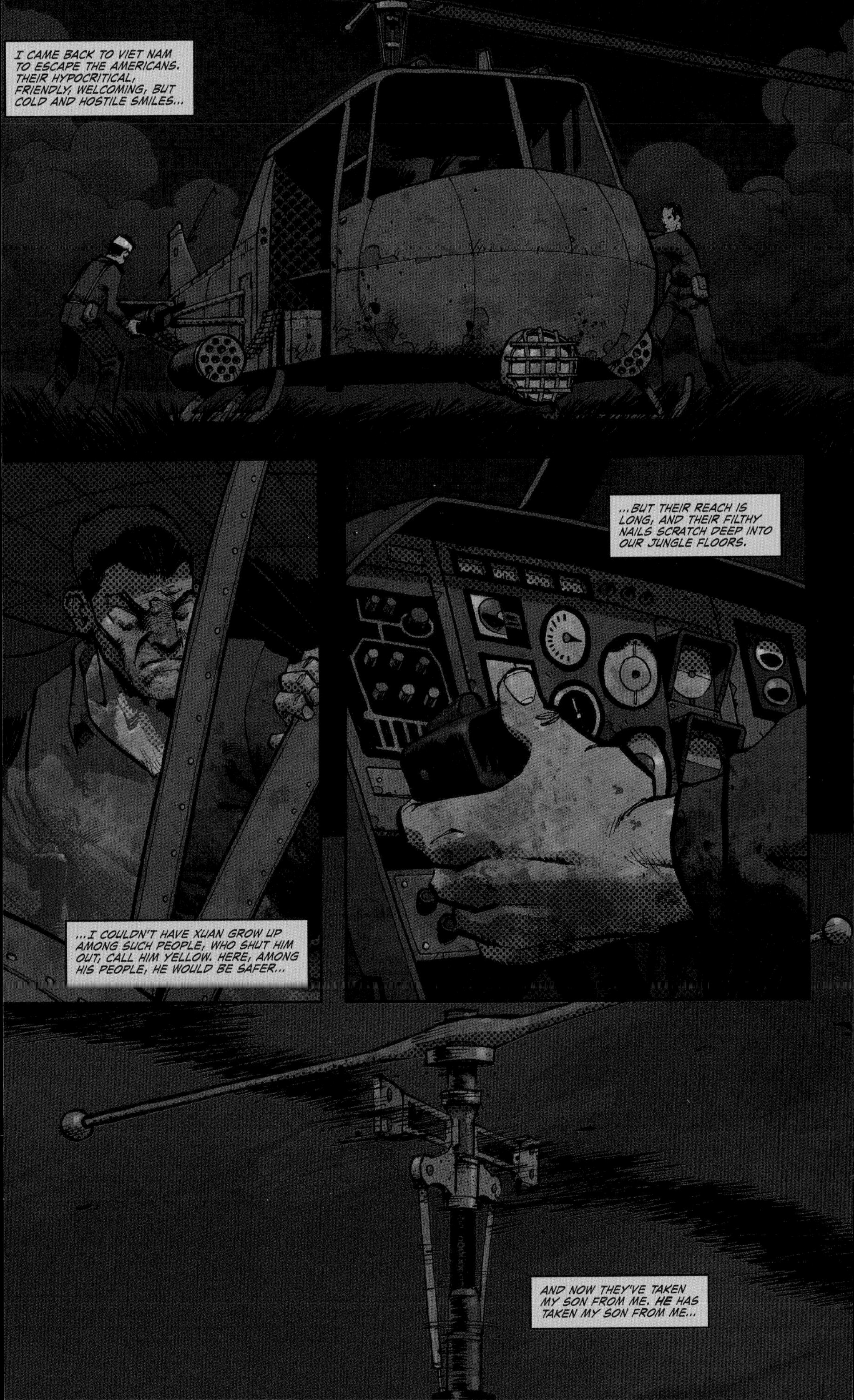
I CAME BACK TO VIET NAM TO ESCAPE THE AMERICANS. THEIR HYPOCRITICAL, FRIENDLY, WELCOMING, BUT COLD AND HOSTILE SMILES...
...I COULDN'T HAVE XUAN GROW UP AMONG SUCH PEOPLE, WHO SHUT HIM OUT, CALL HIM YELLOW. HERE, AMONG HIS PEOPLE, HE WOULD BE SAFER...
...BUT THEIR REACH IS LONG, AND THEIR FILTHY NAILS SCRATCH DEEP INTO OUR JUNGLE FLOORS.
AND NOW THEY'VE TAKEN MY SON FROM ME. HE HAS TAKEN MY SON FROM ME...

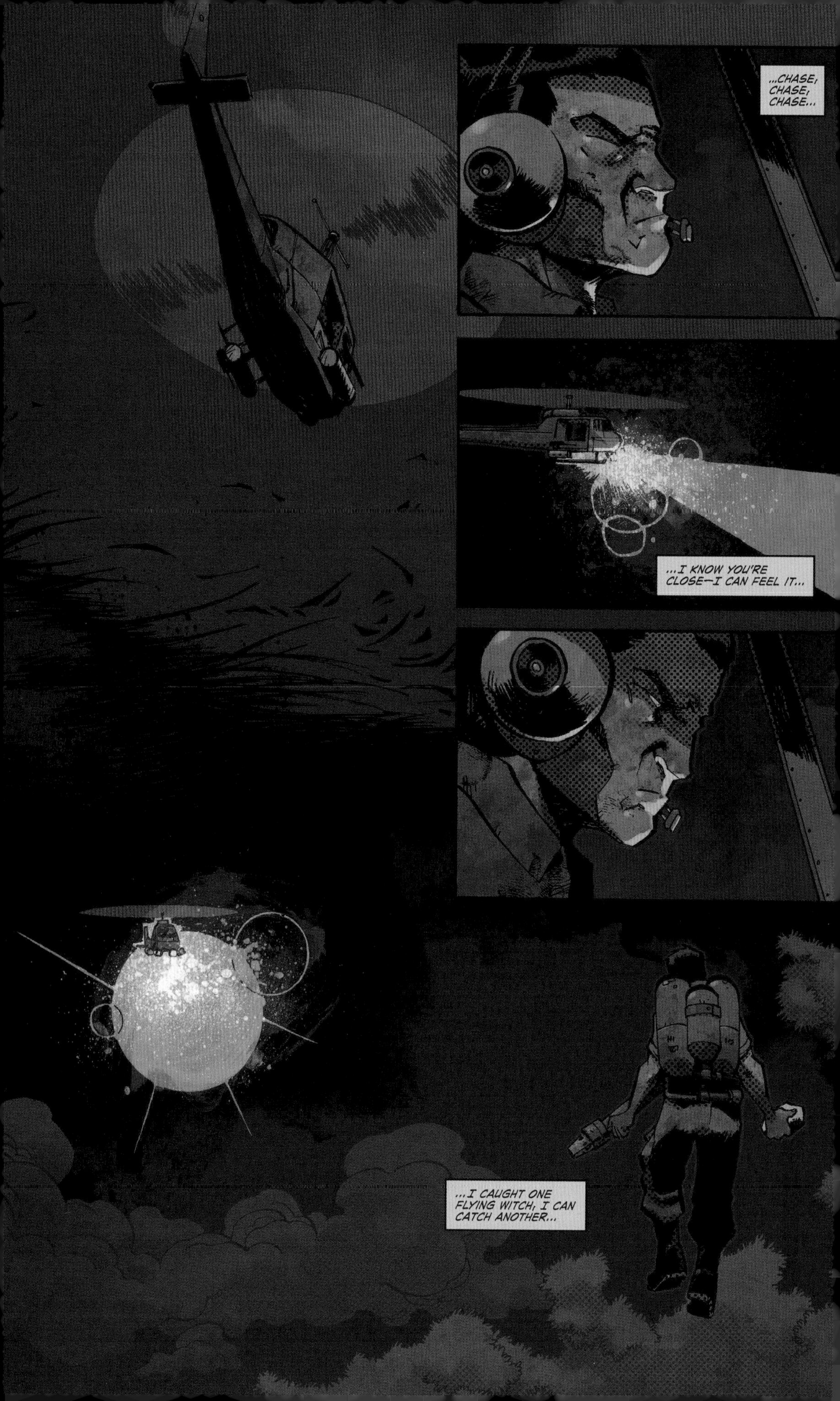
...CHASE,
CHASE,
CHASE...
...I KNOW YOU'RE
CLOSE—I CAN FEEL IT...
...I CAUGHT ONE
FLYING WITCH; I CAN
CATCH ANOTHER...

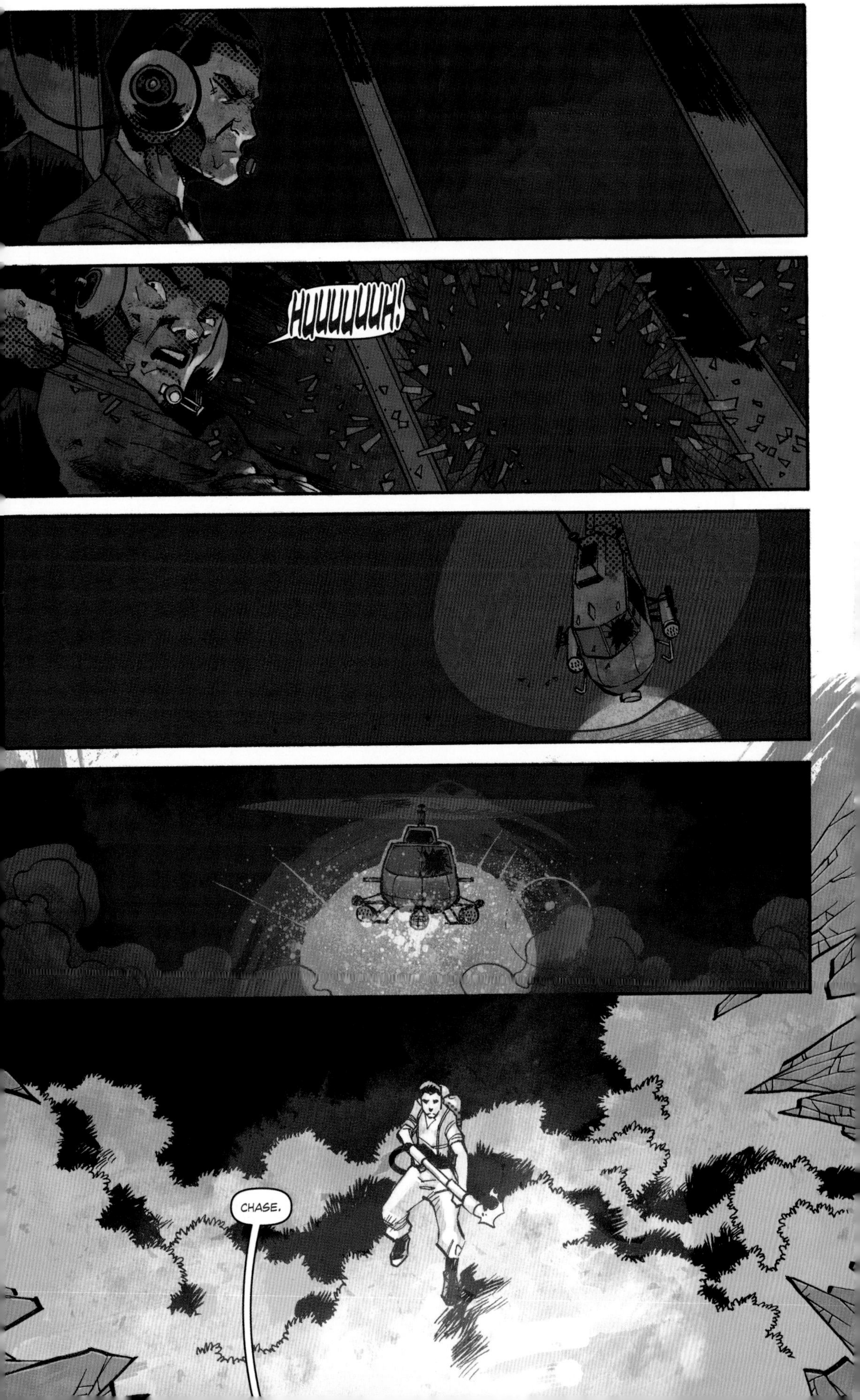
HUUUUUUH!
CHASE.

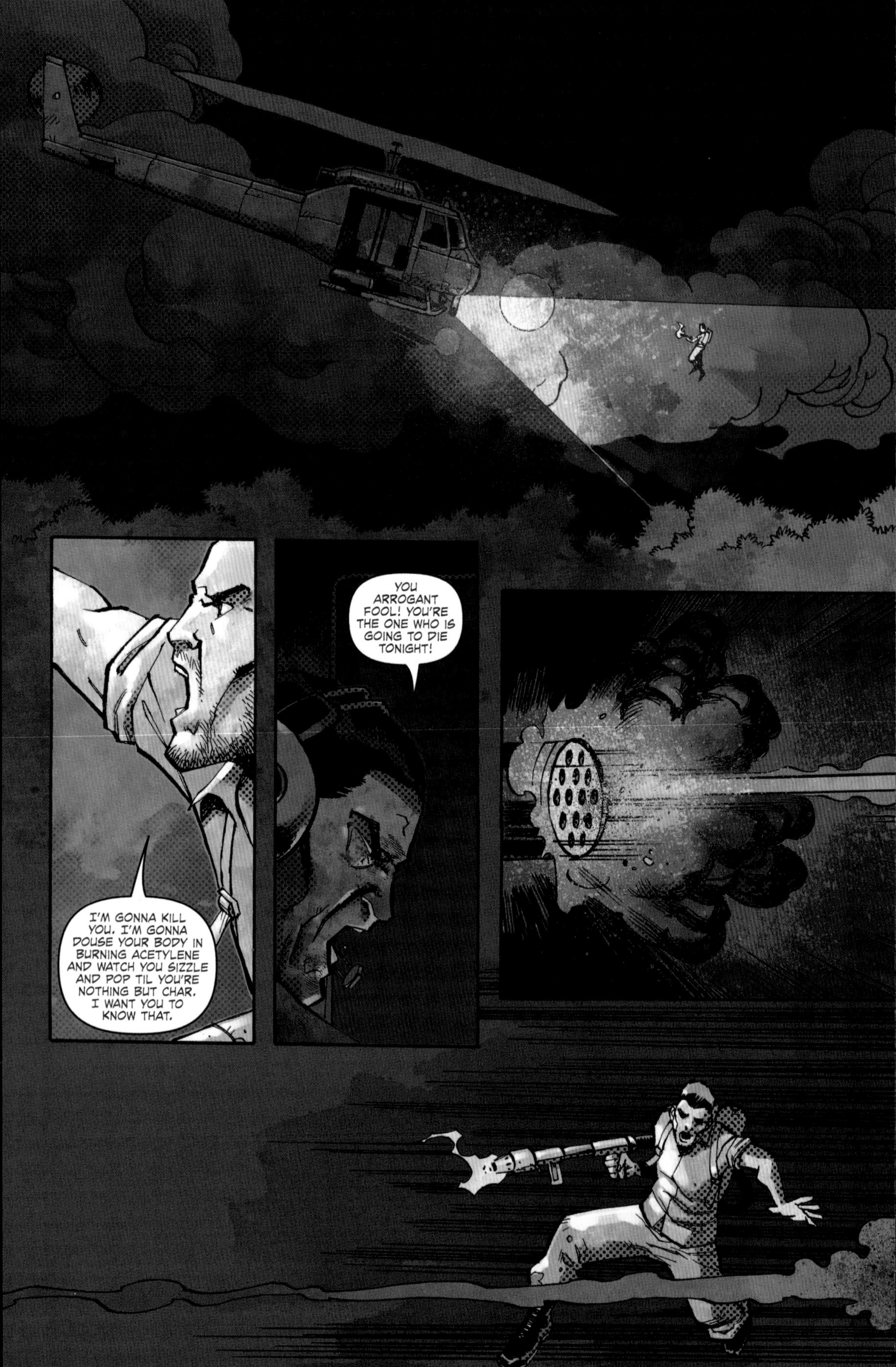
I'M GONNA KILL YOU. I'M GONNA DOUSE YOUR BODY IN BURNING ACETYLENE AND WATCH YOU SIZZLE AND POP TIL YOU'RE NOTHING BUT CHAR. I WANT YOU TO KNOW THAT.
YOU ARROGANT FOOL! YOU'RE THE ONE WHO IS GOING TO DIE TONIGHT!

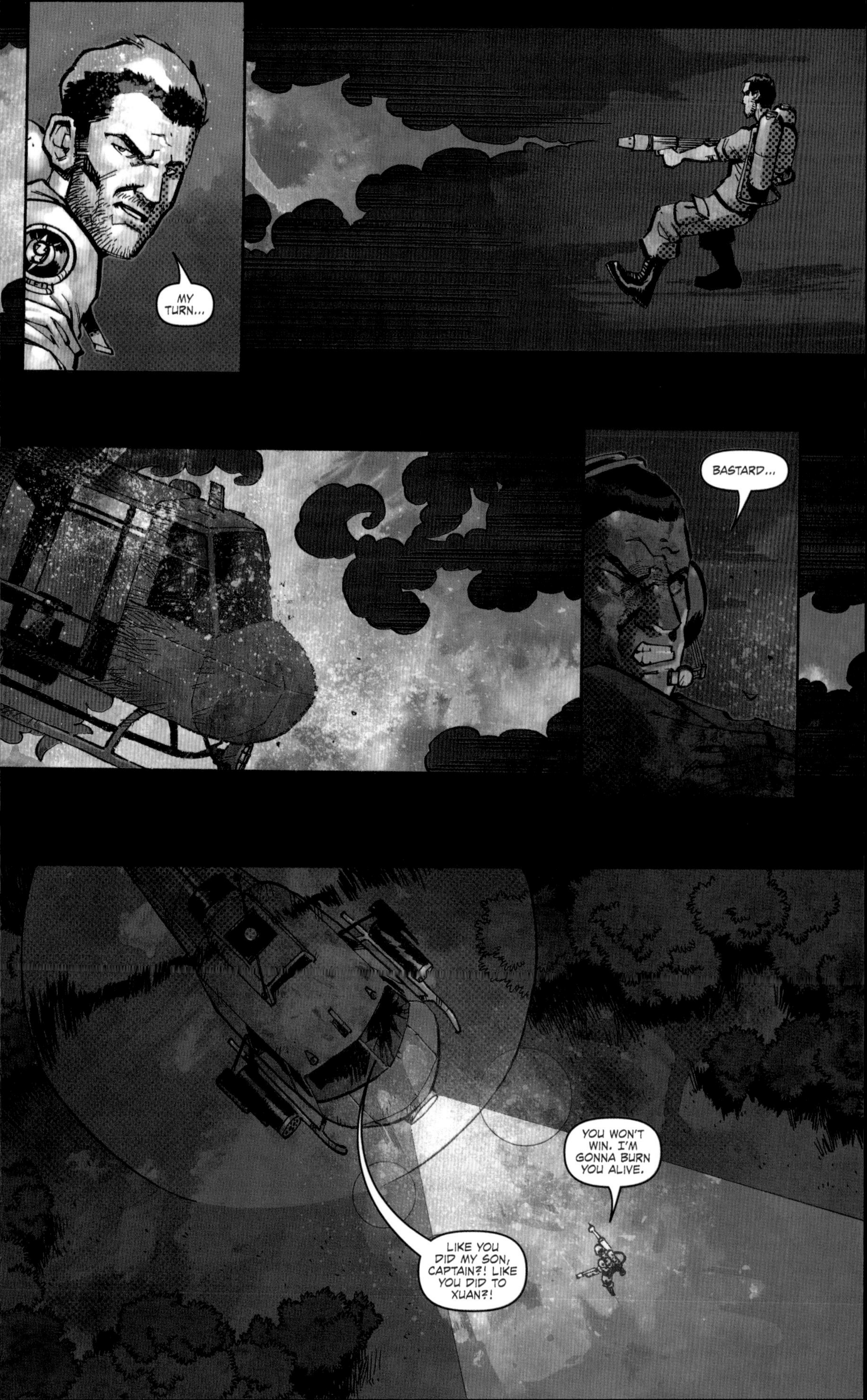
MY TURN...
BASTARD...
YOU WON'T WIN. I'M GONNA BURN YOU ALIVE.
LIKE YOU DID MY SON, CAPTAIN?! LIKE YOU DID TO XUAN?!

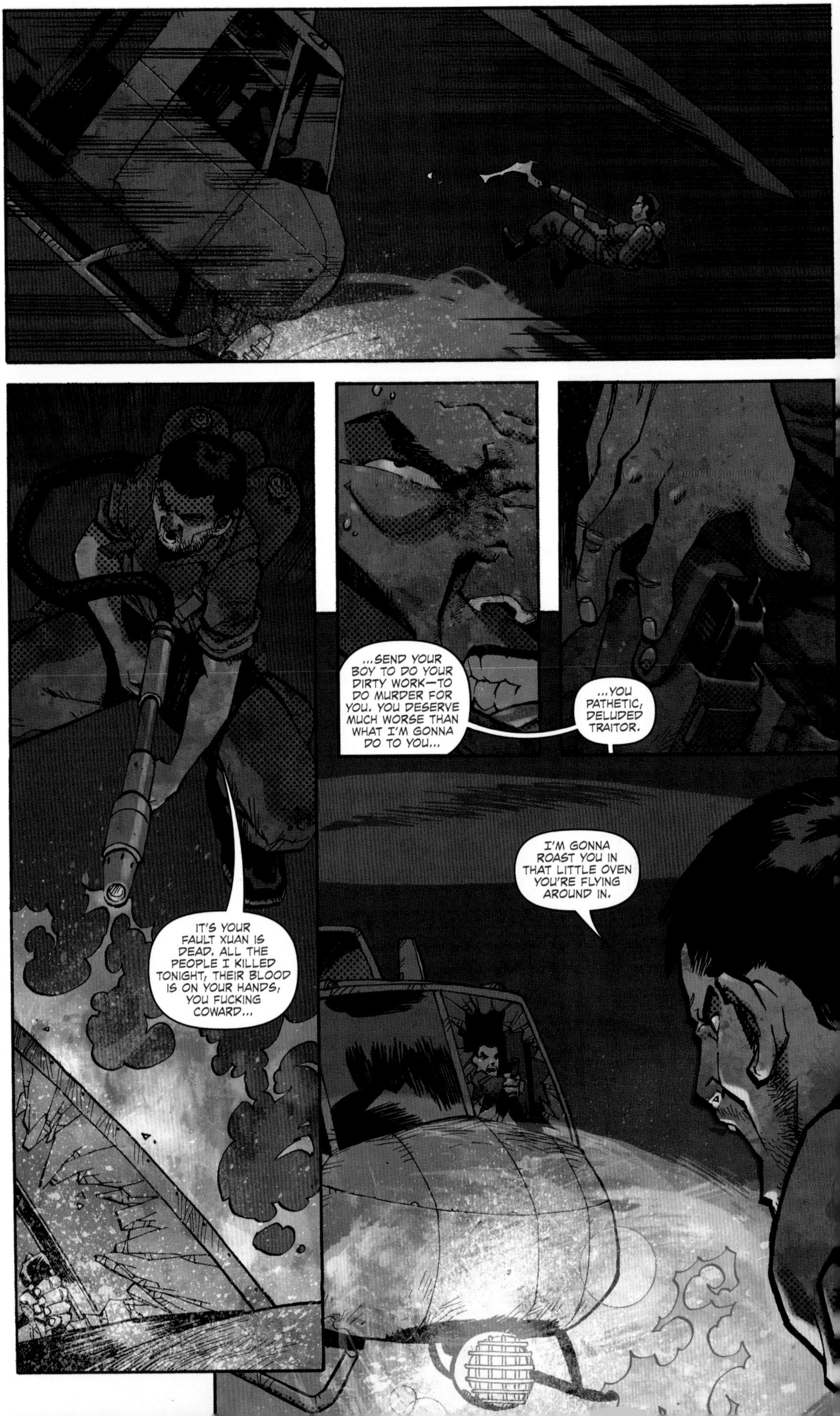
...SEND YOUR BOY TO DO YOUR DIRTY WORK—TO DO MURDER FOR YOU. YOU DESERVE MUCH WORSE THAN WHAT I'M GONNA DO TO YOU...
...YOU PATHETIC, DELUDED TRAITOR.
IT'S YOUR FAULT XUAN IS DEAD. ALL THE PEOPLE I KILLED TONIGHT, THEIR BLOOD IS ON YOUR HANDS, YOU FUCKING COWARD...
I'M GONNA ROAST YOU IN THAT LITTLE OVEN YOU'RE FLYING AROUND IN.

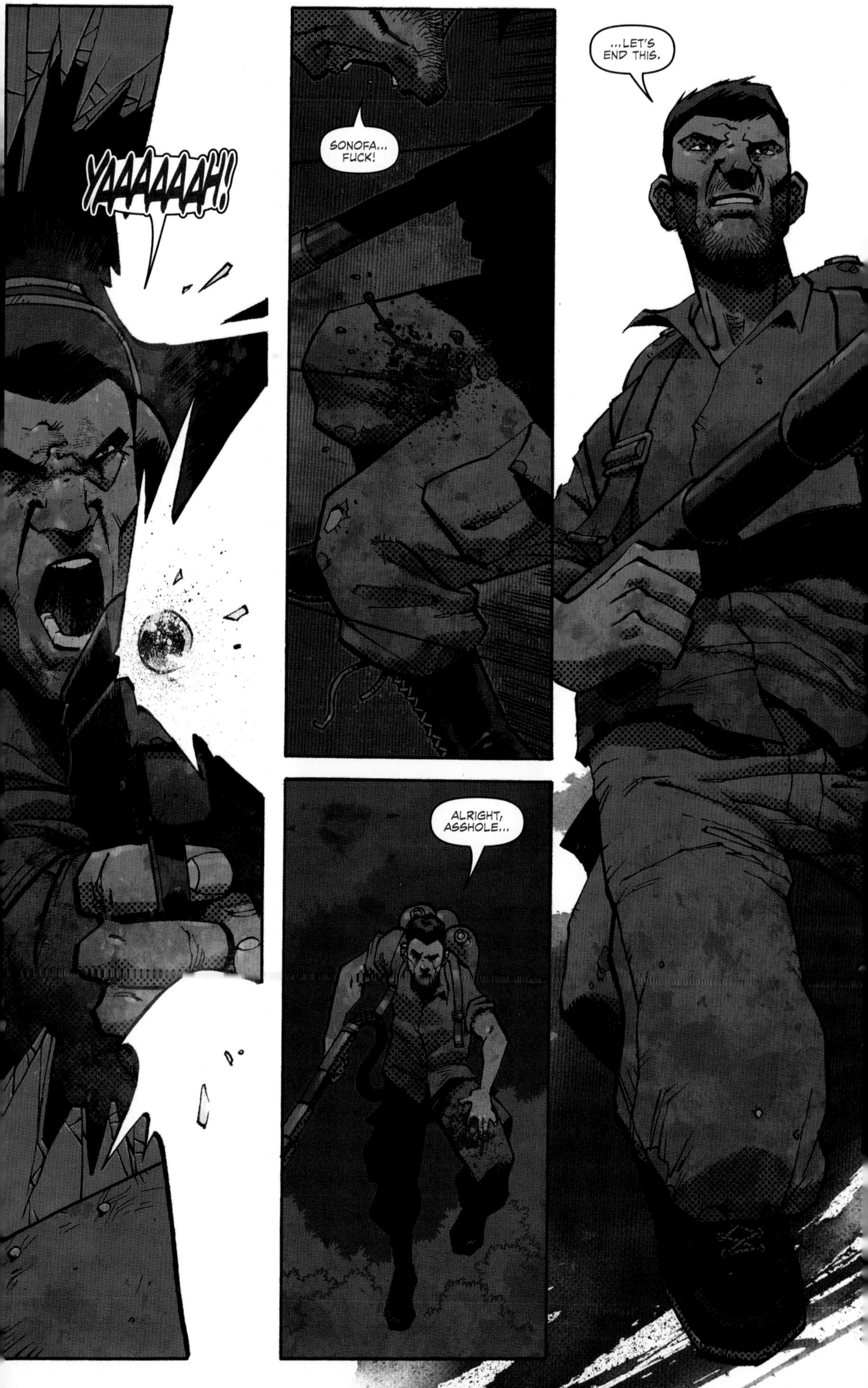
YAAAAAAH!
SONOFA... FUCK!
ALRIGHT, ASSHOLE...
...LET'S END THIS.

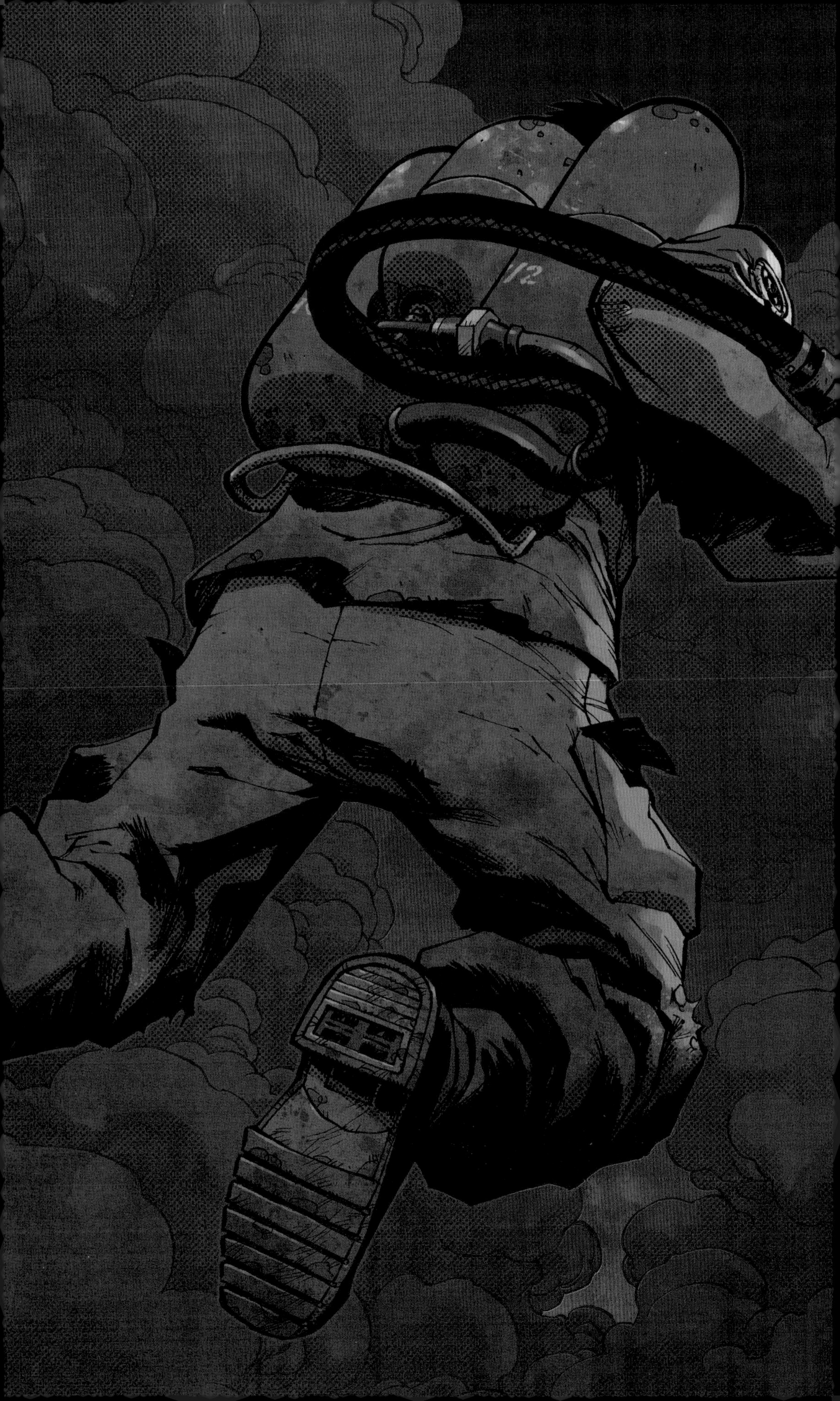

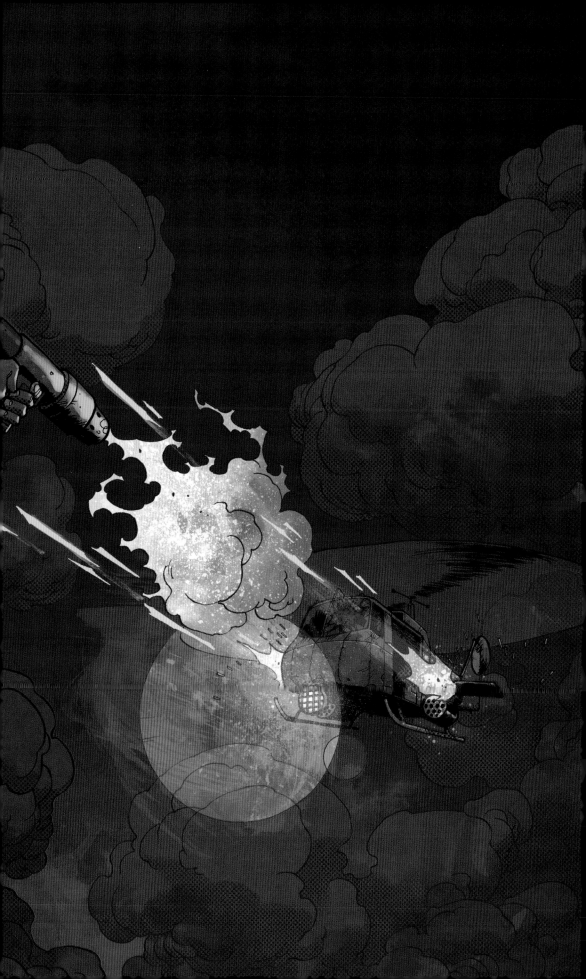

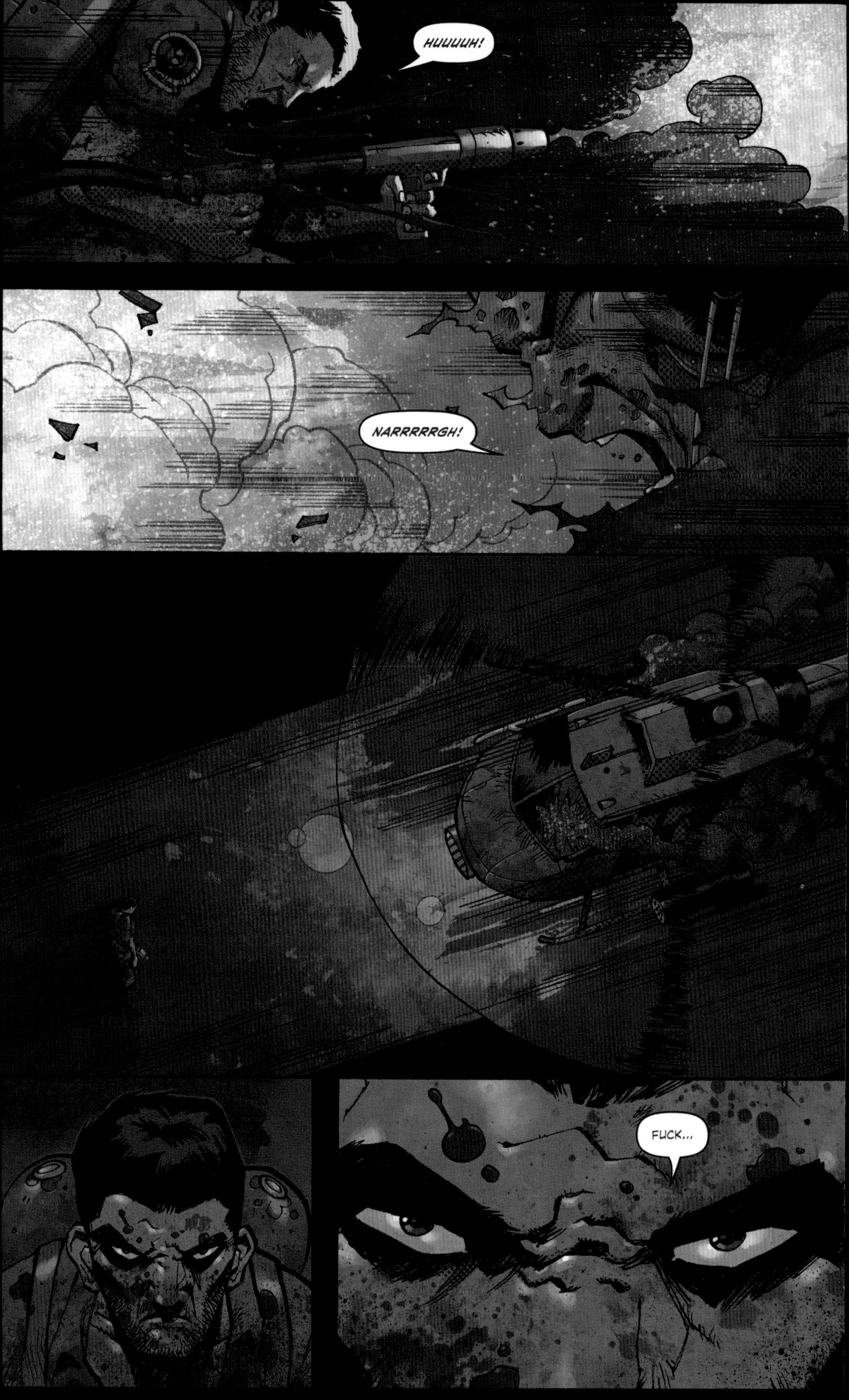
HUUUUH!
NARRRRRGH!
FUCK...

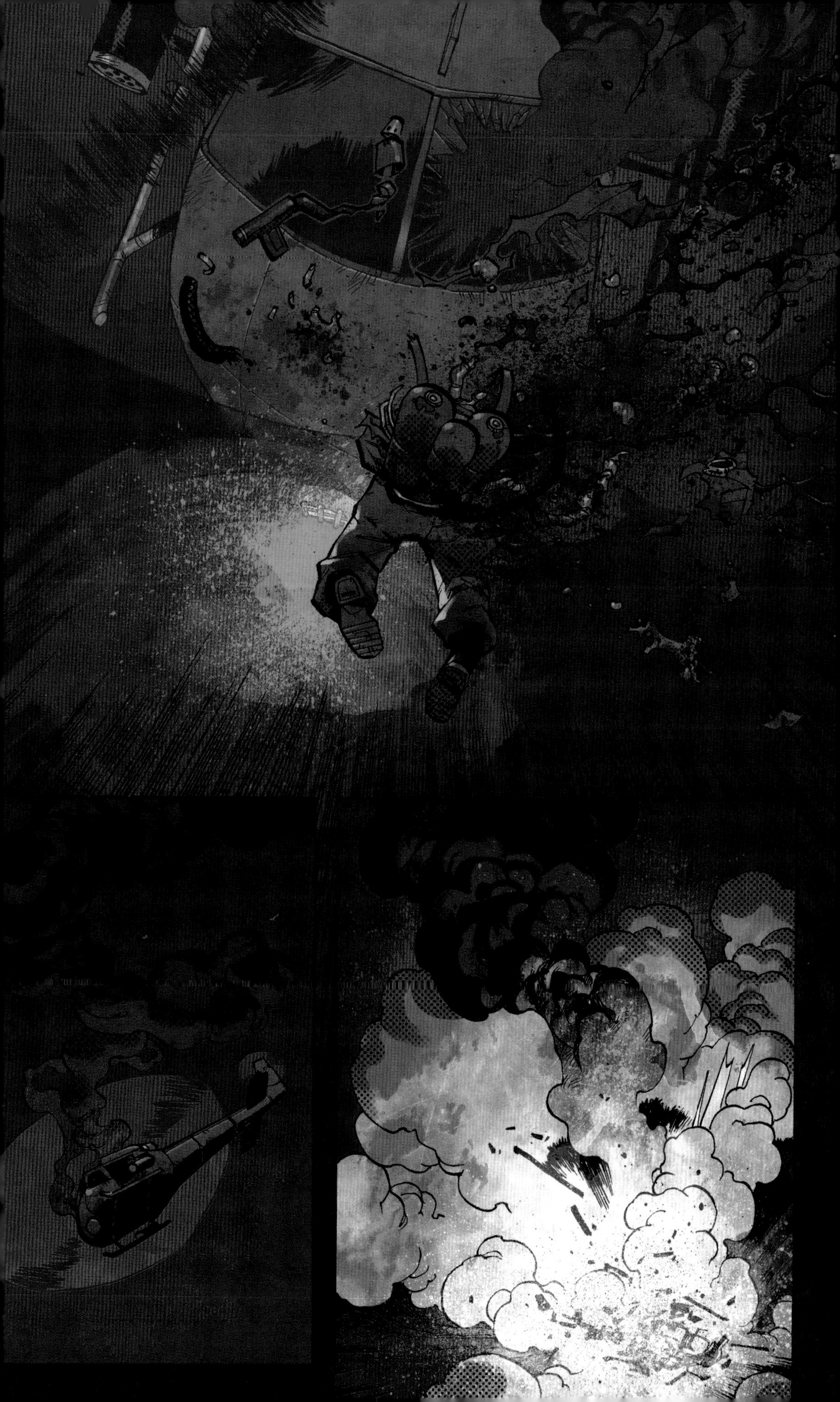

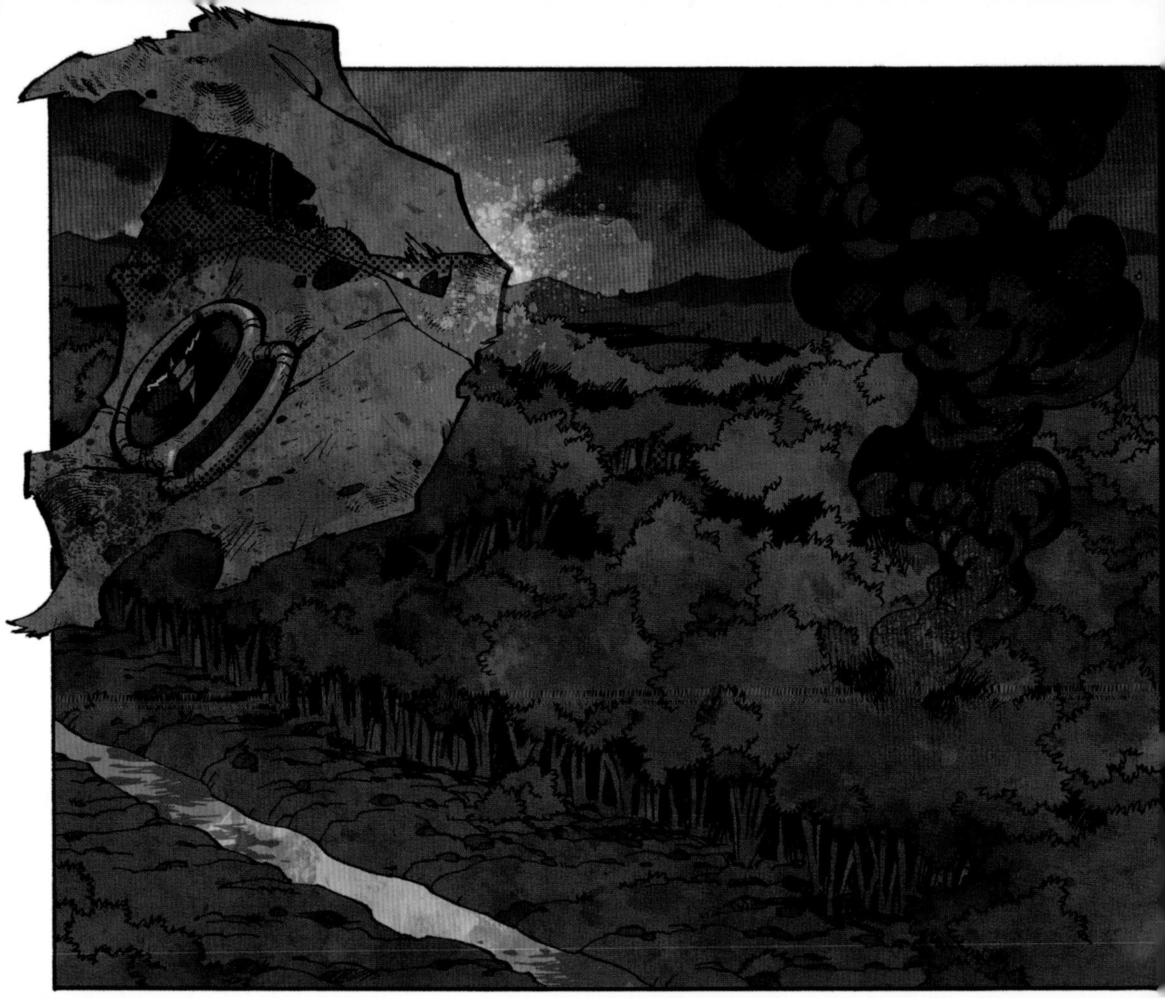

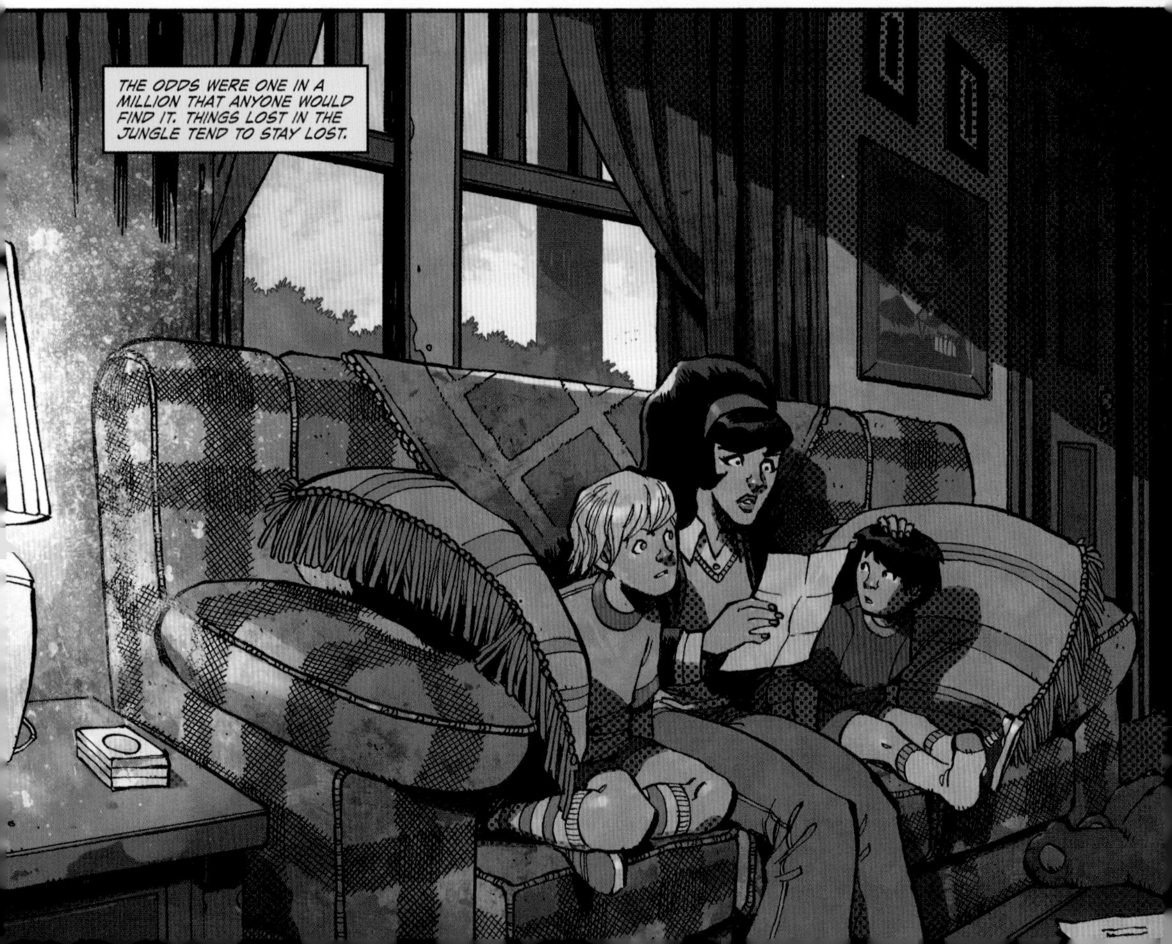
THE ODDS WERE ONE IN A MILLION THAT ANYONE WOULD FIND IT. THINGS LOST IN THE JUNGLE TEND TO STAY LOST.

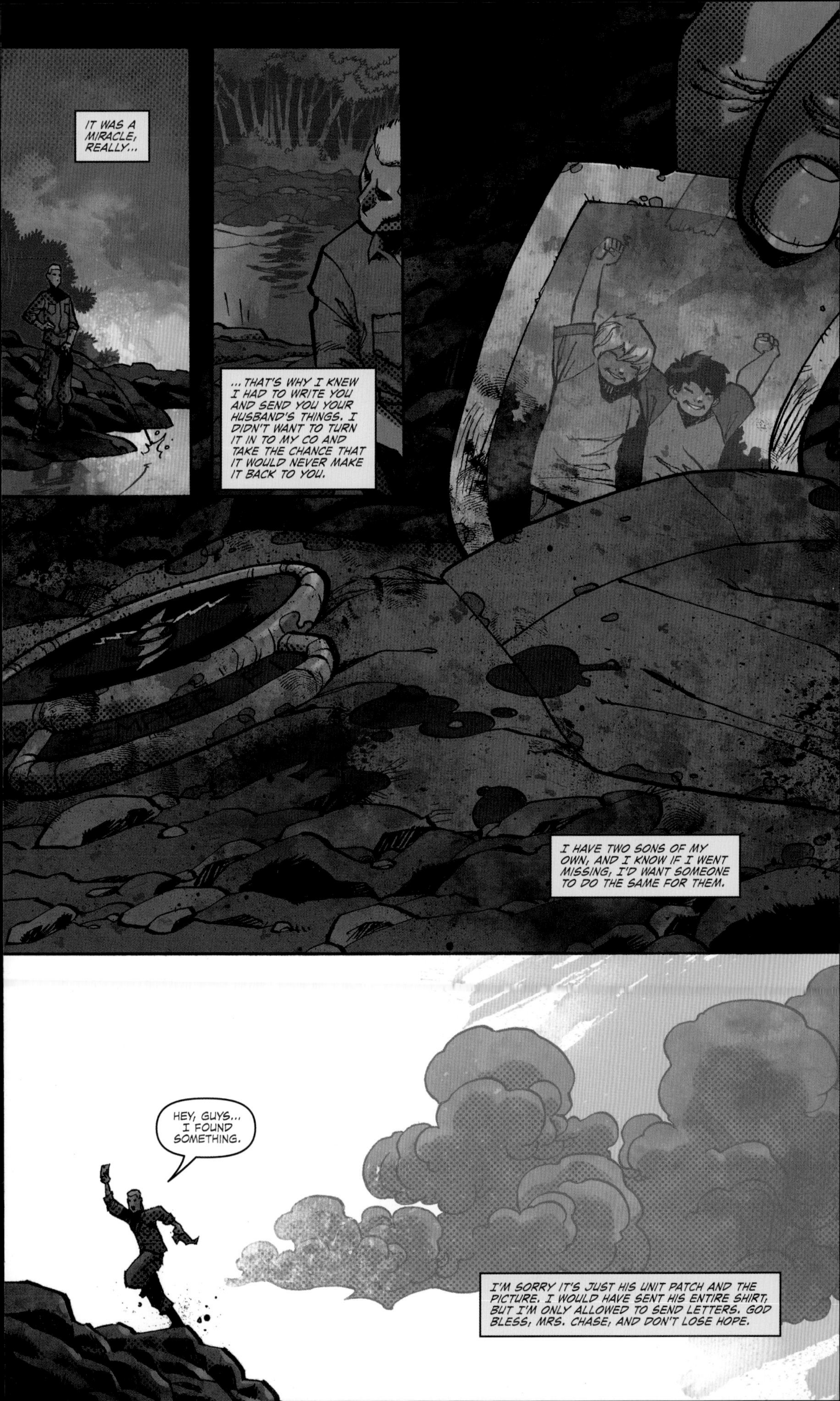
IT WAS A MIRACLE, REALLY...
...THAT'S WHY I KNEW I HAD TO WRITE YOU AND SEND YOU YOUR HUSBAND'S THINGS. I DIDN'T WANT TO TURN IT IN TO MY CO AND TAKE THE CHANCE THAT IT WOULD NEVER MAKE IT BACK TO YOU.
I HAVE TWO SONS OF MY OWN, AND I KNOW IF I WENT MISSING, I'D WANT SOMEONE TO DO THE SAME FOR THEM.
HEY, GUYS... I FOUND SOMETHING.
I'M SORRY IT'S JUST HIS UNIT PATCH AND THE PICTURE. I WOULD HAVE SENT HIS ENTIRE SHIRT, BUT I'M ONLY ALLOWED TO SEND LETTERS. GOD BLESS, MRS. CHASE, AND DON'T LOSE HOPE.

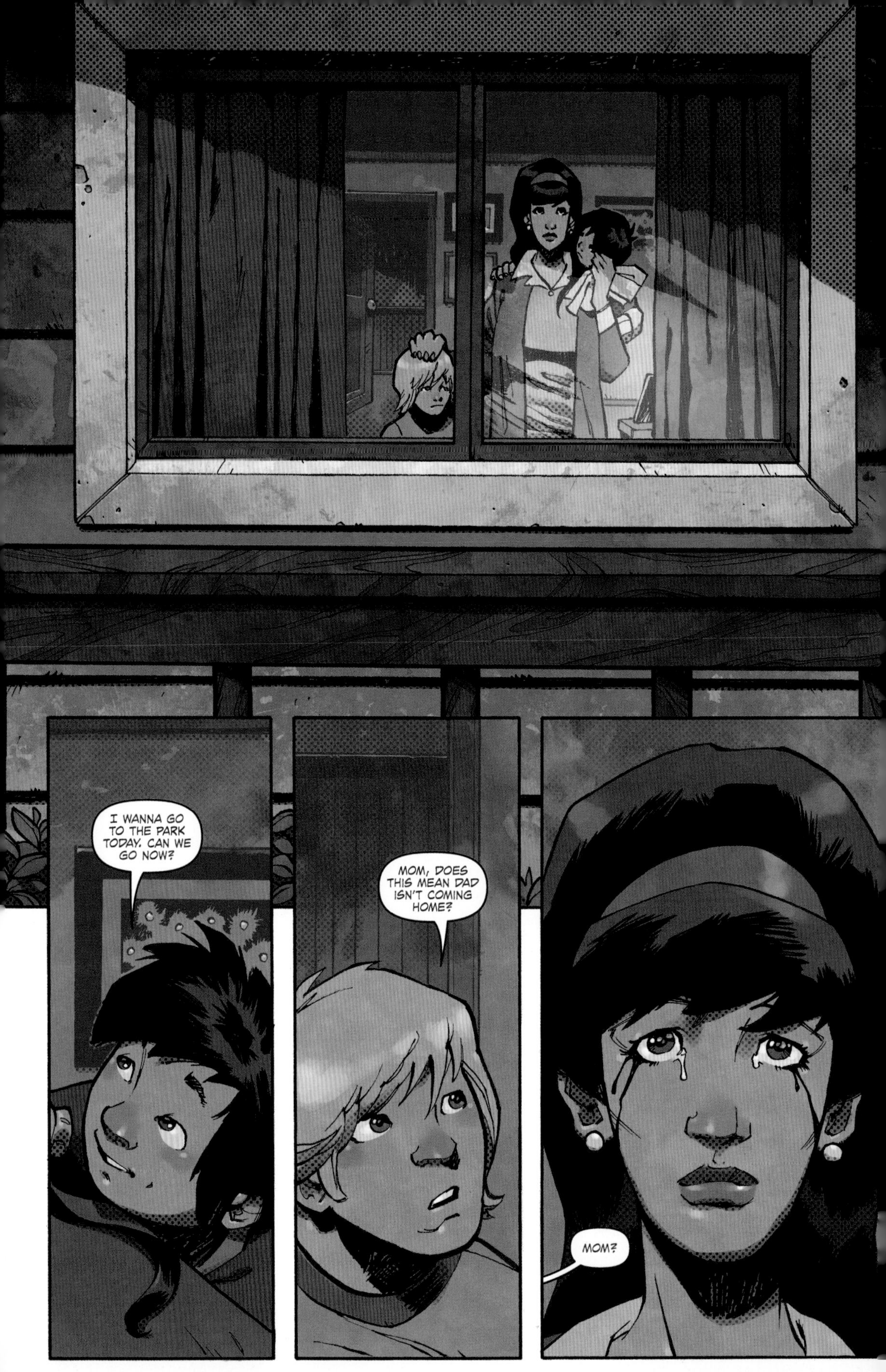
I WANNA GO TO THE PARK TODAY. CAN WE GO NOW?
MOM, DOES THIS MEAN DAD ISN'T COMING HOME?
MOM?

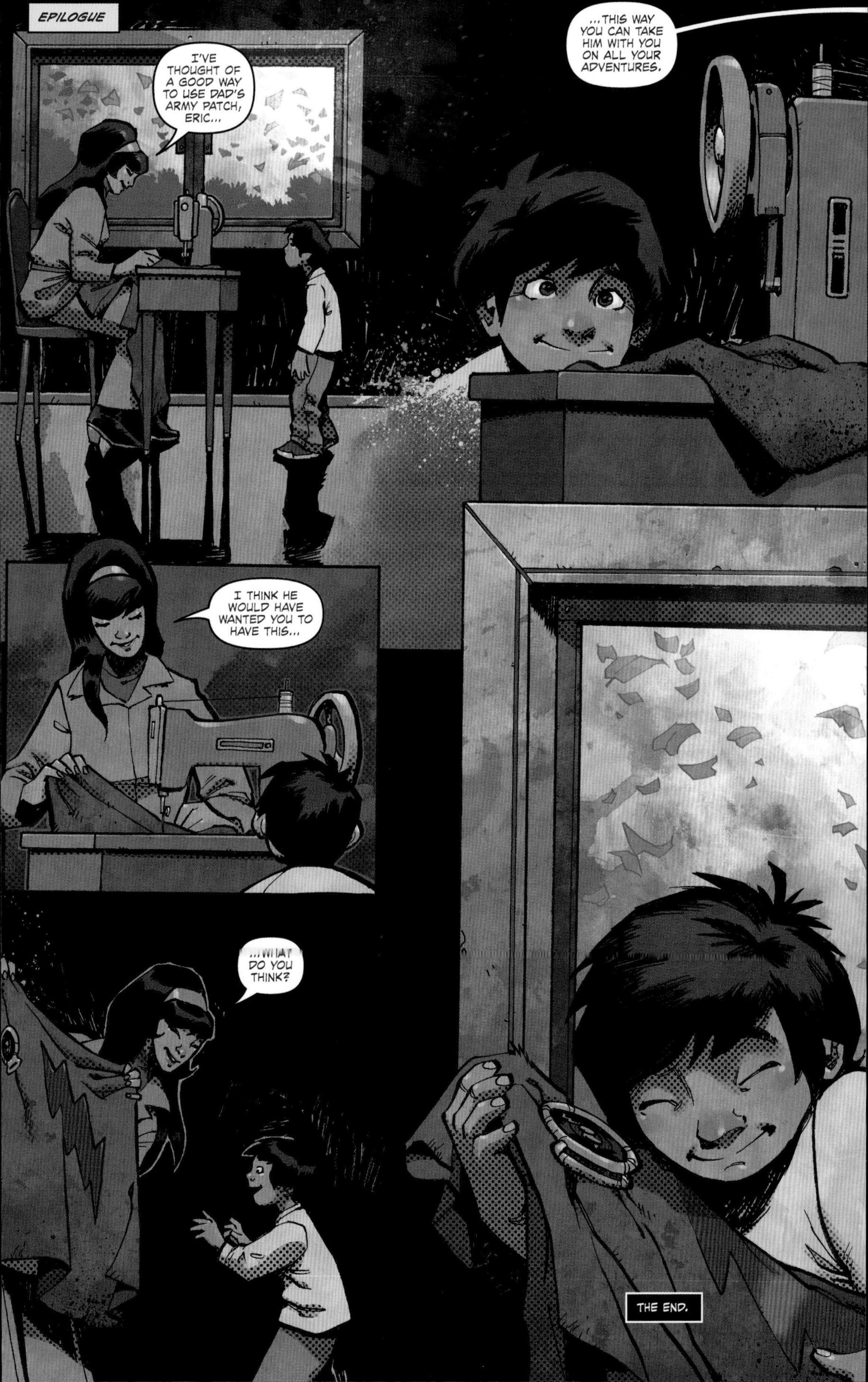
EPILOGUE
I'VE THOUGHT OF A GOOD WAY TO USE DAD'S ARMY PATCH, ERIC...
I THINK HE WOULD HAVE WANTED YOU TO HAVE THIS...
...WHAT DO YOU THINK?
...THIS WAY YOU CAN TAKE HIM WITH YOU ON ALL YOUR ADVENTURES.
THE END.

ART GALLERY
FEATURING NELSON DANIEL

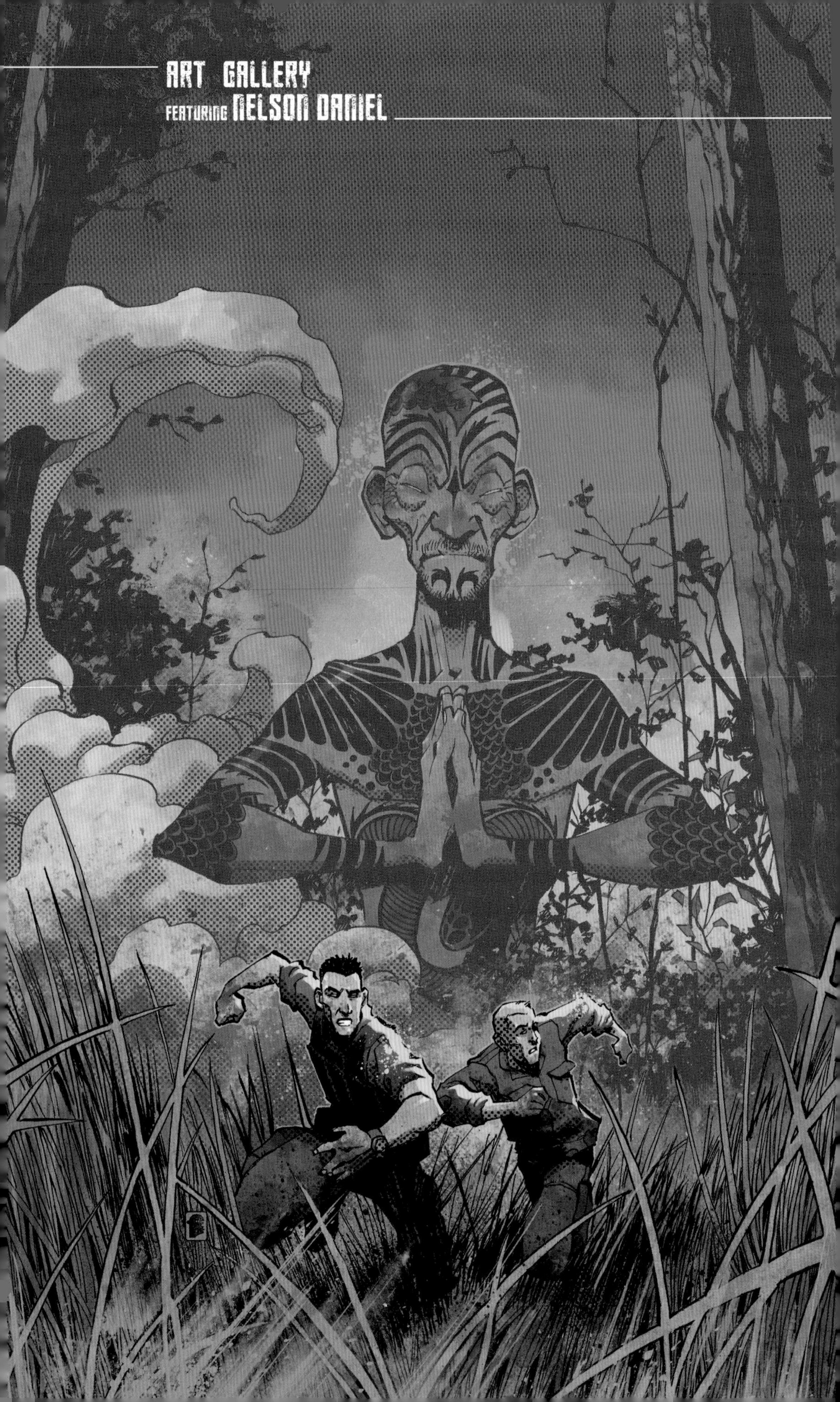

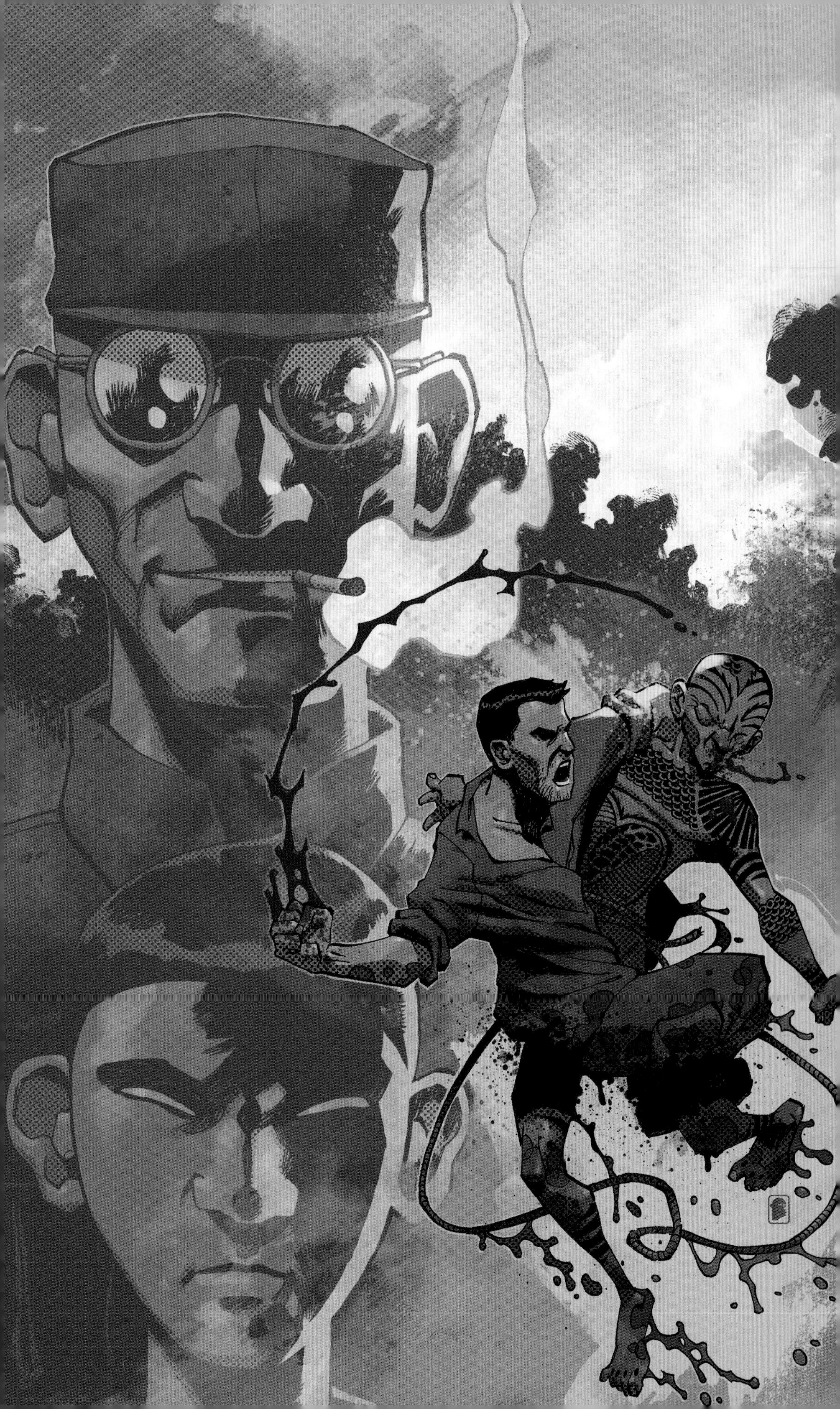

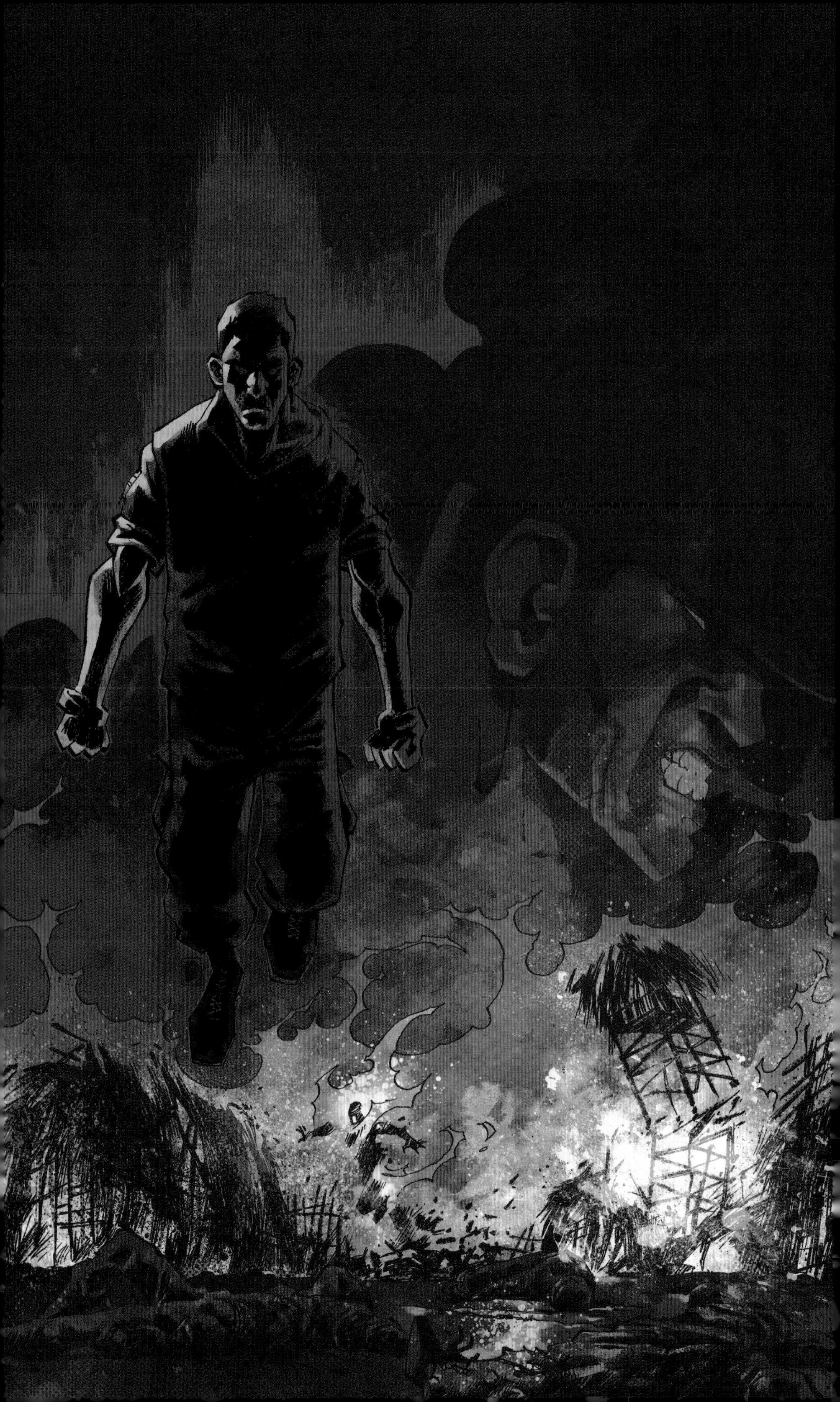

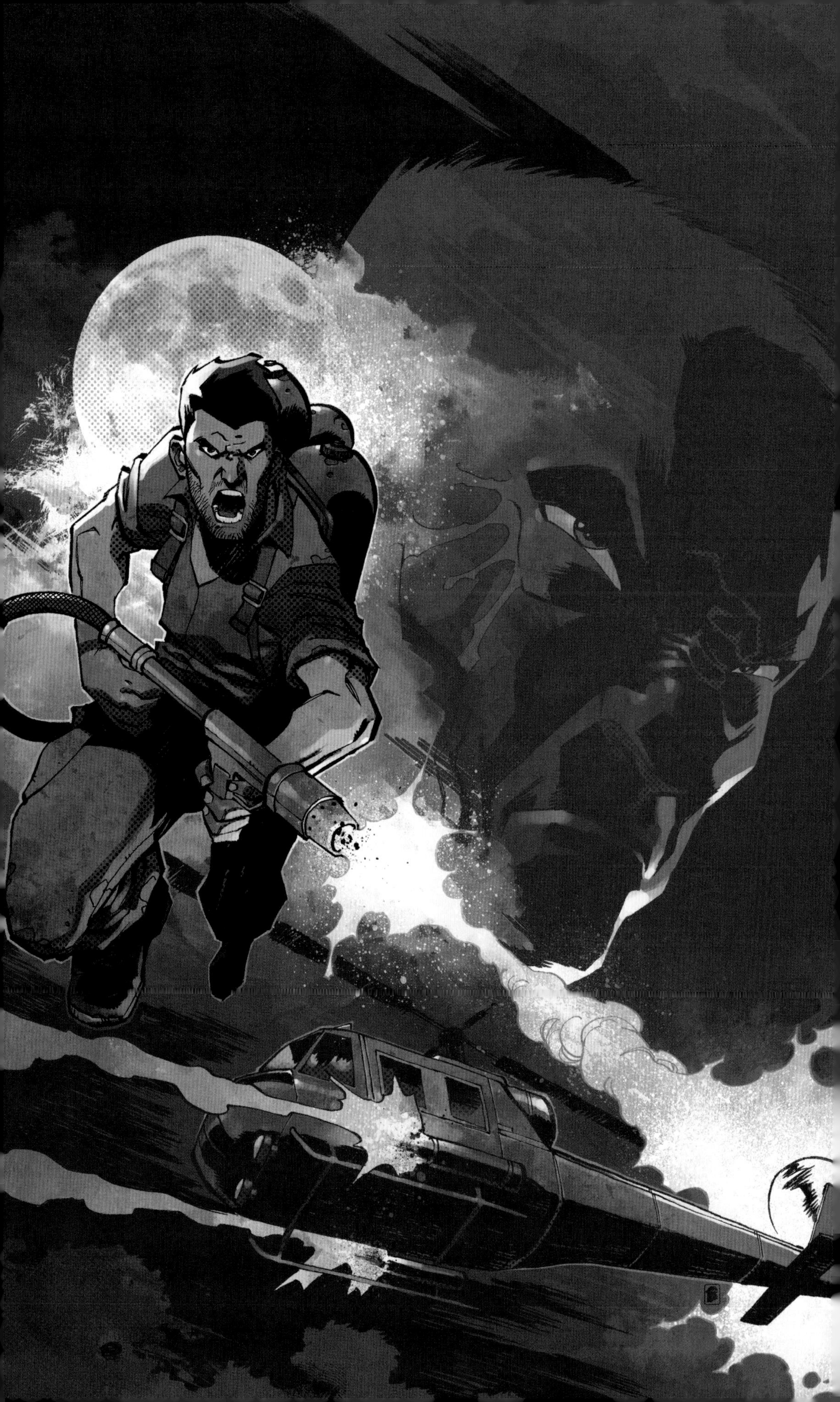

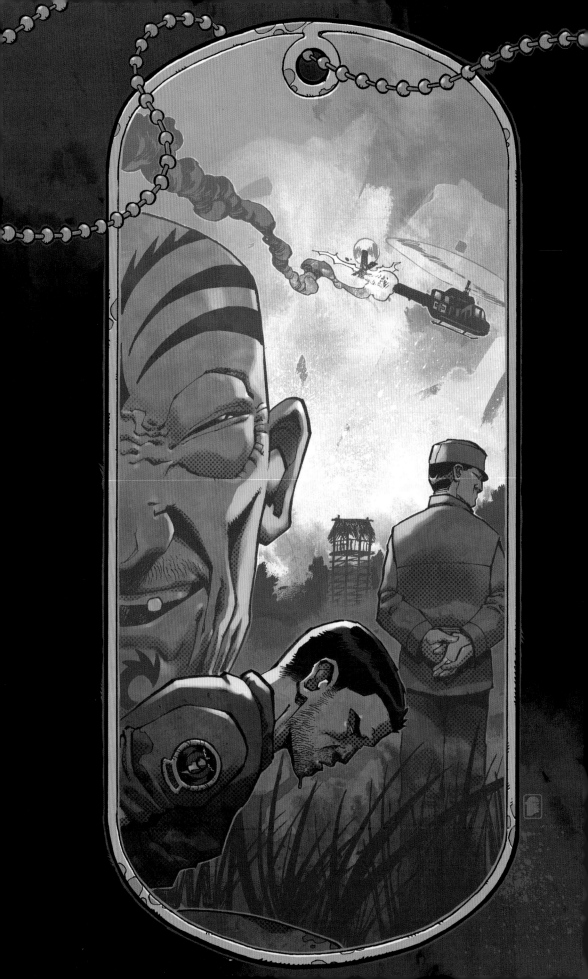

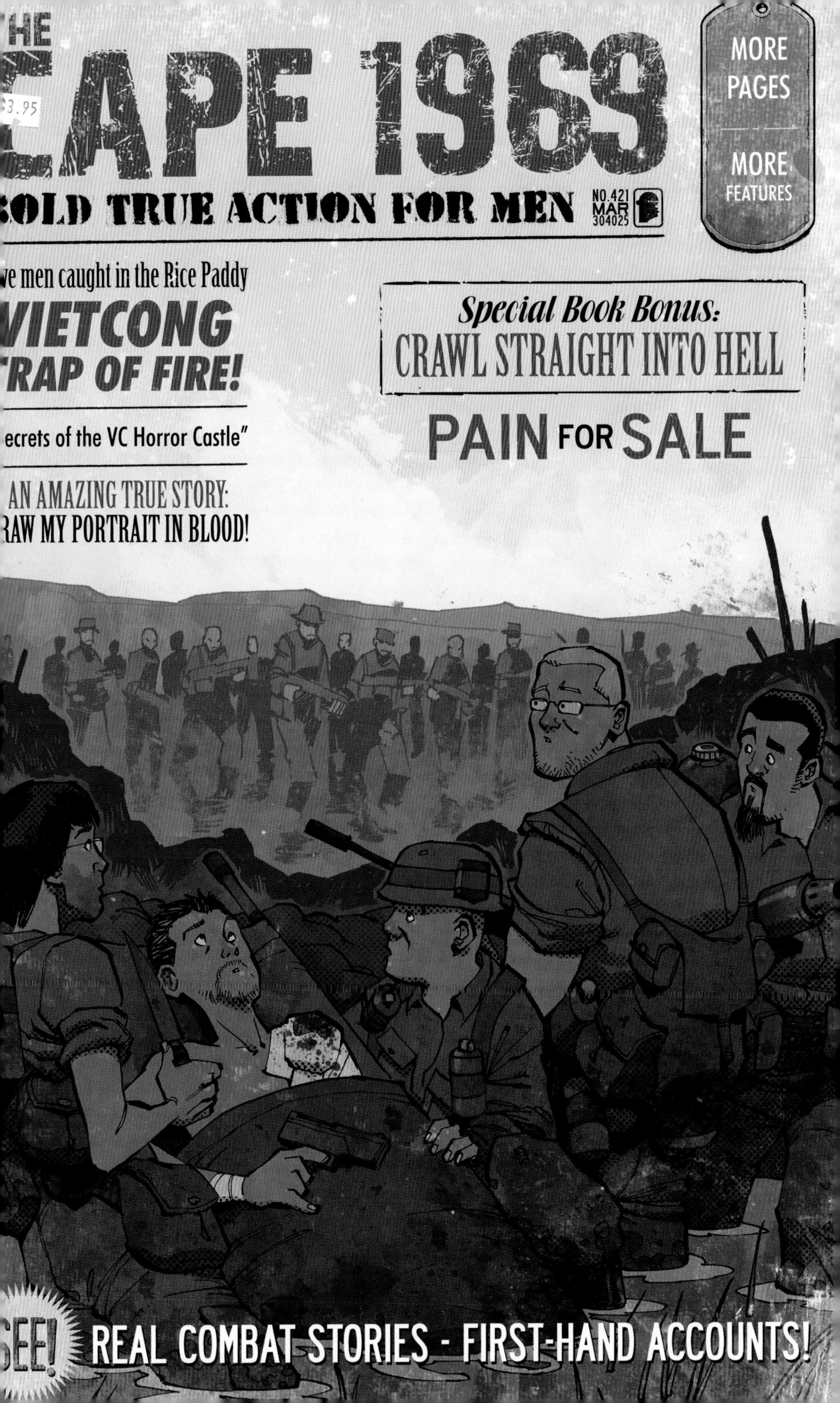
HE
CAPE 1969
3.95
OLD TRUE ACTION FOR MEN
NO.421 MAR 304025
MORE PAGES
MORE FEATURES
ve men caught in the Rice Paddy
VIETCONG
RAP OF FIRE!
ecrets of the VC Horror Castle"
AN AMAZING TRUE STORY:
RAW MY PORTRAIT IN BLOOD!
Special Book Bonus:
CRAWL STRAIGHT INTO HELL
PAIN FOR SALE
EE!
REAL COMBAT STORIES - FIRST-HAND ACCOUNTS!

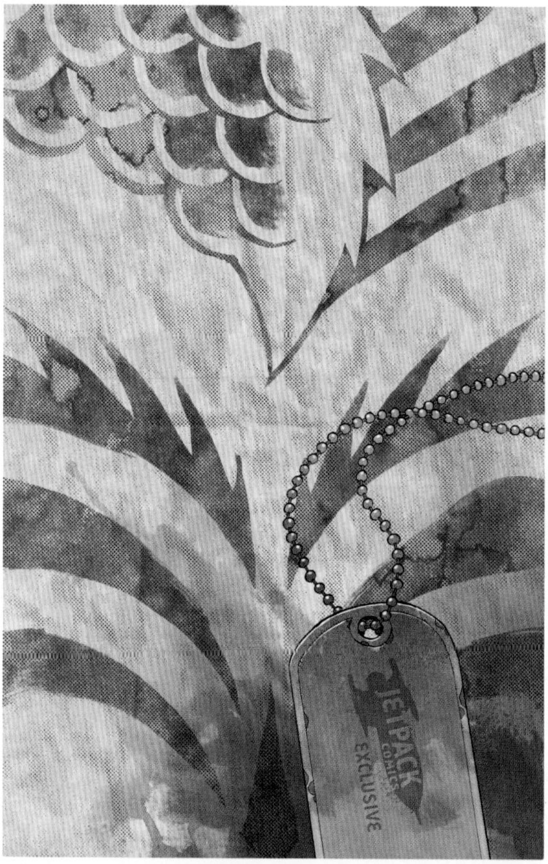
JETPACK
EXCLUSIVE
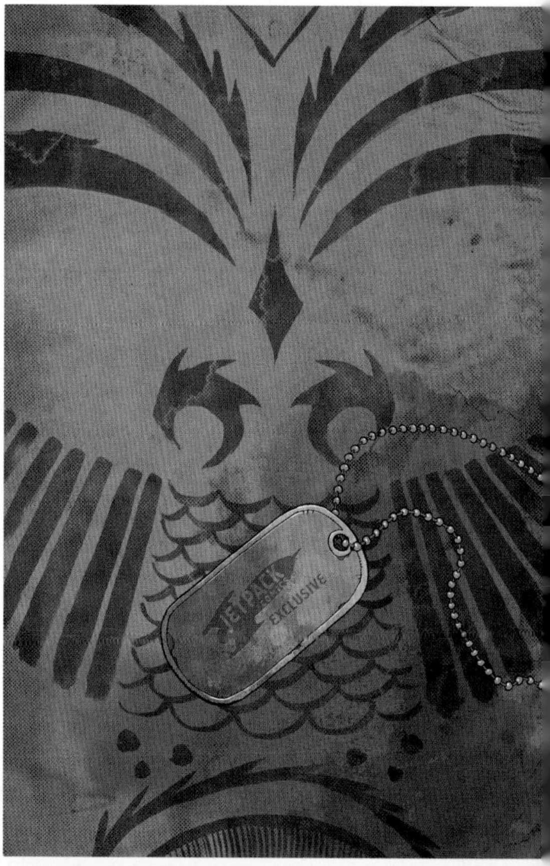
JETPACK
EXCLUSIVE
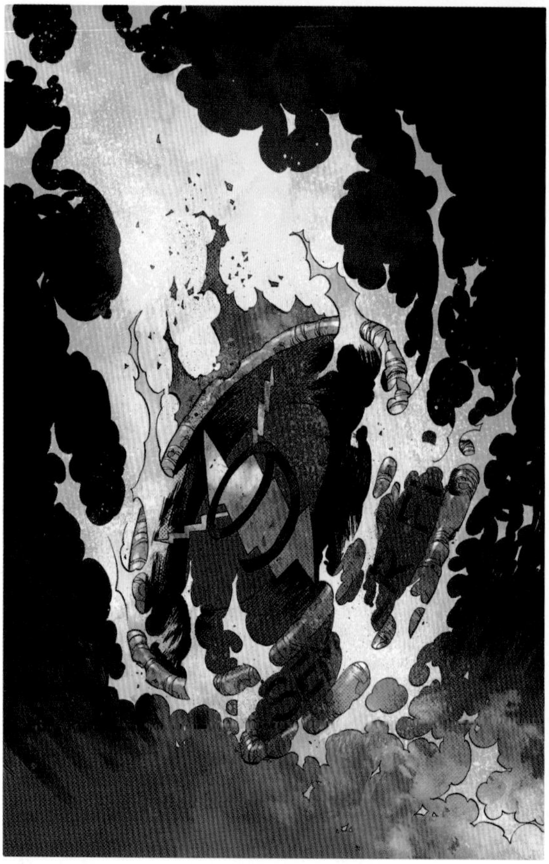
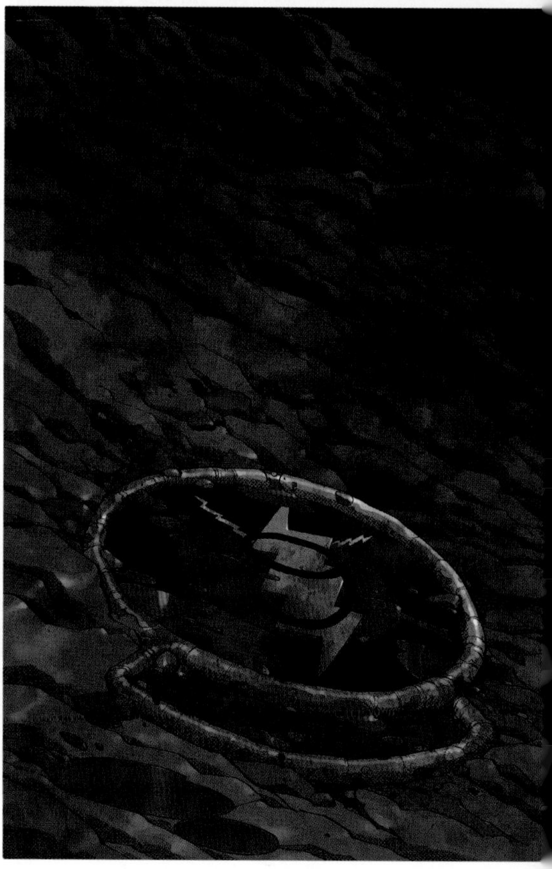

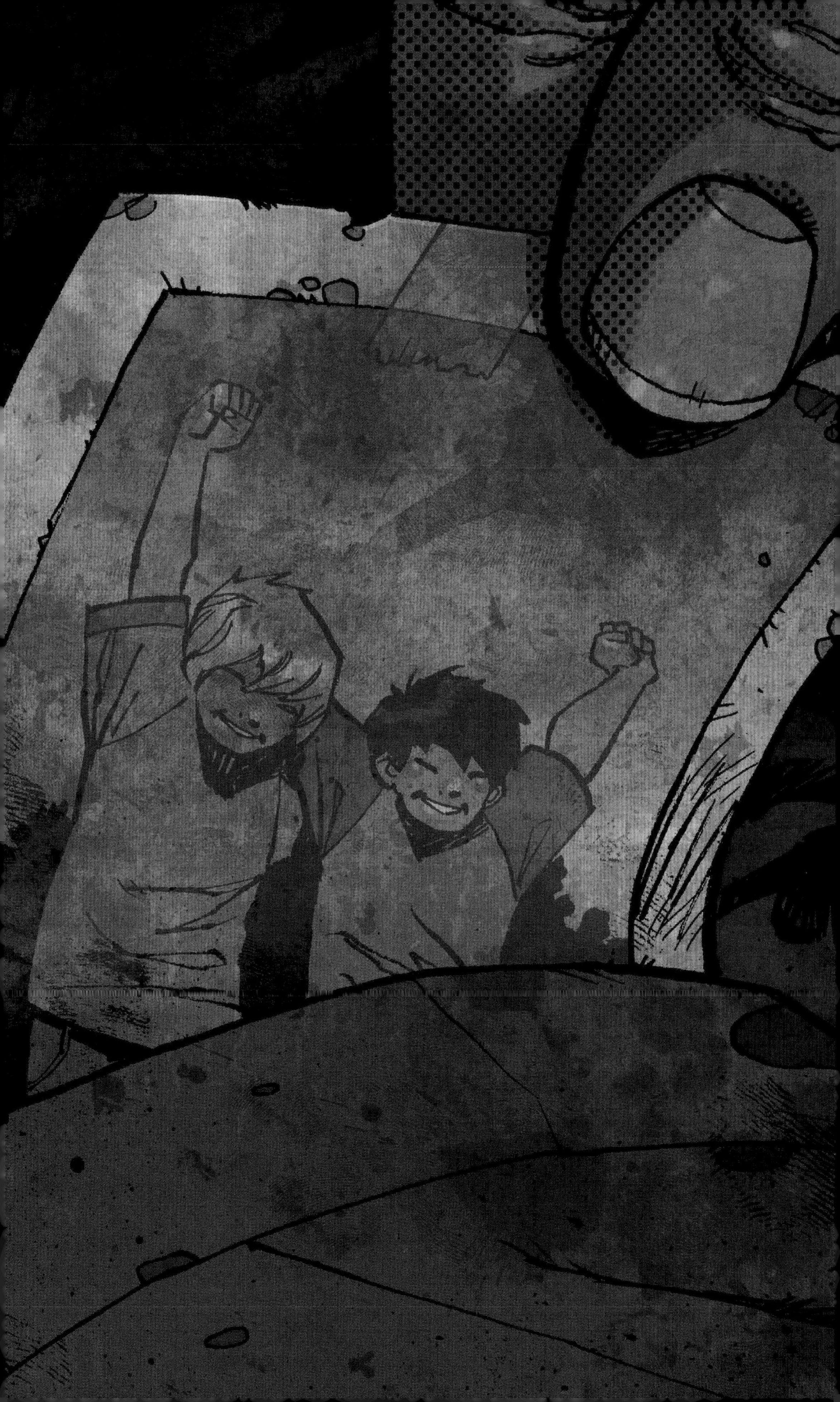

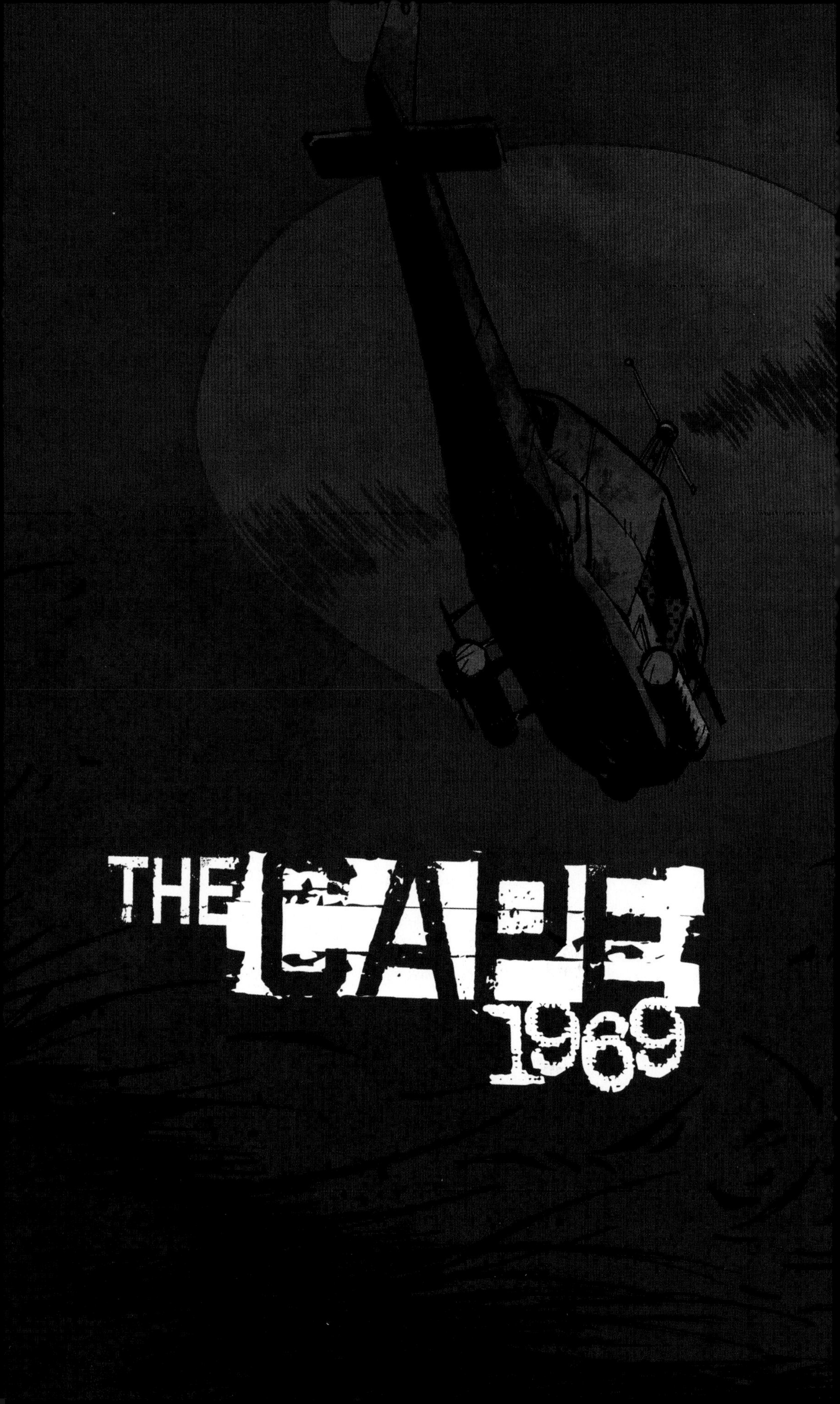
THE CAPE
1969